HADES' ANGELS

An Inside View of Women Who Love Lifers and Death Row Inmates

What Women Can Learn From Their Transformative Journeys

HADES' ANGELS: An Inside View of Women Who Love Lifers and Death Row Inmates and What Women Can Learn From Their Transformative Journeys.

ISBN: Paperback   978-0-9916298-2-4
             eBook   978-0-9916298-3-1

Cover design & production by Ken Rubin

To order additional copies of this book, contact:
Charlyne Gelt, Ph.D.
1-818-501-4123
www.drgelt.com

or

Garden Wall Publishers
Sherman Oaks, California
www.gardenwallpublishers.com
kenmozo@gardenwallpublishers.com

ACKNOWLEDGMENTS

My deepest gratitude goes to the 26 incredible women, my co-researchers, whose lived experience and willingness to talk about it with me, made this "work" a reality. You all trusted me enough to share the intimate details of your lives. Thank you for your cooperation and your gracious way of welcoming me, a total stranger, into your inner and outer worlds.

I thank my dissertation advisor, Dr. Cathy Rives, M.D., for her clinical expertise, her guidance, her belief in me, and in the value of this "work".

Sylvia Cary, MFT, for working with me and jump-starting the dissertation into the idea for a book.

I thank Jackie Parker for using her writing talent to help me pull together the results of my research, the seven common threads, into story format [Part One]. It makes the findings understandable to academics as well as the general population.

To my friend Lorrie Drogin who generously used her life time editing the second section of this book; to my sister, my friend, Judy Masliyah, MFT, a support and a sounding board and to my family and friends who, steadfast throughout this process, never left me but knew when to leave me alone.

To my husband, Stephen, who throughout this process, respected my space, learned to read me, and knew when to do his own thing. You were always there...to hold me, to listen, to give me feedback, and travel this life journey.

Thank you.

FEAR BEING THE UNSEEN JAILER

I dedicate this work
To those who risk leaving the safety of the shore,
To those who seek release from the inner prison,
To those who are open to change.

This book is also dedicated to
the women who the participated in my research and
to the many women I have met along the way
who are so good at doing for others,
but short-change the self,
who want to grow and
learn new tools to move beyond
the self-destructive patterns

And

To my husband, Stephen
Who, in his summer/autumn years with me,
Jumped into the depths of the deep, dark mysteries of life,
Bravely left the safety of the shore for parts unknown,
And has so flourished while in his earnest quest for his truth, for soul,
And who has grown, changed, evolved alongside me.

*"It takes courage to grow up and turn out to be who you
really are."*
                                              --- e.e. cummings

Table of Contents

FOREWORD AND INTRODUCTION

Part I: Common Threads in Story Format

Part II: Hidden Forces: Analysis and Interpretation

FOREWORD

Hades' Angels is the story of twenty-six women who each experienced a transformative journey through their relationships with prison lifers and death row inmates. These women did not know these men prior to his incarceration. This work applies Kohut's understanding of the individual, the soul's drive for potentiality from inner bondage, out of deadness and subjectivity, towards wholeness, to heal their early childhood narcissistic injury and sustain meaning on three levels: personal, interpersonal, and societal.

Their stories fly in the face of all the clichés and stereotypes that assume that such relationships are necessarily neurotic and dysfuntional. After all, what woman in her right mind would "date" or marry a man in prison when he can give her so little and with whom she can never have what society would call a "normal" relationship? Certain prison love relationships turn out to be positive – even "transforming" – for the women involved in them: a corrective emotional experience that is a clear step-up from earlier, destructive "demon lover" relationships that drained them emotionally and dragged them down. By contrast, their inmate relationships actually encouraged them to become more than they ever thought they could be, moving them towards self-discovery and healing.

There are six chapters in Section One which incorporate the historical, emotional and psychological factors that predispose, invite or attract certain women to the prison environment— factors that are part and parcel of becoming involved with an incarcerated man. These common factors are: Early Childhood Narcissistic Injury; Family of Origin Marital Dynamics of Dominance/Submission; Taking on the Family Caretaker/Nurturer Role; Identification as a "Father's Daughter;" Emotional/Intellectual Split; Involvement in Previous "Demon Lover" Relationships; True Self/False Self Split. Section Two breaks down the issues and common threads into factual, theoretical and psychological concepts that offer a deeper understanding of the inner transformation and healing.

In Section One, one Hades' Angels story per chapter is used to exemplify the findings, the seven common threads of the research. It is these common threads that have drawn certain women to become involved with men in prison. Woven together they make a tapestry that describes their historical, emotional, and psychological findings. And further, though personal shame and stigma about the prison relationship is denied by each and every Hades' Angel, it is the very physical circumstances of these relationships, prison, that is the stage set for their transformative journeys. Paradoxically, what is born in that setting is the nurturing, emotional interchange of empathic attunement, which acts as a catalyst for change and healing. Feeling nurtured rather than being the nurturer, is the fertilizing agent that launches a groundbreaking journey of self- discovery, of self-awareness, an unconscious drive towards wholeness, and the integration of the split-off aspects of the self.

The physical environment is part and parcel of that which creates the emotional environment, and vice versa. The actual descent from the outside into the "hellish" environment of a super-max prison serves as a dramatic backdrop, a stage set for these relationships in which the top-dog/under-dog splits are rampant; therefore, it is intrinsic to the lived experience.

When love is not easy or comfortable but is separated by external forces of an unwelcoming, harsh (prison) environment of polarities, split archetypes, what is it like? "Popular" literature pathologizes these women who, according to Isenberg, "can't help themselves and are in this relationship to fulfill their deepest needs, their most complex emotional dependencies, their ultimate fantasies," (1991). A great deal of literature exists about a surge in the male prison population, about the pathology of men who are incarcerated for murder, about the difficulties incarceration imposes upon prisoner's families, the injustices of the prison system, a sensationalizing of women who choose to be with murderers, and a popular pathologizing of the women who stay with these men. Contrary to that "popular" pathology, what Hades' Angels have in common is an unconscious search for that which transforms the ascriptive statements that have defined their inner sense of self. What they have found is far more powerful than turning lead into gold: found in the subtle body, that space in between, is the healing, soothing, transformative energy of feeling loved. They did not seek to change themselves yet they were changed, transformed, and feeling mirrored, held, and understood, was the transformative energy for a "corrective emotional experience".

Perspective: According to Capra's (1983) view of quantum theory, "the basic structures of the material world, ultimately, are determined by the way we look at it; the observed patterns of matter are reflections of patterns of mind." Thus, historical emotional patterns of functioning as they might affect the perception of the Hades' Angels lived experience, such as dominance and submission, were explored in the research and in this book.

A common mistake with perspective is that our own is often fixed, which makes the other a threat. What one perceives depends on our point of observation, who we are, and what we are looking for. One person's view of a situation, even when observing the same thing, can be widely divergent from another. Additionally, our perspective can even shift with new information. Shedding old perceptions enables a different reality to shine through.

Psychotherapists develop the art of listening because people benefit from having their words, actions, and emotional experience understood. Many theoretical orientations exist for understanding that experience: cognitive, behavioral, developmental, analytical, depth. This suggests that the various theoretical perspectives frame, guide, and also limit the listener's unique way of thinking, perceiving, and understanding the other. The interpretation of personal meaning of the experience is therefore the subjective view of the listener. A vastly underutilized point of view is from the perspective of soul. When reading *Hades' Angels* I encourage reading between the lines and listening to these women's stories from the perspective of soul.

Hades' Angels contains relationship stories, which have the potential to be destructive- all the men are prison inmates convicted of violent crimes - but instead these relationships prove to be healing and empowering for the women involved. *Hades' Angels* probes the hidden forces behind relationships. As such it draws on a wider readership, not only those who want to read stories about the Mr. Wrongs of the world, but those who want to learn how women--even those in relationship with prison inmates—are able to heal, to transform and grow so the Mr. Wrongs no longer find their way into their lives.

Why can a nice girl, a former cheerleader, honor student, publishing executive fall in love with a prison lifer? And it is one question that many readers want to have answered for them. *Hades' Angels* shows readers why this kind of relationship happens. The subjects are "nice" women, good women, independent, bright, self- supporting, caretakers/peacemakers, nurturers, who still have a history of failed relationships. Hades' Angels shows readers the unrecognized "shadow" part in the lives of the women interviewed. Their unacknowledged anger and hurt, buried within since childhood, recognizes itself in the mirror of the other. Differently expressed, it is the "unseen magnetic draw" that forms their common wound. "Beauty and the beast" are polar opposites, but in the world of the emotions, the two are psychologically mated.

The reader of *Hades' Angels* will understand how a woman learns to act-in, repress her feelings, and how her historical, emotional and family dynamics are the lens that infuses and defines her adult relationship attractions. She will be able to understand the powerful impact of the family of origin marital dynamics on future relationships. She will be able to understand her own attractions as a result of reading *Hades' Angels*. I show how the unacknowledged childhood wounds affect even outwardly successful clients seen in private practice; the reader will learn to recognize how they impact her life. *Hades' Angels* will not leave readers with questions but will hopefully leave many grateful for the understanding it imparts, freed to acknowledge and face the buried wounds of the past rather than act them out in relationships.

This book utilizes the laboratory of the prison to understand certain relationships that occur in the general population, difficult relationships that present in the therapeutic setting. These relationships describe the transformative journey from emotional submission to empowerment. This book helps us understand how women that society dismiss as worthless, who have connected with the discards of society, get from them what they have always wanted: emotional connection, and emotional intimacy.

For the millions of women who buy books to help them understand themselves and their relationships, *Hades' Angels* will explain both who they love and how they love. I narrate the true-life stories of women who fall in love with and are emotionally healed in their relationships with prison lifers. And at the same time I discuss the hidden forces to help readers see how their own "shadow" parts are reflected in the men they choose to love. The relationship dynamics in *Hades' Angels* helps to clarify what goes on in some couples who seek marital therapy and are unaware of the source of their problems, yet experience themselves as imprisoned or trapped by unseen jailers. *Hades' Angels* reveals deep emotional experiences that repair and transform women with a history of destructive relationships. The backdrop for this inner transformation is the dramatic, threatening and oppressive prison environment.

Today there are hundreds of thousands of women in relationships with prison inmates, and the number is growing. In addition, there is the population of wives and families of the incarcerated who will find real value in *Hades' Angels* because of the insights they will get into themselves and because the inmates depicted in *Hades' Angels* are shown as human beings, able to provide emotional support and serve as vehicles for the emotional growth of the women who love them.

Hades' Angels offers analysis and interpretation and teaches readers how to confront and heal the kind of wounds whose source remains a mystery. *Hades' Angels* demystifies the suffering and offers readers the chance to look into their own lives and learn to confront the true source of their pain.

Chapter One

Hades' Angels in Love

"When an inner situation is not made conscious, it happens outside as fate."

--- Carl Jung

The Long, Lonely Road

It is still dark. I have miles of long, lonely road ahead of me. Mother would turn over in her grave if she knew where I was heading. I can hear her now, 'No one with a scrap of decency ends up even as a visitor in prison. Nice people don't affiliate with people like that because people like that are bad.' What my mother doesn't know is that these past twelve years since I've been with him have been the best of my life, even though he is in prison. I get so excited because I can't wait to see and talk to him. Every time I arrive at the guard gate I'm a nervous wreck, but the moment I walk into the visiting room and see his warm smile, I fall in love with him all over again. One kiss hello and goodbye and that's it. Remember: Don't touch.

--- Hades' Angel Callie

Certain women in this society count themselves as involved with, even committed to, men who will spend the rest of their lives behind bars. I am not talking about women already in relationships with these men prior to imprisonment. I am talking about women who reach out, meet, and then become involved with lifers or men on death row after they have been incarcerated. I call them Hades' Angels.

There are thousands of such women all over the country. We've heard about the more high-profile examples sensationalized in the media, like Doreen Lioy and Nightstalker Richard Ramirez, or Tammi Menendez (interviewed on 60 Minutes and Larry King) who met and married convicted murderer, Erik Menendez, after he was imprisoned. The women in this book are not involved in high-profile relationships.

This book informs you, through the lens of the women who live it, what motivates certain women who rise at the crack of dawn to make that lonely, early morning trek to the prison to visit him. It tells you what motivates certain women, Hades' Angels, to link their own lives with men living in a prison environment: to stand in long lines, to experience the bars, the concrete, razor wire fences, clanging electronic gates, watch towers manned with guns, and then wait patiently for the visiting room guard to call out their name, anxiously hoping to "pass". It tells you why certain women, inwardly armored against verbal slights for associating with an inmate, undergo humiliating physical searches to descend into the deep, dark underbelly of a prison hellhole to spend their lifetime with a prison love they say "fills me up"!

To look at these women you wouldn't peg them as being desperate for a man. They are not fat, ugly, or hooked on welfare. They present as strong and confident, although they may feel fragile inside. They come across as articulate, caring, thoughtful, strong-willed and they are remarkably self-sufficient. In fact, most appear as though they could do perfectly well on their own, yet they choose men with whom they will never have what our society terms a "normal" relationship. Why? What are their relationships like and what is their story? Do certain women somehow benefit from these relationships? My answer is a resounding Yes. Do their partners benefit from these relationships? Yes, again. And can society as a whole ultimately benefit from these relationships? Once again, Yes!

I became aware of this unique segment of society of women who meet, fall for, and then commit to men behind bars---the Hades' Angels---when, under the umbrella of Friends Outside, I began facilitating a support group for families with a loved one in prison: mothers, fathers, sisters, brothers, and adult children. Although the group was intended for families with loved ones in prison, over the years many women came in and out of this group who were not bonded by blood, they were bonded by love.

Being a psychotherapist, the professional part of me was curious as to what psychological factors contributed to the initial attraction to a man who made his home locked away in a 6' x 9' cell. Neither dragon nor dragon slayer, I wanted to understand them and what motivated them. Over time, I became aware that many of these women made profound and positive psychological changes, even healings, as a result of being in their prison relationship. It was as though they intuitively knew they needed to heal from early childhood wounds and the harmful impact of previous unhappy, even destructive, relationships.

This work cracks open the door for the reader to enter into this unique relational world where this unique population find meaning: the inner world, the realm of soul. It also informs us about the internal, psychological world of women who are drawn to find their true love in prison, for life.

Even more surprisingly, many of these women reported similar positive changes in the men they were visiting, though I never met the men and couldn't judge that for myself. There appeared to be a win/win situation occurring: the women, the men (apparently), and on a larger playing field, even society. It seemed as though nobody was getting hurt. These women did not seek to change themselves yet they were changed, transformed, by their experience. I was fascinated listening to them reveal their lived experiences. I wanted to tell about it in order to shed light on what for them appeared to be a "corrective emotional experience". That's when I decided to do the research and to write about it.

Hades' Angels: An Inside View of Women Who Love Lifers and Death Row Inmates is born from this fascination. Initially, it was the topic of my doctoral dissertation; then it became this book. It is based on in-depth interviews with twenty-six of these remarkable women from all parts of the country, each involved with or married to a lifer or on Death Row. Again, I want to make it clear that none of these women were involved with men who were serial murderers or child molesters. I am well aware that not all women involved with inmates have positive transformative experiences. This book is about is the twenty-six women who did.

All for Love

So why would any woman put herself through long drives, the long waiting lines, the expenses (phone bills, gas, food, motel rooms), and then arrive at the prison gate only to find all her efforts are for naught? She may not be wearing the right clothes, or they are the wrong colors, or the prison may be on lockdown. All this obviously makes it extremely difficult to maintain a relationship with an inmate. Yet, these women do it.

What is the payoff?

For many women, the payoff, simply, is love. Surprising as this may sound, it is also an opportunity, although an unconscious one, for personal growth. The prison marriage or romance gives the woman an opportunity to begin dealing with painful emotional wounds buried deep in her psyche: that which got pushed down or split off from awareness. Her prison journey becomes a journey towards wholeness and individuation. How does this happen? What do these women learn in this prison setting and how does it impact their lives?

Asha Bandele, though not a Hades' Angel, is such a woman -- a poet, intelligent, beautiful, educated, and black. Invited by her professor to visit a New York maximum-security correctional facility, she met and fell in love with Rashid, a prisoner there, and later married him. In her book, The Prisoner's Wife, she states: "Rashid and I, convict and student, gangster and poet, resident host and visiting performer. He gave me something I never had: romance. No-one, and I am not exaggerating, no-one has ever treated me like a woman who ought to be handled with care."

Other women like Asha Bandele believe they have fallen in love with an inmate because "he helps me live from the inside out." One Hades' Angel comments, "He encourages me to be all I can be," and in return, she believes she sees the part of him the world doesn't see: the man's true inner soul. These women set aside their own comforts, "open their ear to the great below" and descend into the depths of Hades, prison, to nurture a prisoner because as they say, "he fills me up emotionally." To those Hades' Angels aware of an empty, dark, isolated, lonely place within themselves, these visits feel like remedies. They get caught up in the man's prison experience, issues, and sometimes the chaos of his prison life. The woman may question her choice of partner, yet may remain unaware, unconscious, of what lies beneath her unusual love choice.

Historically, Hades' Angels are caretakers and nurturers who learned in childhood that their own needs were unimportant. Early on, they internalized messages about the self: "You are never good enough; you are never smart enough; you never do it right." They also internalized destructive family beliefs that kept them anchored in destructive relationships: "Women are worthless"; "women are nothing without a man"; and "women exist only to take care of men." Women who believe these deeply ingrained messages as true, think they are not good enough or not entitled to receive love, which leads women to accept crumbs, so they suffer their lot. Hades' Angel Michelle told me, "I was deceived by my first husband, and deceived by my second husband. Finally, I had to examine what I believed in."

What Hades' Angels Can Teach the Rest of Us

Destructive relationships figure prominently in a large segment of the general female population, inside and outside of prison where the hidden, unknown, or un-nurtured aspects of the self play a critical, though often invisible, role in one's choice of mate. Many women find themselves in relationships with the kind of men who probably ought to be behind bars, but aren't. In my clinical practice in Los Angeles, I treat many women who are involved in destructive relationships, silently imprisoned behind invisible glass walls: women whose full potential is locked away inside their inner emotional prison. They enter therapy hoping for enlightenment about the self, build healthier relationships, and be freed from their destructive life patterns. They want to change their lives.

Demon Lovers

There is some unseen subtle body, an intangible energy, felt in the dynamic between certain women and the type of man I call a demon lover (Woodman, 1982). It keeps these women stuck in toxic emotional environments. As a psychologist, my focus is on awareness and insight as an avenue towards emotional growth, wholeness, individuation and transformation. Similarly, for the Hades' Angels who seek love relationships inside an arena behind bars, narcissistic healing and transformation often occurs. Somehow these women transcend the limits imposed by their early childhood wounds and their previous abusive "demon lover" relationships and find comfort, even happiness, with their prison partner. How this happens may hold lessons for women among the general population who want to learn to change their relationship dynamics.

For example, Joyce, a patient on the outside, thought that marriage and financial self-sufficiency would be her escape route from the negativity, put-downs, and physical abuse of her family. That premise proved faulty. Not long after marriage, her husband's affairs first gave her an embarrassing disease then his physical abuse brought on an emergency abortion. To her demon lover husband this seemed the perfect opportunity to run away with his girlfriend. Joyce was abandoned, discarded, alone, and left to pay the hospital bill.

Lucy, also a patient on the outside, was married to an alcoholic who simply refused to leave. Lucy spent her days caring for their two young daughters and worked nights at the hospital to pay the bills. Meanwhile, her husband languished in bed until noon or hung out at the neighborhood bar where he explained to anyone who listened how to get a woman to support her man. Linda, yet another patient in the general population, worked full-time and turned over her paychecks to a spouse who never tired telling her how inept she was handling money. Unbeknownst to her, while she was working, he was molesting their children, and he threatened to kill their mother if they told her. When Linda discovered the truth, she reported him – and ended up losing custody of their children because the judge found her "neglectful" of their welfare. The husband got off with a warning. As you will read in another chapter, when Hades' Angel Lisa Heart came face to face with her husband's indiscretions, it was a really jolting experience.

Such chaotic, toxic, and traumatic events in the lives of these and other women often stem from historical patterns of control, dominance and emotional submission, and family belief systems leading to learned helplessness that devours the soul. These negative messages have a trickle-down multigenerational effect. Women caught in these traps know exactly what I'm talking about. Believing they cannot survive without their husband's economic support, some women perpetuate this dynamic by choosing financial security over emotional freedom. Others continue unconsciously in patterns of emotional and verbal abuse because it is familiar; not all that different from what they knew at home growing up. "It becomes a real comfortable shoe," says Hades' Angel PJ. Such women are painfully aware of their quick willingness to sacrifice their fragile sense of self, allowing themselves to get eaten up alive in order to be loved.

Like a virus, family emotional injuries, lack of love and affection, faulty boundaries, or an inappropriate sense of entitlement can pervade and infect the family system. When the most primary relationship, the family, is dysfunctional it casts dark, ubiquitous shadows over one's entire life. In families where mothers model how to lie down and play dead, their daughters need no formal training to teach them that women are worthless. The impact of these messages get played out in one relationship after another, including relationships with the inmate spouse until a healing energy motivates change.

Women who get drawn into destructive "demon lover" relationships describe being sucked in by some unseen energy or magnetic force. That draw makes them feel special and wanted; they get hooked. However, what they don't know is that they are being singled out by the kind of man who sees a healthy filly; harnesses her energy, her strength, and even her finances for his own purposes; then uses, abuses, and drops her.

It is no surprise that these are just the kind of women who can end up as Hades' Angels, unconsciously drawn by unseen internal ties they don't understand to connect with men doing serious life time. Some early narcissistic wound fates them to bind themselves to a prison relationship that society assumes hopelessly pathological, even stigmatizing. Therefore, it is a huge surprise when many Hades' Angels end up having a "corrective emotional experience" with partners living inside prison walls. Here, the outer reality becomes a "holding environment" (Winnicott, 1958), "a stage prop to the inner world of Spirit" (Lozoff, 1985). Perhaps on some unconscious level they knew exactly what they were doing.

Shamed for Wanting

When love is a mysterious quantity, dreamed of but never felt, it breeds a longing for it. The child left hungry for love, yet shamed for wanting it, survives by denying that very neediness. Denying that desire exists is a survival tool that protects the fragile part of the self, as is walling it all off and withdrawing from the hurt and the anger for not getting it. When, if ever, do those invisible scars, those protective walls come down? When does giving love, all the while knowing it will never be reciprocated, become too heavy for the lonely heart to bear? When does one courageously declare it's time to turn the page, time to say, "Enough, stop!" when called crazy, put down, chastised or abused?

What will gently coax the wounded part of the self from hiding? What turns daily life crises into turning points?

As I learned from my twenty-six Hades' Angels, the unconscious can undergo a sobering jolt out of stuck, on behalf of change. There is no guarantee that this will happen, but it can happen. Hades' Angels begin their inner journey, which psychologist Carl Jung calls "the transformative journey," while "held" by an inmate who lives inside that mix of evil and safety: prison. When inside prison that is their lived, outer reality.

The Transformative Journey

The transformative journey is a common theme expressed through characters in movies, myths, and fairytales all over the world. It is an inward journey, a process, and in traveling that road we gain access to unknown parts of the self. Myths and stories are valuable metaphorical models that describe this internal process that pushes us forward, in quest of healing the early childhood narcissistic wound, and a search for meaning (Jung). Hades' Angels unconsciously begin their search for meaning through their prison relationship and in the process, confront their dark side, their shadow, their evil twin.

There, but for the grace of God, go I.

--- Hades' Angel Louise

Inanna's descent from the upper world, into the depths of the intuitive inner world may be understood as a metaphor for the transformative journey in the search for meaning. Ascension from this into-the-depths experience creates a "heaven quake". In modern language, when awareness of the cut off parts recognize and dialogue with one another, the splits can become integrated into a sense of wholeness.

In Hispanic cultures, it is said one is blessed when death sits down beside you because it teaches you to live from the inside out (Pincola Estes, 1992). As such, it is a transformative experience. In living with death, one values life; it becomes an opportunity leading to change. Hades' Angels experienced countless life crises where they were the only stable factor in an unstable environment. From their stories, you will discover that crisis, though covered by a facade of calm, perfectionism, achievement, and self-sufficiency, was their way of life. Through their inmate free-mate relationships, they, like Inanna, connected with the darker aspects of the self, and learned about living from the inside out

Transformation results from a deep, internal shift in our mind-set, changing our values, our priorities, and how we see ourselves. Transformation is far different than behavioral change that adapts and accommodates the external environment; it turns our world upside down. It catapults us into a position of centeredness about who we are. From this emotionally centered position, we question the meaning of our existence and challenge old belief systems that have kept us locked in destructive behavior patterns.

He helped me look at life in a whole new way.

--Hades' Angel Danielle

Hades' Angels sought ways to deepen their identity as they searched for meaning in their lives. After years of hiding their pain, and continued attempts to maintain the status quo, the facade, and even outward success, they finally decided to relinquish their surface identity, their mask. Their house of cards collapsed: they let go of their persona, who they thought they were; questioned their roles in the family; questioned the belief systems with which they were raised; questioned their relationships; questioned the direction their own lives had taken-- and found them wanting.

Turning points became opportunities for deep change. Hades' Angels forced themselves to see the self in the looking glass. Bravely, they began to break down old structures, old belief systems, and ways they identified with their "false self". They, current day Inannas, descended through underworld prison portals into the unknown, discarded their weighty persona, and suffered a "dark night of the soul".

Hades' Angels say that as the result of their prison relationships, they are experiencing meaning in their lives and are uncovering their own true potential. They believe they value themselves more now… that they are more now than they thought they possibly could be.

About Twenty-Six Hades' Angels: Search for Meaning

All of this came about because I, like Alice in Wonderland, was curious about and needed to understand the women I saw returning to the prison, week after week, and month after month to visit their inmate spouses. Because of a committed relationship with a man inside, they kept being drawn back into it – probably for life.

"Who in the world am I?" asks Alice in Wonderland. "Ah, that's the great puzzle," responds the white rabbit. Cautiously, Alice enters that hole and then views life from a different perspective. She undergoes numerous physical changes, a metaphor representing our attempts to alter and adapt to outer reality or the needs of others: she makes herself bigger or smaller; still, she can never quite fit in. Pressured by time and chaos, a silly, chattering, no-sense rabbit leads her through difficult and even threatening terrain. Along her journey, her yellow brick road, she meets many characters, understood metaphorically as the split-off aspects of herself: the cat, Queen of Hearts, the Duchess, the Mad Hatter, etc.

Curiosity was my white rabbit. Wanting to find out more about this great puzzle, like Alice, I peeked into a small hole in the wall, followed it down twisting paths, and entered into the unknown, from which I tried to understand Hades' Angels experience. It is not surprising that Alice gets lost because inside, her spirit is lost and she cannot find a way to live in her repressed outer reality. Hades' Angels understand that everything operates within that imprisoning outer reality. Until Alice learns to listen and value the guidance of her intuitive self, she remains lost. Suffering is a "state of mind" that spirals us downward and, like Alice, we must go it alone. Many a wounded modern-day Alice masks the self to fit someone else's mold, into a world that makes no sense or meaning.

> *To know what you prefer instead of humbly saying Amen to what the world tells you you ought to prefer, is to have kept your soul alive.*
>
> --- Robert Louis Stevenson

In selecting my twenty-six Hades' Angels (initially there were thirty, but four withdrew), I traveled all over the United States interviewing them in depth. This is when I first began referring to them as "Hades' Angels". I began to explore the question of what lies behind the decisions we each make about how to spend our life-time, and with whom. It is my belief that – at least in part – the past patterns can determine one's future, and bringing them to consciousness, understanding them and questioning the belief systems that keep us stuck, we can change the landscape of our future. When the true self is freed, unshackled from an invisible destructive inner prison, we can learn to live fully in the present moment.

The Hades' Angels range from ages 42 to 67. Each volunteered to be interviewed. All met their man, lifer or death row inmate, after his incarceration. As they so generously opened up to me, I helped them tell their story, including telling the world about their unusual relationships, without judging them. Last, it is important to say that I speak only for the women in my study, not for the men whom I met solely through the eyes of their women.

I listened to these women with all my senses. I felt each story, each unique experience within my soul. When I told them to make up names for themselves, many chose creative, whimsical, and often telling pseudonyms. For example, Dimples was chosen because as a child she was told to "smile at all costs." And indeed, those dimples masked a great deal of shame and pain that she carried around with her all her life.

The Numbers Keep Rising

According to the Sentencing Project, the United States is the world's leader in incarceration with 2.3 million people currently in this nation's prisons or jails -- a 500% increase over the past thirty years. U.S. prisons, jails grew by 1,000 Inmates a week from '04 to '05 (White, 2006). According to an earlier Justice Department report, 127,000 people, or one of every eleven offenders in state and federal prisons, is serving a life sentence. Just how many of these men "on the inside" have a woman in their lives they met after they entered prison is a difficult statistic to track down. But they are a remarkable group of women and this book is dedicated to them. Many chapters include their portraits and explore their experiences. Hades' Angels stories inform about dignity and of people going against the grain while searching for meaning in a place where that must be a rare quality.

Hades' Angels is divided into two parts. Part I, chapters 2-6, uses a story format to describe the women's historical and emotional common threads, their joys, their sorrows, and the dynamics of their relationships. Part II, chapters 7-13 breaks down the issues into the following:

Chapter 7, <u>Redemption Motifs in Myths and Fairytales</u> explores how themes of descent, suffering, and heroic journeys, embodied in myth, fairytales, and metaphors, are similar to Hades' Angels real-life journey of individuation.

Chapter 8, <u>Nine Ways Hades' Angels Met a Man in Prison</u> details ways Hades' Angels get involved with their inmates in the first place (none knew the inmate prior to his incarceration). I discuss the Internet, personal ads, mutual friends, newspaper ads, church groups, college courses, etc. Portraits of Hades' Angels Ann and Maria are included.

Chapter 9, <u>A Visitor in Hades</u> describes what visiting a prison is like: the visiting room experience, the rules and regulations; the frustrations; the "stigma by association"; a prison wedding; and a portrait of Hades' Angel Cretia. I discuss briefly the prison crisis and the emotional environment so you will have an understanding of what these women are exposed to. I explore some intriguing questions, among them: How are these relationships maintained? What about sex? How do friends and families feel about these unique relationships? What are the payoffs, if any?

Chapter 10, <u>The Anatomy of the Hades' Angel</u> explores seven common threads that link Hades' Angels together, along with the theoretical and psychological concepts that explain these unique attractions, and a portrait of Hades' Angel Dimples.

Chapter 11, <u>Turning Points and Transformations</u> explores inner change and transformation, the true self unmasked, and how one's identity, goals, and life purpose get re-evaluated. This chapter discusses the crises, events, and insights that encouraged Hades' Angels to redefine their relationship with the self and others. A portrait of Hades' Angel Michele and Betty Jo are included.

Chapter 12, <u>The Future for Hades' Angels</u> describes how Hades' Angels use their new found sense of self on multiple levels – in their personal lives, in relationships with others, and in relationship with the world, such as prison advocacy and prison reform, and in helping others. A portrait of Hades' Angel Sabrina is included. It also addresses a proactive approach that links the issues and the outcomes of this work to the general population.

Chapter 13, <u>Help and Self-Help</u> provides resource links and self-help exercises to increase awareness of past and present relationship patterns and move forward. Readers may explore such topics as, 1) Identifying the invisible wounds, family roles and belief systems that bind and blind you; 2) Learning what gives you your sense of identity; 3) Identifying your "shadow side"; and, 4) Determining your relationship goals.

The Epilogue states my hope about the impact of Hades' Angels Transformative Journey for women in the general population who are in destructive relationships with men who are not incarcerated.

The Big Questions

Back to the big questions: Why would a woman take up with a man when there's little or no chance of a "normal relationship," or a happy future, either inside or outside of prison? What draws women into these relationships in the first place, and what maintains them? What contributing historical, emotional, and psychological factors do these women share? What internal and external events drive them towards embracing such a difficult relationship and descend into Hades to spend their life-time with a man already doing life time?

This book sheds light on these atypical relationships, and examines the physical, psychological, and emotional factors involved. It hopes to awaken the general population to the existence and worth of this unique population of wives and girlfriends who enter these committed relationships. These women do for others – and they do it freely. In the environment of a prison visiting room, or in visits separated by a glass window, connected by telephone receivers, or in letters of correspondence, certain women experience a "corrective emotional experience" (Alexander, 1961): a transformative experience. What is the catalyst for their transformation? Could it be the transformative energy of love? Are there universal lessons for women on the outside who have similar kinds of wounding?

The Healing Power of Love

Sounded from church and political podiums is an often talked-about, even cost-effective but underutilized resource that can create change: the healing power of love. It is built upon the most basic tenets of our Judeo-Christian thinking, and is freely given by church groups and -- in this case by Hades' Angels. Now let's take a look at the common wound.

Hades' Angels

Chapter Two

In the Beginning: Eve's Tale
The Common Wound

A man and a woman sit at a barren table speaking intimately, gazing into each other's eyes. His are blue-green, keenly intelligent, hers are brown, almond-shaped, exotic, revealing her Lebanese ancestry. "My angel," he calls her.

It is Saturday, the day Eve and Dean wait for all week, their special time to be together. Although they are not quite alone, they are used to the noise, to the presence of others around them, couples, noisy families at similar table talking and arguing, playing cards or board games. They are used to the sounds of the metal gates clanging open and shut, the sudden blaring announcements over the loudspeaker. Above them are video cameras. Stationed around the room on raised platforms sit the prison guards. After nearly six years Eve and Dean have even grown accustomed to the abrupt appearance of a guard at their table shouting commands. *No touching. Hands on the table where they can be seen.* They often forget, reaching out to touch the other's hand, or face.

For a few precious hours each week Eve and Dean are completely devoted to being together in the kind of intimacy that most couples would envy. In spite of all the distractions they are attentive only to each other, fully absorbed, speaking and listening, nothing held back. For nearly six years this table is the closest thing to privacy that Eve and Dean have known. It is their marriage bed, their family room couch, their kitchen table, the space that they make in the crowded prison visiting room, where somehow they have been able to develop and sustain their love. How have they managed this level of connection in a relationship without sex, without a home, in the confines of a maximum-security prison?

At first glance we could say that these two don't fit the stereotype most people hold of inmates and the women who choose to love them. Dean is a man of presence, an artist as well as mentor to many of the younger prisoners; he is respected inside the prison, even by the guards. And he is respected outside as well. Recently, one of his paintings was shown in a gallery in Boston. In another city, his work has earned him a prize as emerging artist of the year. For five years Dean has been teaching classes in emotional awareness to other inmates using the acclaimed prison program Houses of Healing developed by Robin Casarjian (1995). Dean's classes have become so successful that psychologists from the outside have come to the prison to observe them firsthand.

Eve, an attractive, passionate woman in her late forties with a pretty face and a forthright demeanor, is a registered nurse. Married briefly when she was in her twenties, she is the mother of one grown son. Eve is self-supporting, self sufficient, a devoted member of her church. "No one gets it," Eve says of her relationship with Dean, not her family, not her friends. Even the guards have occasionally asked why she doesn't have a man "outside." Dean has already served twelve years of a life sentence handed down after three separate robbery convictions--unarmed robbery. His finger and a menacing rage were the only weapons he used. Even with his good works his chances for parole are slim.

And though Eve still struggles with the restrictions of an inmate/freemate relationship and speaks of a time when she had an affair with a man outside, she believes that after the kind of love she has shared with Dean she can never settle for less. She tells me that Dean says their connection is deeper than any sex he has ever known.

What they have is intimacy. A kind of emotional intimacy that, as a psychologist who deals with relationship issues, I know is precious and hard won among partners. It is the elusive something we all hunger for, an emotional closeness that is a challenge for all of us, including long-married couples. Eve and Dean have never made love. They see each other only six hours a week and in public, one kiss at the beginning of a visit and another at the end.

Eve was not looking for a relationship with an inmate, she says. Eve believes she was "given" Dean. Like many of the women you will read about in this book, Eve first got to know Dean through corresponding with him. But before she even learned of him, she had been sitting in weekly meditation with her church group, and over and over what kept coming to mind were her fears. The criminal mind was chief among them. She could not fathom it. And so, silently, each time Eve meditated she asked for help to understand it.

Several weeks later her pastor posed a question to the group: what would they do if they knew Jesus were about to appear on earth? "Go into prisons", Eve responded immediately, "Go into the prisons and teach them what we are learning about acceptance and love." After the discussion a Board member approached her. "Funny you should speak about prisons because we received a letter from an inmate this week." The writer had selected their church because it was the only one listed that advertised meditation and he was already a practitioner. "I think this letter is for you," the Board member said and handed it to Eve. As soon as she read it she was struck by the inmate's intelligence. "This is marvelous," Eve thought. "Whoever he is, he is a really smart man." And so she wrote back, mindful that she had in some sense asked for this, asked to understand the criminal mind. And so their connection began.

Correspondence is a way many of the Hades' Angels first come into contact with their inmate love. But opening oneself up by putting thoughts and feelings and ideas to paper can lead to the possibility of a woman being seduced, used, and manipulated by a seductive, socially-appealing but false image. It is easy to be hooked by a smooth line and not know it, especially if the woman is emotionally vulnerable and "under-nourished". When the writer Joyce Maynard was in the midst of a divorce, shaky and lonely, desperate for connection, she answered a letter from an inmate who was an admirer of her newspaper columns.

His letters were persuasive, full of respect and affection. She began to write back and ultimately a relationship was born. The man was able to convince Maynard that he was deeply concerned for her welfare and for the welfare of her children. He was a skilled seducer. "I know you like I know my blood," he wrote at one point. Only after he began to make plans to visit her did Maynard grow alarmed, call the prison and discover the truth about the man she had opened-up to through letters. He was serving two consecutive eighty-year sentences for the savage murder of his parents.

This kind of manipulation happens even to women who are intelligent and sophisticated. A woman who lives from the upper world -- the head -- split off from her emotions may find herself especially vulnerable. Correspondence can feel like it touches the soul. It can become the container that holds the undernourished parts of the woman's self, her vulnerable feelings. Once "hooked", women like Joyce Maynard feel they are free to reveal these feelings to the man who is writing to her so persuasively, a man she believes "knows" her.

Eve was also a woman who had lived her life largely out of touch with her own feelings, one who experienced life from the upper world of her mind, but what she received in response to her letter to Dean was not layers of scam. Nor was it simply "the criminal mind," which she had "asked" in meditation to understand. What came to her in Dean's letters was a man who was as open and eager to learn about her, as he was to share himself. Dean was driven by the genuine need for connection, and though Eve did not yet know it, so was she.

From the very beginning, through her correspondence with Dean, Eve began to tap into her inner world, a world that was openly received and then reciprocated. This was a new way of relating for Eve. All her life Eve had been a do-er, used to giving to and doing for others, not exploring and sharing her private self. In psychological terms we call this being split off from her own feelings and needs. In her relationships as well as within herself, Eve paid a high price for not knowing her true self.

Eve had been married briefly in her twenties to a man who was intellectually gifted and angry, an alcoholic, unable to be a good father or husband, who exploded in violent rages, gradually becoming more and more alienated from life. Eve admits that she too was an angry young woman but learned to control her anger. The marriage ended after only three years, leaving her to raise her son alone.

Eve had other disappointing relationships. In all of them she felt unmet, unrecognized. Even her beauty, Eve felt, was not received in her culture. She was not a demure southern girl, but dark, vibrant, direct. The men in her life accepted her—they did not know her. She was hungry to be known and appreciated--to be loved by a man who could see who she was.

Instead, Eve repeatedly found herself serving the needs of her lover, hardly aware of her own. By profession Eve was a registered nurse. Her work consisted of healing and helping others. By the time she came to know Dean, Eve had nursed three of the older people in her family, including an aunt and her mother in the years before they died. And Eve had been a single parent.

Like her mother and like the women in her culture, Eve's way of loving was to serve, to be of help—to ignore her own needs and feelings. Rarely did she express them. Rarely did she expose her vulnerable core. And when, through writing to Dean, she first got a taste of this kind of open sharing and receiving it struck an immediate chord deep within her. Weeks before she had even set eyes on Dean, Eve was already experiencing a heart-to-heart connection with another and coming to experience a part of herself she had not known before-- her feeling self.

In addition, Dean was an artist and a deep thinker, exactly the kind of man she had always been drawn to. How could this be, Eve wondered? A man who was in prison for life who seemed to possess the very qualities she had been seeking? She felt compelled to continue the relationship. She wanted to know this man. But before she went on her first prison visit, Eve had sought out and read the transcripts of Dean's trials. "I really didn't take any of this lightly," she explains, "I called. I got a copy of his trial transcripts. I wanted to make sure he was someone who had not lied to me about why he was in jail." She learned Dean had told her the truth. Sixteen convictions for robbery. No weapons found. And so she agreed to go on her first prison visit, eager to see this man with whom she seemed to have such a connection, wondering what she would feel once she went into the prison and was face to face with him.

But from the moment they met, Eve says, there was a powerful draw. She was "hooked". Even the ordeal of entering the prison, the waiting, the humiliating searches, the tense atmosphere were not enough to deter her. She was thrilled by Dean, the man!

The question of what draws us to those we come to love is such an intriguing one for us all. It is the perennial subject of the great operas and literature. All cultures have been fascinated by it. What attracts us to someone? Why is the pull so incredibly strong? Overpowering? What is it that makes us fall in love with one person and not another?

In my private practice I see many women who are wrestling with this issue in their lives. Successful women, bright, independent, self-supporting, who either lose themselves in relationship, or find themselves drawn to men who disappoint or use them, who hurt them or drain them dry.

As therapists we understand the mystery of attraction lies buried in an individual's past. For it is in childhood within our original families (what psychologists call the family of origin) where we learn the emotional lessons that will determine who we are attracted to and how we will love. Even though the partners we later come to choose may hurt us or cause us great suffering, there is a powerful unconscious draw that pulls us to them. We have something deep and important in common with these partners. It is this mysterious something that causes us to unconsciously form a perfect psychological fit. What we share is something that is often difficult for most people to understand. It is powerful and often hidden. It is something we carry from childhood--an unseen, unconscious wound.

And, as I would discover, it was the unseen childhood wound in Eve that would explain why she--an attractive, respected member of the community--could form a perfect psychological fit with a man in a maximum-security prison who was serving a life sentence after numerous robbery convictions.

Eve grew up in the South in a big, extended Lebanese- American family with a father who was very passionate, intellectual, and artistic, and a mother who was quiet, practical, and withdrawn. Her brother was nine years older and according to Eve he lived almost in a separate world. Eve describes her home as one in which there was not much conversation but a great deal of fighting. Her parents were people who understood reality so differently, she explains. Her father worked hard all his life but earned little money. Her mother followed the tradition of her culture, where the woman served, but Eve's mother was also in business with a brother and sister and was quite successful, earning more money than her husband. "Your mother should have married a rich man," Eve's father would tell her. Early on and all through her childhood Eve was her father's confidante, the one to whom he would regularly pour out his heart.

"In the eyes of my mother's family, my father was not good enough," Eve explains, "but I could see what my father was. He was artistic, intellectual; he loved people. He was passionate. He told stories. He cried. He sang and made music. He poured himself out to people and that was his outlet. He spent lots of time in the Lebanese community where we lived. And my father drank. He was an alcoholic. I can't tell what my brother or my mother knew about my father. I knew my father felt trapped. I was the one closest to him. I was Daddy's little girl."

Eve's earliest memory is of waking up and having her father hold her close and sing to her. Their connection was always very deep. "It was a connection of the soul," she says now; "I felt completely safe and completely accepted by him."

On the day that we spoke of her father Eve explained that she keeps in her car a cassette from her childhood of the two of them singing together. They sing the old southern folk songs her father learned as a little boy. When she tells me this she is moved to tears. Her father is no longer alive. She cherishes every memory. Their connection is still powerful for her. And though she speaks of her mother lovingly she admits her mother was not able to be close to her in the way that her father was. Her mother was busy, she was working, or she was caring for the house, cooking the food. There was little conversation between Eve and her mother, certainly not intimate conversation, not the kind that Eve had with her father.

What she received from her mother, Eve says, were the qualities of patience and loyalty and long suffering "in the very best sense of the word. My mother never got to assert herself and her ideas. People were always walking all over her because she was trained to serve. It was part of her culture."

It wasn't until later, when Eve began to talk about "her prisoner" Dean and the way he responded to violence inside the prison, that Eve revealed to me an aspect of her family life that she had quickly glossed over when speaking of her childhood. In her home she, too, had been exposed to violence. It was difficult for her to acknowledge. "What kind of violence?" I ask. There was always fighting in her house, Eve explains. Her parents' arguments were loud and frequent, the atmosphere in her home charged with tension. At any moment a battle between her parents might erupt. The shouting was terrible, unrelenting. Her brother left home at eighteen, leaving Eve, at nine, alone with it. He did not return for years.

A child who is exposed to this kind of constant arguing between her parents experiences an emotional trauma. The effect does not wash away but stays within. The fear of what will happen next. The fear that she will be abandoned, or that the violence will be turned against her.

The child witnesses her parents' pain and grows up "swallowing it" as if it is her own.

Eve mentions this aspect of her family life with reluctance. She loves her parents and appreciates their good qualities, which are many. She is especially concerned about her father's pain. The pain he felt because he was an outsider, a creative man who did not get the chance to express himself fully in his life. She does not focus on, or even mention, her own pain. Eve is reluctant to say any more about the chaos she experienced in her home, the anger and pain it had caused her, the guilt and the shame she must have carried. She does not talk about what it felt like to be a little girl who was so absorbed in the pain and the needs of her father that she has nearly forgotten herself.

But when a child has to hide a part of herself to meet the emotional needs of a parent, it causes a deep psychological wound. She builds invisible walls, closes down to protect the self, shuts down her feelings, discounting them even to herself. The helpless child then creates a mask to hide behind. She learns to keep quiet about her own needs and often finds a way to belong -- to adapt -- by becoming indispensable to the family. To belong, the child creates or takes on a caretaker/nurturer role. In Eve's case, she became emotional caretaker of her father. From this role, emerges an overly self-sufficient false self. This competent false self acts as caretaker and protector not only of her parent, but in so doing, care-takes the wounded part of herself. The anger and pain she feels are locked away. She grows up out of touch with key parts of herself that are necessary for a healthy relationship. She will not be a woman who is free to express her needs. What she learned from caretaking her father was to meet the needs of another.

A child who has been wounded in this way is left emotionally un-nurtured. She becomes the woman who is unaware of her feelings, the kind who will offer nurturing to others but will not expect it back. She will not know how to nurture herself. Eve coped with her childhood wound by burying her angry feelings. She pushed them down — repressed them. This is how many women who are wounded in childhood cope with their angry feelings. And a woman who is wounded and acts-in provides a perfect psychological fit for the man who has also been wounded in childhood but has reacted to his wound by acting-out. This buried pain recognizes itself in the mirror of the other. Differently expressed, it is often the unseen draw that forms their common wound.

When a woman is drawn to so-called bad boys, or to men who act out in rage or who commit acts involving uncontrolled aggression, it is likely the unseen common wound that is the cause of the attraction. On the surface the man may appear to be her polar opposite -- he is "bad" and she is "good," but in the world of the emotions, the two are psychologically mated. She has an unacknowledged, internalized sense of shame about things that don't show in the external world. She hasn't done anything "wrong", but having been raised with her own natural instinctual emotional needs denied she grows up feeling different in herself. She feels something is missing. Deep within she carries the critical sense that "I am not okay." This forms her part of the common wound that binds her to her lover, her angry man, her prison inmate. He acts-out in response to his wound. She acts-in.

To change the pattern of her attraction and "learn" to choose a different kind of man, a man who will be a healthy partner, a woman must become aware of her wound, learn to recognize her needs, and unearth her old childhood pain. She must go into shadowy territory. Until she does this she will be drawn to the same kind of man and the same kind of relationship pattern, one in which the hurts she suffered in childhood will be unconsciously repeated and acted out in her adult relationships. Until she can define and accept her needs she will continue to choose a man who will not meet them. She will find herself caught in the pattern of serving the needs of others.

This kind of healing requires her to go deeply into herself, to the parts she may have forgotten or "disowned" long ago and reclaim them. Facing her buried anger and hurt, her fears of being abandoned, is a journey which demands a great deal of courage. And it is this journey which Eve unknowingly found herself on once she went into the prison to meet Dean face to face.

From the beginning Eve saw that there was substance in Dean, and that was something, which in her words "is hard to find. Period. And because there was substance in an extremely difficult situation, and he also showed amazing inner strength and discipline --- and produces, I was excited."

Eve was pleasantly seduced by Dean in the most fascinating way — the artistic, the intellectual. And by his eyes, blue-green, riveting. By his stillness and presence. Very quickly, as their relationship developed, she began taking his art work around and showing it in galleries in their city. And Dean started using her as his subject. She encouraged him to go from a realistic style to the more expressive so he could get his feelings out. A woman whose beauty had not been "received" by the men in her culture had now become the model of an artist. Dean quit smoking out of gratitude to God for Eve's presence in his life. Through her he was known, he was valued. He was affirmed. He blossomed.

Riding in on her high horse to fix a wounded man as so many women who are wounded in this way often do, Eve not only encouraged Dean's work and took it into the world, but from the time she was with him, Eve also helped Dean to understand the idea of service. Dean became a mentor in emotional healing; teaching the prison classes in emotional awareness that would help many other inmates and which would, in a period of five years, bring him so much attention and respect. And too, Dean began writing. A story of his was later published in a collection of prison writings.

Eve revealed to me that this is not the first time she has done this with a man she was involved with. Years before she had also given this kind of creative support to another man with whom she had had an extended relationship. "If only they could have gotten it when they were younger," she reflects. "And what if Eve could have gotten all this when she was younger," I wonder. And then I think of her father: artistic, intellectual, a man who felt trapped by his life. "And you know,"

Eve says, "In a way, I reclaimed my daddy all over again. I am giving Dean the support my daddy never had."

"Give him the support, he gives others support. Give him the idea of a prison ministry, and he runs with it," she says. This is a wonderful satisfaction for Eve who believes in the idea of service. It is her creed. It is also her emotional style. Give to others. Help others fulfill their needs.

I ask Eve how she feels about doing so much to encourage Dean. After all, she has a full-time nursing job. "I am giving out, giving out, giving out. Well that's where this affair came in." And then she describes the affair she has had while she was "with" Dean. Eve is a passionate woman. She does not want to be celibate. Dean understood, she explains. He accepted her need. He assures her he will be released from prison. She believes in him. The laws have changed. He did not use a weapon. He has supporters who are helping him. Eve, too has hired lawyers to help argue for his release.

The relationship with "the man outside" occurred after Eve had experienced five deaths in her family. "Three of them I took care of; one of them was my mother. I had had it. I needed a break."

"Understand," she says, "I'm putting out, you know. Not that I resent anything that I have given to Dean, because he takes it and he does wonderful things with it. The truth is I can give more than what I get. And I have to generate most of my inspiration myself."

This is the do-er Eve. The wounded child who earns love by being indispensable, who takes care of the pain and the needs of others. Who *reclaimed her Daddy* all over again by helping Dean, an artist and an inmate, bringing his art into the world.

Eve took a trip with the man outside. He was newly divorced. He was nothing like Dean, not artistic, not intellectual, but she was "tapped out" and he was kind-- and there. Eventually he decided he wanted to see other women. He had been married for twenty years. He did not want to commit.

Dean "waited" through this affair. Eve did not stop coming to the prison. Their relationship continued. Eve was calling the shots. They stayed present to each other through it. The relationship grew.

What does Eve get from this relationship, I wonder? Eve tells me that in Dean she sees a man who has gotten used to abuse and who is desperate for affection. A man who "has been dealing with superficialities and who has a lot more potential than that; who wants to go deeper. I see a man who casually, guiltlessly hurts people, including me, but never intends to. And he really wants to learn."

"So he has been hurt?" I ask, noting once again that she does not speak of herself. That she seems to have begged the question of how Dean nurtures her. She nods. It is sometimes difficult to discern whose pain Eve is talking about, Dean's or her own. I feel an abiding sorrow within her. When I ask Eve if she connects with that part of Dean she responds, "Of course. Always. I have always connected with the wounds of a child."

We sit in silence for a moment then Eve looks at me, "What he gives me is emotional support. I think it's big." Another pause before she continues, "His sorrow is deep. It comes from being exposed regularly to violence and ignorance and fear and having to center himself to face those things fearlessly with courage and love and kindness."

She explains how Dean can be the most still of any other person she has known. Eve too has faced insanity and had to be still, "at least twice." With her husband, and in her childhood home where she first experienced the anger and the emotional violence she does not like to speak of.

"I think that we touch deeply-soul. If there is a problem in this world it is that we can't be still, and that we are controlled by our fears." Both she and Dean, Eve explains, see it as a goal to be able to face violence and anger in another and be still. Be untouched. Not be afraid. "Both of us are extremely weary of being afraid. Just tired of it."

I imagine the conversations Eve and Dean must have had in the nearly six years they have been together. I think of how Eve must have spoken to Dean of the hurt that she experienced as a child. How he would be still, taking it in, knowing full well what she meant.

"What have you been afraid of?" I ask. "Well, when one sees as a child anger and frustration and violence, hears violence in those who have authority over them, it's very fearful."

With me she is still careful, still tentative to uncover the wound. When *one sees as a child, she says, not when I was a child.* As open as Eve is about some aspects of her life, the affair she has had, the husband who suffered a breakdown, her tears for her father, the way her mother was "walked on", how she is used to "giving out and giving out" until she is empty. Eve does not like to talk about what she experienced as a child, the pain of it, the hidden wound that does not heal.

I ask if there is something about the underlying tension in the prison that feels familiar. She admits that it is not unlike the atmosphere she knew in her family's home: the threat of violence, the emotionally charged atmosphere. This is something I will hear over and over again from the women I speak to. For the Hades' Angels, the atmosphere in the prison is familiar. It reminds them of home.

So many of the clients I see in my private practice come to me because in the face of emotional tension and anxiety they lose their sense of self, and they give in. They become once again the submissive child. How they grow past it is something I will come to respect. "I'm trapped. I feel sadness at the inhuman environment," Eve says of the prison. *"It's like a step backward into your childhood. It's no control."*

But in the midst of this, Eve marvels, shifting the subject, Dean has learned to be centered. Eve admires him for it. It gives her courage, she says, courage to do the same.

Over the years Dean has told her stories about times when he has had to take a stand against violence, when he was attacked in the prison. "And I understand full well how he was able to rob banks with his finger. There was not a weapon ever found because this man's mind is dangerous. It's so powerful. And you know, a powerful mind will scare someone with a weak mind."

But Dean has not been able to use his focused mind on the outside. Only in prison has he been able to write, paint, teach, and meditate. If he is released will he be able to focus his mind constructively? If he and Eve live together as husband and wife, will they be able to maintain the emotional connection that sustains them in the prison relationship?

Many studies reveal that the vast majority of men who are incarcerated had childhoods marked by continuous violence. Eve tells me Dean has revealed that his father was abusive and an alcoholic; his mother, also an alcoholic, kept him away from his father as much as she could. Dean was close to her, "he was his mother's boy." For five years Dean has been writing his life story. He has written about his mother's pain.

The anger and violence a child experiences does not disappear over time. It stays within. It waits to be healed, or it festers. Some people act out in response in anger and rage, like Dean. Others, like Eve, make themselves indispensable, serving others, tending to their needs, denying their own feelings, acting in.

What Heals Eve's Wound?

Like many of the Hades' Angels I came to know, Eve recognizes Dean's wounds, his pain, his need for nurturing and support, but she does not recognize her own. In some ways her needs are the same as Dean's: to have her pain mirrored, to be listened to deeply, to be heard.

"It is very old world," she says of the way they relate, "Many hours of talking. Just talking." There is a comfort in that. The sound of the voice talking to you, the sounds which hold you softly, like a song.

Most of the Hades' Angels I speak to will tell me that when they met their man inside they had the sense of meeting their soul mate. Often, when a couple is drawn together by a common wound that is just what it feels like. But to heal the wound it is not enough simply to meet the soul mate, both must be heard, both must be listened to deeply, free to expose their vulnerability and to express their pain without fear that it will later be turned against you. This is what will set the stage for internal change.

Eve feels heard, listened to with empathy by Dean. That is the gift that the prison relationship offers to her, and to others outside prison, who are open to it. Without the distractions of life "on the outside", with only the bare table as their meeting space, without the seductions of sex, the only real connection Eve and Dean can have is through talking and listening and presence, through the very things we all crave in relationship. And it is the thing Eve has most needed.

"Dean knows how to love women," Eve says, "It's such a relief you have no idea. It's such a relief to know that there exists a male counterpart to which I can be feminine. To which I can be vulnerable."

Something has happened with Eve because of this relationship. She had been a caretaker for all the people in her family, meeting her father's emotional needs when she was a child. The men in her life have been variations of her father. Dean is the first man who would simply be still and listen to her speak from her truest self, one with whom she could finally let down her guard and allow the vulnerable parts of herself to be seen.

The restrictions of the prison relationship allow Eve to deal with the tension and anxiety that letting her emotional guard down arouses. Could she bear this tension "on the outside"-- without these limitations?

The love between Even and Dean seems to have had an impact even on the intractable prison establishment. "I get away with stuff now because inside I am always laughing at the guards. We steal little kisses and we do this and that, and now when they come our way and say, "Hands on the table!" we don't even take it personally anymore. It used to be a big deal. Most of the guards know Dean on the inside and know what kind of man he is. They know what kind of responsibility he has had. And many, many guards have said, "I just wish I could let you all go into that room and go at it."

But Eve is a very passionate woman. She has been forced into a situation, or has put herself into a situation, where the physical passion has had to be on hold. Though she is aware that this is the very condition that has enabled their relationship to develop in other ways, Eve is not one to ignore her passions. When she met "the man outside," Dean was afraid of what would happen between them. He said, "I am going to be right in the middle of it." And Eve responded, "This is going to be about me, not you."

Now that relationship is over. And through it, Eve still continued to love Dean. She was not going to be stopped from seeing him. She wants a full relationship, she declares. She does not know what will happen if Dean spends the rest of his life in prison.

"The few hours I get to be in his physical presence each month are still magic for both of us. And the two kisses we are allowed get sweeter by the years. My imagination makes up for a lot, but I would rather imagine making love to the blue-green eyes of the strong man that loves me, than to have intercourse with a man whose eyes hardly see me."

Chapter Three

Early Childhood Narcissistic Injury

Hades' Angel Callie, a legal secretary in her late forties, is a petite blonde with a kind expression and round blue eyes. Gentle and feminine, Callie has a softness about her that is comforting-a woman who would not hurt a living soul. For twelve years she has been married to Melvin, a former Black Panther serving seven years to life for murder in a maximum-security prison. Melvin has been incarcerated thirty years.

Callie had correspondences with imprisoned men before she "found" Melvin—the man she refers to as "God's gift to me." But it all began "on a lark" when Callie went with a friend on the long drive to visit her friend's inmate boyfriend. Callie remained in the car all day—in beastly hot weather. "Next time, I'll get you someone to spend the day with, so you don't have to be out in the heat," said the friend. "Why would I want to go in there and spend time talking to a prisoner?" Callie asked. "You'd be surprised," said her friend. "There are some interesting men on the inside. I think you'd like it."

Callie was an outwardly free-spirited, adventurous woman, mourning the death of Andrew, an ex-boxer she had lived with and supported financially for eighteen tempestuous years. Andrew, a black man, was an alcoholic. The last year of his life he became sober and then died of cancer. Callie was heartbroken, but clear. She would never again be with an alcoholic, a man who could never stay present long enough to "see" her or recognize her needs.

Born into a conservative family, Callie was the good girl who had become the family rebel. "If you knew my whole family, you'd say, 'Where did she come from?'" She first rebelled against the "family rules" by dating black men - long before it was, in her words "the thing to do." But a relationship with a prison inmate was something even free-thinking Callie had never considered.

It took correspondence and meetings with several different inmates before Callie found Melvin. After one conversation she knew he was the one. And three weeks after their first meeting, Melvin asked Callie to marry him. She said yes.

"I know it sounds hard to understand. But I just knew from the start it was right. And on the day that Melvin proposed I was asking for guidance, listening to the radio on the long drive back from prison, and thinking of Andrew, asking him, actually, what he thought I should do. On came this song, 'Please Release Me.' I took it as a sign. I had never married Andrew because I never felt the kind of connection that I felt from the moment I met Melvin. It was a soul-connection, and so after just three weeks of knowing him, even with the chance he would never be paroled, when he asked me to marry him, I said yes."

Melvin had had many relationships with women while he was in prison, but they had all been tempestuous, marked by arguments and charges of manipulation. And his first wife, the mother of his children, had divorced him while he was in prison but kept close ties to him. She was later killed. Callie was different from any woman Melvin had known. She was generous and open. She was not a game-player. He liked that a lot. Melvin, Callie says, was a good listener. He listened to her deeply. He was interested in every detail of her life. With Melvin, Callie felt treated with compassion and respect.

Women visitors, entering into the depths of the prison, bring the outside, inside, and thus are generally treated with respect. Into the cold, harsh, all-male environment these women bring a sense of connection, softness, and a glimpse of the feminine, which is prized. Melvin let Callie know how much he appreciated her. Hungry for affirmation and acknowledgment, she responded; it was what she had longed for all of her life - to be listened to deeply and seen.

Although Callie's childhood would appear to have been stable, something was deeply amiss. Her father worked three jobs to support his family: as a teacher at an army base, tutoring after dinner, and a third job doing labor on weekends; and Callie's mother, "a really strong lady," stayed at home and cared for the children and everything else in the household. Her father was rarely there. "I don't remember my dad ever hugging or kissing me," Callie says, "He teased me verbally, but he just didn't know how to show his affection. I think once we got past the baby stage, he didn't know how to relate to us. He was usually at home an hour a day. The rest of the time he was working; we hardly saw him."

Callie and her two brothers saw their mother as the source of love and security, but from earliest memory Callie never felt safe. If she ever expressed an emotion her mother immediately shut her down. "I guess," Callie says, speaking of herself in the second person and with obvious difficulty, "you really did take care of yourself."

"You're higher than a kite today," her mother would say whenever Callie expressed her feelings. "It could set your teeth on edge," Callie says. "She said it to me to the day she died." Everything had to remain on an even keel. Emotional expression was forbidden in the household, and Callie was always expected to be proper and good. Callie learned to go inside herself for safety and comfort. "I could get really angry and carry on a conversation and you'd never know I was mad. As a little girl I just had to turn it all inside." What she was truly, her true self, was completely dismissed.

Callie fell in love in high school and married at twenty and supported her young husband while he was in college. The marriage was a disaster. After the divorce, Callie's "free-thinking" rebellious nature shone forth. At twenty-four, she fell in love with Andrew. A black man was a shock to her conservative family, though her father surprised her by accepting the bi-racial couple. "If you love him, then that's it," he told Callie. "I just never saw color," Callie says. Her brothers were astounded, and her mother, who had been raised in the South, disapproved. But even as a very little girl Callie had a propensity to choose a partner who would act out her forbidden emotions--her kindergarten boyfriend was the bad boy who nearly burned down the school.

For a child to grow up psychologically healthy, she needs a positively toned emotional environment, one in which her feelings and needs are received and mirrored by the parent. All babies, Kohut tells us, are born into a state of "primary narcissism", when they imagine they are complete, perfect, and all-powerful. When the parent responds empathically, acknowledging her child as "an independent center of his/her own initiative," a healthy sense of self develops, one in which a child can learn to recognize his/her own feelings (Kohut, 1978).

But if these feelings are denied, or worse, if a parent repeatedly humiliates a child for her normal instinctual needs, these feelings intensify into a sense of shame. This gets inwardly directed, or outwardly enacted as anger and rage.

Without empathic attunement a "developmental arrest" occurs. Deprivation or emotional trauma at this delicate moment causes severe psychological wounding in the child. Without the crucial "mirroring" of the child's internal state, a narcissistic injury results — a wound to the developing self. The child then reacts, according to Kohut, either by flight, shame-faced withdrawal — running away from her feelings - or by acting out in uncontrolled rage. As she grows up, she becomes a person who either cuts off from her feelings or acts them out aggressively. In either case she does not have the ability to recognize them, and as a result she also cannot find her true voice. As an adult she chooses partners just like her parents, who will be unable to see, feel, and know her - whether they are men in the general population, or men who are held behind bars, for life, for crimes of violence.

Part of the reason that a Hades' Angel is drawn to her incarcerated partner is that through nurturing and mirroring him in that most containing of environments — prison — she feels she gets mirrored by him in return. Unconsciously, she is attempting to work through her own unmet needs, creating a "corrective emotional experience" for herself. Even in the drab, dark, cold, hellish place of prison with a man convicted of a violent crime, Callie and the other Hades' Angels discover an emotional climate in which an empathic interaction between humans can take place. It is this empathically attuned emotional experience with Melvin that enabled Callie to feel and acknowledge the emotions that she was forbidden to feel as a child. And by acknowledging and reclaiming what was lost over time she was able to transform her wounds and to heal them.

Callie's earlier relationships all reflected the same lack of emotional attunement she had experienced as a narcissistically wounded child. She would always choose men who carried a great deal of pain and anger, who acted out in rage and addiction and refused to see or know her, or were unable to do so. She married young, right out of her parents' house, supporting her first husband as he went to college, but overnight, she says, he seemed to change: turning cold, rejecting her reality when she tried to explain her feelings—even telling her she was crazy. Then he dropped out of college, and took a job in the same company where she worked. His coldness to Callie increased. She could not understand it. She had done everything "right", given everything she had. Callie was living a nightmare, one from which, as a young naïve woman she could see no escape. Eventually, her husband left her for another woman. Callie was stunned, unable to understand what had happened. Feeling betrayed, Callie vowed never to marry again.

For many narcissistically injured women this is a common pattern. They fall in love with a man who seems wonderful and loving at first but who then seems to undergo a complete change — a change they cannot understand. Trained not to want but only to meet the needs of others, they ultimately discover that they are receiving nothing in return.

I see this pattern frequently in my private practice, as well. Recently, Angela, 42, a design artist came to me emotionally devastated and penniless after her twelve-year marriage to a studio cameraman had ended. "Peace at all costs. That's what I learned from my mother," she explained. "Matt made a lot of money and at first I felt it to be the root of our problems. I didn't learn until twelve years of marriage that he was an addict, a gambler, and an alcoholic. When he left me, I had to borrow from my abusive father to pay my bills." Angela wanted to understand why she seemed to repeat the same pattern in relationship never knowing who the man really was until it was too late. Friends kept telling her she was "too nice." In fact, Angela says, when she is in a relationship she feels excluded *from who they really* are until she gets all used up. A little deeper digging revealed that Angela lived out a family myth: "you have to give to get, and if you have strong views contrary to the man in your life, swallow them." And so Angela had given everything she had until she was drained dry, all under the guise of wanting nothing back.

Callie began to get a sense that something was wrong with her choice of partners in her second relationship. Andrew was sweet and kind when he was sober, but most of the time he was drunk, unavailable to Callie in the same way her young husband had been. Again, she worked to support them both, becoming a legal secretary and eventually obtaining a responsible job. But there was physical violence in the relationship. She had never seen a man hit a woman until Andrew hit her. "I was so shocked," she explains, "that it didn't even hurt me. My whole head was relaxed and I just rolled with the punch." This happened twice; both times Andrew was drunk, both times Callie kicked him out of the house and then let him back in because "He begged and begged." Months later she snapped. "This time, I just knew he was going to hit me, so I pulled a knife on him and told him if he thought he was going to hit me, he'd better kill me because I'd end up sharing a hospital bed with him." One hundred seventy pounds, and six feet one — an ex-professional boxer, the petite Callie tossed Andrew across the room. "I lost my mind." Callie had acted out in rage, having reached the point where she could not take the abuse. "Growing up we weren't allowed to show anger or anything. Because expressing anger makes you a bad kid."

After joining Al-Anon, Callie began to recognize that she was a co-dependent in this relationship and learned how to cope as the partner of an addict. Eventually, she saw it was hopeless and left, taking everything with her. But five years later she met Andrew by chance, and feeling his pain and her love, took him back. They had one year of living together while he was sober, then he got cancer and died.

Narcissistically wounded women are expert nurturers, giving to others and asking for nothing in return, trying to earn love through submissive and pleasing behavior. In relationship, a narcissistically wounded woman will do almost anything to be loved. Nearly all of the women I interviewed, as well as many of my clients, have paid dearly for this, tending to believe their partners unflinchingly. Often they do not expect to be taken seriously. One loyal wife and mother ended up HIV positive before she was able to free herself from a husband who, for over twenty years, had been chronically unfaithful and dishonest about his many liaisons, about money, about every aspect of their lives. Another, a night-duty nurse, turned over her paycheck to her husband whom she trusted. She later lost custody of her children for "neglect" when it turned out he had been molesting her children while she was at work. He got off with only a warning.

The effects of such chaotic and traumatic marital events, which result from the kind of emotional submissiveness and learned helplessness in which many narcissistically wounded are caught, can be tragic, and they permeate the generations that follow. There are so many, many women out there who know exactly of what I speak, know of that hole inside, and know of their quick willingness to sacrifice their fragile sense of self for someone else. Sometimes it seems as if a woman will allow herself to get eaten up alive in order to be loved.

Even when a narcissistically wounded woman is able to look at what has brought her down this emotionally exhausting path she is often hard-pressed to unravel what has caused her husband or partner to hurt her. Kind, loving, understanding of his faults, never getting angry with him, he walks all over her, and she does not see that it is about her. She is the source of her own pain. To own it, to find her way out, and to prevent the pattern from reoccurring, she has to face the shadowy, unknown aspects of herself: her long-denied, forbidden feelings.

Looking into the mirror at the shadow self is a terrifying experience because it leads to the crumbling of old protective walls. The courageous Hades' Angels in this book allowed themselves to become vulnerable by breaking through their own armor, while protecting and caretaking the preciousness of the self.

It was with Melvin that Callie was finally able to see her shadow self - the parts she had been suppressing since she was a child. Before they met, they wrote letters, which led to phone calls. "He had this really, sexy, wonderful voice on the phone, and I liked what he had to say," Callie says. When he asked Callie if she wanted to come visit him, she said yes right away. She wanted to see what this charismatic man looked like.

When she sat down with Melvin in the visiting room that first day she was flooded by his presence: a mature man who had come into his own. He had a self-awareness that had come from hours of participation in emotional self-help groups in the prison, an openness and great warmth and charm. Melvin had been infraction-free for fifteen years, a near impossibility in a maximum-security prison. In prison he was a man in control of himself having grown beyond the swagger of his youth, the "player" who used women, the careless and violent gangster, the drug addict. He had a loyal family "outside" who loved him and worried about him, and visited regularly: a mother, sisters, children, even a young granddaughter. But Melvin was looking to connect with a woman who would be able to receive him simply as a man. Callie's sweetness delighted him. She was someone he could speak the truth of his life to in a way that he could not do with anyone else. Within three weeks, Melvin proposed. Throwing the last remnants of her good-girl image to the winds, Callie decided--to everyone's surprise--to marry him.

Unlike many of the Hades' Angels, Callie and Melvin were allowed conjugal visits. (Since 1996 conjugal visits are no longer permitted in the state where Melvin is incarcerated). One week after they married, Callie found herself facing a weekend with a man she realized she hardly knew. "In my generation you have sex first, then you marry." Suddenly, Callie was full of reservations. Melvin was a man she had barely touched, someone whose physical habits she didn't yet know. "What if I did not like his smell?" she recalled. But after their weekend together Callie's fears were allayed; and their connection only deepened because of their physical intimacy. But these visits were infrequent and at the whim of the prison authorities and had their own challenges. Toward the end of a weekend, she would watch Melvin withdraw into himself, a familiar coldness crept over him, the coldness of emotional withdrawal. But Callie was able to understand it had nothing to do with her; it was Melvin, putting on the emotional armor he needed to return to prison. So, in spite of their occasional sexual relationship, the real work of maintaining their emotional connection remained: the weekend visits in a room crowded with strangers. "The din of the visiting room," Callie says, "is impossible to imagine. There you are trying to talk with your husband and you can hardly hear yourself."

Still, they made the most of their time together, and their relationship grew. "He's very open. He talks. He loves you inside. He wants to know what's going on with you. He's not self centered," she explains. Once again, I note that when Callie speaks of herself she chooses the second person—Callie is not "I" but "you".

Her family had great difficulty accepting the relationship. Her father had died, but her brothers and mother voiced their fears. A convicted murderer? A former Black Panther? What could their pretty sister possibly be getting out of it? What if he was ever released? He was a murderer, didn't Callie have the sense even to be afraid, her mother asked.

Callie couldn't explain it. She knew it would be something they could not understand, but all her life she had tolerated their conservative views and their lifestyle and never spoken a word, never confronted her mother who had always shut Callie down. What was it that drew her to Melvin? Was it her old pattern of "receiving" very little in return for her love and devotion? Or did she instinctively sense that what she most needed would be given to her through this most unlikely of loves? The healing of the split comes alive in women who fall helplessly in love with men who are stigmatized by society as violent criminals. The shame and stigma that may be split off, repressed, or hidden in the women recognizes the woundedness in the men whose shame and stigma are public. Shame and stigma denied meet shame and stigma in an open forum: prison.

What Heals the Wound

For Callie, as for Eve, all the time she has spent face-to-face with her inmate husband has enabled her to focus on the parts of herself that had been crying out to be recognized. "You can't hide how you really feel. You're sitting there at a table with this person and you're looking at each other and you have to deal with it. With Melvin there is more communication than I ever even knew was possible with a man," Callie explains.

In the din of the prison visiting room, surrounded by hundreds of others, video cameras, and the ever-watchful guards, Callie and Melvin are able to create the positively attuned emotional environment that, in the course of their twelve year marriage, has enabled Callie to express the full spectrum of feelings by which she is able to realize her true self: "Always before I had to be good or the best or not show how I really felt because what if they don't like me?" The fear of what might happen if she revealed her feeling self had controlled her since childhood. It was what kept her from full relationship with others and with herself. "With Melvin, though, I almost feel like I'm learning how to be myself."

For Callie, as for other narcissistically wounded adults, feeling and expressing their emotions involves great risk, for it brings up the painful childhood legacy--the deep fear of rejection and abandonment: If you have your own feelings and dare to express them you will not be cared for. You will not be loved. "Melvin can always just tell me, you know what? I'm tired of you, bye. But I feel like I can be me and he's still going to love me."

Her relationship with Melvin has enabled Callie to create the reparative emotional experience which allows her to own and feel the whole spectrum of her true self. Not the child "higher than a kite today", but the woman who can be angry and still be accepted, be happy and not be "too high". "Always before I was afraid that I wasn't going to be loved if I actually had a temper tantrum, for instance, or disagreed." But inside the walls of a maximum-security prison Callie has at last found the conditions and the person with whom she is able to expose the different aspects of her self, allowing her true self to be seen by someone "who loves me the way I am."

For the narcissistically wounded woman being seen, heard, and known for her authentic self helps her reclaim those parts of herself that she had to split-off or deny in order to survive and adapt in her family of origin. "Since I've been with Melvin I can express myself. I've never been able to do that before, never. I had to justify. I always had to say, even if I was very angry, 'this is why I'm angry.' He likes me no matter what I do. I can tell him to fuck off, and it's okay."

Having finally become a woman "at the center of her own independent initiative", Callie now trusts her instincts and does not retreat when she is challenged. For the previously submissive Callie this has given her the strength to stand her ground in relationship: with Melvin, but also with her boss, an attorney. "I call them on their behavior. And I've never been comfortable doing that with any man. If Melvin doesn't like something I do and he starts going off on me—and he's right—I'm not going to argue. But I'm not going to let him get away with things either. He's so used to someone not fighting with him he's surprised. It just takes the wind out of his sails."

Melvin, too, has the chance to look at himself and his reactions, instead of simply ignoring his woman, or exploding in anger. "A man can love you and still not pay attention to what you say or have respect for you. We respect each other," Callie says proudly. Through this relationship both of them have changed and grown.

Melvin was given a sentence of seven years to life, but the political climate in his state, which is "tough on crime", makes it impossible for a man who was convicted of murder to be released, even after his exemplary record of the past fifteen years. Callie says she has no fear that Melvin will ever do anything to anybody ever again. He was a boy on drugs when he committed the crime for which he is serving time. Now he has matured and grown to see life very differently than he did in his youth. "He values life more," Callie says, "he values his connections to people." They have celebrated their twelfth anniversary, and through their connection Callie has gained the love of members of his family, as well.

Callie brings his "beautiful granddaughter" with her on visiting day, helping her to dress so that she will pass inspection. She stays in close touch with his mother. One year after they had been married, Melvin's mother called to tell Callie that she had some mail for her. "My son wrote to me but all he talks about is you." Before Callie came into his life even his mother was frightened of him because "he was so mean-looking and depressed and just down. And she thanks me all the time. I told him in our first year of marriage, 'you know what, when you come out that door, you leave that shit behind you, because this is the real world. I'm here.' He comes out with a smile on his face now. He doesn't have to be a tough guy. Maybe he has to do that out there--be tough to protect himself; I can't interfere with that. But he doesn't need to bring that to me. His mom says, 'Ever since you he looks so good and healthy, and he's got a smile. That's the child I raised. You brought my son back.'"

Friends and family know about her marriage, she doesn't keep it a secret, but when outsiders ask, she confidently tells them the truth: "He works for the state and I can't talk about it." Generally, Callie feels no shame to admit that her husband is in prison. Her boss at the law firm where she works knows about Melvin and has even tried helping her in her effort to obtain his release. Twelve years later, her brothers both say they cannot understand the marriage, but then again, they had never approved of her life choices. She acknowledges that Melvin shouldn't have done what he did, that he deserved to be punished. "He killed somebody, but that's between him and God, and he's got to live with that every day. Every day of his life! The man I fell in love with is the one that I know today. She doesn't know the man who 'was such a player that he'd have walked right by and never noticed me thirty years ago.' Melvin has never tried to hide what he has done. And that has given me the chance to really know who he is."

When I ask Callie if she feels this relationship would have been worth it even if Melvin were never released, she says, "Even if it all ended right now, it was worth it. Worth it for all that I have received. For what I am today. My house is empty and my bed is empty, but I don't feel alone emotionally."

Chapter Four

The Father's Daughter

When Hades' Angel Jamie, a successful, vivacious professional in her late forties, married "one of those slime balls", an inmate serving twenty-five years to life for armed robbery, her action seemed incomprehensible to everyone who knew her: her friends, her family, her college-age daughter, but especially the officials in the Department of Corrections where Jamie had worked as an administrator for sixteen years. Her marriage to an inmate caused Jamie to fall from the good graces "of the big people--to lose the prima donna status," she had worked so hard to attain and so enjoyed.

Why would a woman with a fine education, an outstanding reputation and so many options live with such contradiction? What could possibly cause anyone as intelligent as Jamie to make such a seemingly irrational choice?

As a father's daughter, Jamie's achievements in the world had come at a high price. A self-confessed workaholic, she operated solely out of what psychologists identify as her masculine energies. She was goal-oriented, defined by achievement, closed down to her feelings, out of touch with her body and with her instinctual feminine core.

Divorced for twelve years, Jamie had not one but two thriving careers: as a psychotherapist, with a degree from a prestigious university, and as the owner of her own parole advocacy business. But when she met Darren in the course of her advocacy work, a forgotten longing began to open within her, and she began to feel stirrings from a part of herself that had been blocked off all her life. Something was awakening within her.

In Jungian psychology, the term "father's daughter" describes a woman who is allied with the patriarchy, who values her thinking rather than her feeling processes. Unaware of her own identity apart from what she can accomplish, the father's daughter lives primarily from the consciousness of the upper world--her head. She grows up to meet the demands of the outer world, but in the inner world, her life's blood--her creative, intuitive nature--is being drained by her own need for goals, achievement, her perfectionism. Books and knowledge wall her in and wall her off from her emotions and from her hunger for the internal life which she has given away.

Like the goddess Athena, sprung full-blown from the head of her father, the father's daughter is prepared from childhood to "do battle" on behalf of the masculine, the patriarchy, to serve her father's standards of success in the external world. To please her father and to meet his emotional needs she learns to disconnect from her feelings: she learns, in the words of the psychologist Mary Loomis (1995), to control, suppress, or sever the connection between her intellect and her emotions. Instead, she focuses on achievement in order to earn her father's validation and praise. Growing up with a domineering father and a mother who is submissive to him, the father's daughter becomes emotionally armored against her deepest instincts, which are never recognized or prized.

Such a woman was Jamie. Jamie was not seeking a romantic relationship with an inmate when she first encountered Darren. Not one to cross over the lines, Jamie was a rule-follower and had been that way since she was a child. Every day Jamie "crossed over" as an advocate, an outsider coming into the prison. She heard the clanging shut of the prison gates, spoke with the guards by name. When she entered the prison she was treated with respect. Nothing in her experience had prepared her for the lines she would cross when she entered into a relationship with Darren, or the way she would be belittled and mistreated as the girlfriend, and later, the wife of an inmate.

But like the other Hades' Angels and their inmate loves, Jamie and Darren had a great deal in common psychologically: a similar role in their family of origin, a similar discipline and drive; they were both highly intelligent and, in their own ways, devoted to serving others. They, too, would turn out to form a perfect psychological fit.

Darren, like Jamie, was highly accomplished; in prison, he had learned to focus his energies and had achieved a great deal. He was working on a Ph.D. in sociology, had written and published fifteen books, mentored many young inmates, teaching them discipline and guiding their educations. Jamie would discover that Darren was also a person of great compassion with a generous heart; and Darren had experienced a violent childhood. Even as a boy he had tried to protect his mother and his brothers from his alcoholic father. Later, he turned his anger outward and acted out his rage in a non-violent offense, which had earned his long sentence.

It was through her work that Jamie first connected with Darren when he wrote to her requesting that she represent an inmate friend who was coming up for parole. With a reputation as the best parole advocate in her region, she received many requests, but for Jamie this was a first. She had never been hired by one inmate on behalf of another. What an articulate, compassionate man, she thought as she read Darren's description of his friend's situation.

Before entering prison work Jamie describes herself as "pretty much like everybody else. Prisons…the families, the inmates, they didn't cross my mind. What the family goes through…I just wasn't aware." But Jamie had developed a perspective that was rare in the system: she looked at the inmates she worked with as human beings first. "I want to understand--not to condone the offense--but to understand how this person got to this place to do what he did." As an advocate she was discriminating: rejecting nearly half of those who requested her help representing only those inmates who she believed were psychologically ready to live on the outside.

Months after her advocacy work on behalf of his friend was complete, Jamie received an unexpected package. Darren had sent her his own file and asked her to review it. Jamie learned that Darren's robbery attempt had been done in a wrongheaded effort to help someone he knew out of a difficult situation.

Intrigued by the case and the man, Jamie went to the courthouse and did further research, reading through Darren's entire trial transcripts. As a psychotherapist she recognized that Darren had been acting out the pattern of family savior—a role she knew well--she had lived it in her own family. But when Jamie wrote to Darren describing the next step, a clinical interview, Darren refused it. Without a psychological interview she couldn't take on his case.

Two years passed before Jamie heard from Darren again. This time he had obtained a grant to establish a rape prevention program in the prison, and he wanted her to serve as an advisor. Obtaining a grant was an impressive accomplishment for an inmate, and working on it would help her expand her own expertise. Curious to finally meet him, Jamie made her first trip to the prison.

When she sat down opposite him in the visiting room that Saturday she failed to notice Darren's attractiveness or their similarities: how fit and athletic they both were, how neat and well-groomed. The observations went right past her conscious mind. What she saw in Darren was a man with a strong, quiet presence, low key and polite. As they began talking, she was impressed by his scholarly nature and how knowledgeable he was about the prison culture, and by his discipline. Under the most difficult circumstances Darren had built an impressive work life. She realized she could learn a lot from working with him. After those first hours together, Jamie agreed to serve as his advisor on the grant. The very next week, she was back, and their relationship had begun. As far as Jamie was concerned, it was strictly work. Work was her comfort zone, and it was Darren's as well. Week after week, as Jamie and Darren worked closely together developing the program, she began to see beyond the label "inmate" to Darren, the man. Except for the prison jeans and blue shirt, he seemed like a colleague.

Jamie had encountered many intelligent professional men in the course of her life, attorneys and doctors, but too often she had gotten the sense that "the man was above and the woman below." With Darren she felt comfortable equality. "If it had been the old con, you're

gorgeous, I probably would have said, well, gee, thanks a lot, goodbye."
Later, thinking back on those early days she observes, "If I was being
seduced I was being intellectually seduced." At the time, however, she
was not aware of it. The father's daughter does not know when she is
being set-up. She doesn't recognize the possibility.

In all of her previous relationships, the ten-year marriage to her
first husband, a six-year relationship that followed, and with the men
she dated Jamie always insisted on maintaining control. "The men in
my life knew that whenever it came to making decisions the only answer
I was able to accept was 'yes, dear.'" She always chose men "like my
mom", she explains, "who did anything to avoid conflict with me
because they would say I was going to win anyway."

Unable to allow herself to be vulnerable or emotionally open,
Jamie was a woman used to doing not being, not a woman at home in
her feelings--a true father's daughter. Her entire identity had been built
on her professional achievements within the prison setting, and so she
kept herself tightly in check. As a trained psychotherapist Jamie
recognized that she was a not a person who was comfortable "engaging
emotionally." She did not know how much of herself she was missing,
the hunger for her own feeling self that existed within her, or the journey
that it would take her on once that hunger was aroused. But that is what
opened to Jamie on the afternoon weeks into their work when Darren
looked up from the piles of papers spread out on the table between them
and said, "Why don't you trying taking off your professional hat?"

"What do you mean?" she asked, and she froze inside. It would
take Jamie a year and a half—the entire length of their "working
relationship" before she was able to bring herself to step out of her
professional role.

Like Rapunzel, the father's daughter waits in the tower for the
right man to say, "let down your hair." And that is just what Darren
did, requesting that Jaime let down her guard, and so he climbed up.
In this "magnetic energy field" what happened for Jamie was an

awakening of her instinctual feminine nature, the part of herself she had learned to abandon when she was a child.

Nearly all the Hades' Angels I met turned out to have been raised as father's daughters, as are many of the women in my Los Angeles women's groups. Successful, accomplished, like Jamie, because they are distanced from their own feelings and needs, they can become easy prey to men who know how to offer just the right kind of validation of their hidden feminine and then harness the woman's strength for themselves. Father's daughters can appear tough, but when it comes to their emotional lives they are extraordinarily naïve. The adult father's daughter often finds herself drawn into relationships with men who turn out to be just like her father--critical and controlling. Emotionally, she lives for crumbs. One such woman, a film producer in my Los Angeles women's group, described her ten-year relationship with a man who is no longer in her life, "You would not believe how long I could go on just one small kindness. How many weeks and months of abuse I could endure on the strength of one kind act or word."

For a father's daughter, even sexual intimacy can bypass feelings. It does not lead her into her emotions, but away from them. To a woman who doesn't want closeness, sexual intimacy can become completely overwhelming, and she risks losing herself to the man she is with. Another of my clients, a beautiful actress who had worked all her life to build her successful career, met and fell head over heals in love with a wealthy contractor who seduced her in every way possible. He bought her expensive gifts, romanced her, and with a vampiric energy, sexually devoured her. Sex with him was different from anything she had ever before felt, she said. "It was like going into his cave. We would stay there for days." She gave herself over to this man completely--a total seduction through sex. When he asked her to move with him to a remote state she agreed, giving up her career, leaving the family she was so fond of and who had been so supportive of her. Then, months later, on the day of her wedding, he abandoned her. She came to me in the aftermath, trying to understand what had happened.

For a father's daughter the inside and the outside don't match. Goal driven and controlling like the father, the father's daughter is emotionally fragile and submissive, just like her mother. She has learned to survive in a man's world but not as a woman who is fully aware of the strengths that lie dormant in her repressed feminine nature. The feminine within her remains starved for recognition, for praise and affirmation. Outwardly she lives her life in control just like the father; inwardly she is emotionally submissive just like her mother.

Jamie managed herself by making sure she was always in control in relationships, never allowing a man to "touch" that vulnerable place within for fear of what would happen to her if she "let go".

Jamie's Family of Origin

Although she had become a courageous, independent woman, Jamie had been a little girl who was afraid to do anything wrong. The only girl among three brothers, she was the academic star. In her family Jamie's father "ran the show." If he was angry or dissatisfied with her, as he often was, he cut her off, refusing to speak to her for days, weeks, and sometimes longer. Early on she learned not to disagree with him, afraid of his disapproval and his anger. Jamie was pulled by her father, the powerful one in the household, "earning" his love through valuing the things that he valued: success in school, and accomplishment in the external world.

Although Jamie and her brothers could go to their mother knowing she loved them, she never made waves and they learned early that their mother had no power in their family; she simply went along with whatever her husband did. When he went for days without speaking to his children, she said nothing.

It is not her mother that a little girl in such a family looks to for approval. And it is not his subservient wife that the man in such a family considers his emotional, intellectual partner but the little girl who he is shaping to be his ally—his little warrior. Though Jamie was not the oldest child, her father was always enlisting her support to help him get what he wanted in the family. When she did this, she felt she was privileged, her father's special child.

"I was the peacemaker, the go-between, the hub of the family wheel. Every family problem went through me," she remembers. When Jamie was away in college, her father would call her if he was angry with something one of her brothers was doing and tell her to do whatever it took to make her brother change course. If her brother didn't listen, her father would accuse her of not trying. "Go back and get it right," he would say. If her brother still wouldn't change, her father would take out his anger on them both, cutting off contact and threatening to take them out of his will. In the days and weeks of silence that ensued, Jamie lived hollowed out with a deep sense of powerlessness and hurt. There was no one to turn to. Her mother threw up her hands. Jamie felt abandoned. There was nothing to do but wait out her father's rejection and anger for days, weeks, even months, until he agreed to speak to her again.

In her family, Jamie says, no one ever said, "*I love you*". "We were all very good at knowing how to get angry. The hardest, scariest thing to do was to be soft or open with someone—to be intimate on an emotional level."

Eventually, her brothers stopped talking to her about their lives. For years Jamie suffered in silence and isolation, carrying the burden as her father's emissary, his unwilling emotional and intellectual partner. She did not "think" about how she was feeling, whether she was hurt, the fact that there was no one to support her emotionally, or that her father was asking too much of her. She shut off this part of herself, becoming a young woman, a successful "workaholic" adult.

Years later, in the course of her training as a psychotherapist, Jamie came to understand her role in the family and the ways she had been used to meet her father's needs. As an adult Jamie had been unable to build good relationships with men. Still tied to her father, he remained her "father god" (Woodman), with whom no man could possibly compete. And because Jamie was cut off from her connection to her body, "severed" from the experience of her emotions, half of herself was unknown to her. Jamie's "feeling nature", which she viewed as weak and submissive, was a stranger to her, and all of her life she avoided emotionally intimate situations, preferring "control".

In none of her relationships, including her first marriage, had Jamie experienced real closeness or emotional intimacy, and the fear of touching these vulnerable parts of herself remained with her long into adult life.

When she was in her twenties, living on her own, her parents separated, and her father contacted her, demanding that Jamie get her mother to come back to him. This time Jamie refused. Her father erupted, blaming Jamie for her mother's leaving. Jamie stood her ground. She was not going do his bidding. After her parents' divorce and her mother's remarriage, her father stopped speaking to Jamie for a long time. She would call him and hear only silence on the phone. After months of this he finally relented and accepted Jamie back into the fold.

It took Jamie many years to understand that her father had tried to make her responsible for his life. "I had to look at a lot of hard truths in my own family," she says. The work that she did in becoming a psychotherapist helped her to see how her father had unconsciously used her as a way to meet his emotional needs, and she came to understand that he might never have had anyone to teach him how to be close. Anger was his style of communication, and control was the way he expressed his love. Anger and control were his defenses against his own fragile feelings and inadequate sense of self.

But Jamie was now able to refuse her father's demands, which did not end just because she was an adult. She even learned to joke with him when he went too far. In her professional life, first in the Department of Corrections, and later, as a parole advocate, Jamie became a champion of powerless men who acted out against others in response to their anger and hurt. She had "shifted" her role from the unconscious girl doing Dad's bidding, to the professional woman in control who, today, recognizes the professional rescuer in herself.

In spite of her self-awareness, Jamie was still shut down to her feminine energies, continuing to operate throughout her adult life out of the masculine energies that had fueled her as her father's special child. It was through her relationship with Darren that Jamie was finally able to claim the missing, shadow aspects of herself. Like Sleeping Beauty, the masked self lies dormant, waiting to be coaxed awake, to be kissed into the light of consciousness.

What Heals the Wound

For a year and a half Darren kept challenging Jamie to take off her professional hat. Eventually, drawn by his commanding intellect and his generous heart, and "protected" by the limited nature of their relationship, Jamie gradually began relating to Darren not as a professional but as a woman; and another kind of relationship began. "He drew me out to be whoever I was beneath the professional armor," she explains, "I was not the person that everyone usually knew me by. Very few people really knew me."

With Darren she found that she could be playful and silly, She could cry. She didn't have to be "so together" all the time. Darren too began to relinquish the tight control he held over himself. Jamie discovered tremendous depth to Darren, something that very many people would not suspect. "Everybody thinks he's nice and he's very respectful. But he holds his own. He could be very endearing and not in a manipulative way."

Through it all, Jamie never lost sight of the fact that Darren was an inmate. "He deserved prison," she says, "He is responsible for where he is." But she was able to see past his identity as inmate to the compassionate part that the system does not recognize. Darren spoke of trying to protect his mother and brothers from his violent, alcoholic father and how he had survived by anesthetizing his emotions. He mourned the older brother who was so damaged that he had to be institutionalized. From a very young age Darren was put in a role he was not qualified for. Jamie explains, "Both of us sacrificed our own wants and our own selves to help another": he, for his mother, she, for her father. That shared role gave Jamie a sense of trust and of "knowing" what was inside Darren and allowed her to get close.

By the time their work on the grant had come to an end, Jamie and Darren had developed a bond that went beyond work. But in order to continue to see Darren, Jamie would not only have to reveal the nature of their relationship to the prison establishment, she would have to apply to visit Darren simply as a woman.

Once Jamie stepped out of her professional role, she became subject to the same treatment as the "groupies", girlfriends and wives and family members of inmates. She was seen as a lowlife the moment she walked into the prison: searched, and questioned, suspected and belittled. She found herself subject to whispers and comments. What did she want with "the slime?"

For a woman who was a respected professional, this abrupt change in status was a shock, but Jamie was opening in ways she had never allowed herself to experience when she lived under the "armor" of control as a father's daughter. She bore the insults and the questions and continued to see Darren every weekend she could. Through her relationship with Darren she was experiencing, for the first time in her life, what was true within for herself.

Over time, there were many surprises for Jamie. One was the sheer pleasure of touch, of holding hands--something that was entirely new for her. In the past, she says, if someone had reached for her hand she would have been uncomfortable and immediately pulled away. "I know this is weird but Darren is the first man I ever held hands with, and I think it's extremely intimate." Darren's simple acts of kindness touched her deeply, the way he reminded her to use her seatbelt, asked about a doctor's appointment, told her to be careful when she closed up her office late at night.

Darren, too, was freed to express aspects of himself that he had never shared with another. Sometimes when speaking of the people he cared for and what they had gone through, Darren would cry. "His tears were always for someone else," Jamie says. He told her how much harder prison had become now that he knew her. Before they met he had lived anesthetized. Now that he was feeling his life, it was harder to shut down.

Above all, it was the emotional intimacy that she and Darren built between them--the very thing she had avoided all her life—that Jamie came to cherish, even the intimacy borne of many hours, face-to-face in the crowded and noisy prison visiting room. There were no conjugal visits at Darren's prison. Without sex, Jamie found, she and Darren had the opportunity to get to know one another in a deep way. "Other couples have distractions. They can go out to dinner with friends, go to a mall, see a movie, walk into separate rooms," she explains. She and Darren had six hours together every Saturday and Sunday. They could not run away when something was not right between them. They had to stay together and work it through. Difficult as this was at times, it fostered the kind of intimacy that allowed them to really build a relationship, even when they disagreed, one that allowed them to feel nurtured by each other, understood and cared for at a deep level, something she had never before known.

For the first time in her life Jamie did not mind that she was seen at her most vulnerable. This father's daughter, formerly a respected professional in the prison setting, became the wife of an inmate with a gentleness in her heart and tears on her face in the visiting room. Her emotional armor had come down; through her relationship with Darren she was finding her way to her inner life. Finally, kissed by emotional connection, she had awakened to her own true potential and that potential included what psychologists refer to as "the dormant, split-off feminine aspects of the self."

"It is the ultimate in femininity to let go," Jamie says. "It was something I never imagined I would be able to do."

For six years Jamie and Darren wrestled with the question of whether or not to get married. Darren resisted wondering why Jamie would want to tie herself to a man who might never be released from prison. But for Jamie, Darren was already in her life emotionally, even if he was not there physically. She would work all week, but she lived for the weekends, especially now that her daughter had gone to college. "He's where my life is," Jamie explained. Darren made her feel whole. "He's my soul mate, my kindred spirit."

There were times when Darren lost trust in her, times when they argued. The issue of anger, a big one for them both, was something they had to contend with. Learning to deal with the emotion rather than cutting it off, withdrawing, or closing down as a defense, was not easy for either of them. That they were doing this together became deeply rewarding for Jamie.

In the end they decided that whether Darren received parole or not, they were going to commit to being together. Even her daughter approved of the marriage, amazed at the changes she was seeing in her mother and impressed with the man Darren was. As for Jamie's friends, they had no idea that she had the capacity to be so full of feeling. Even her best friend was surprised to learn that Jamie had another self buried under the self-sufficient persona she had always shown.

"When a Corrections Officer I had known for years asked me how could I marry an inmate, I said, you just answered your own question. It's a label right now. He earned it through his behavior. One day he's not going to have that label. I didn't fall in love with the inmate part of him. I fell in love with the person that he is, and with me he is a very compassionate, caring person."

For Jamie, as for the other Hades' Angels who shared their lives with me, it is by descending into the prison and giving herself compassionately to "the beast" confined within it, that she opens not only to her inmate love, who bears wounds not unlike her own, but to the wounded parts of herself. All the Hades' Angels are drawn by unseen internal ties they don't understand to connect with men who are doing serious time. They see the hidden parts of themselves, what Jung calls the shadow, in their inmate love. And the empathic relationship with 'an other' allows them to recognize and have compassion for the wounded parts of themselves. Compassion for the self is an essential component in healing, and one that is difficult for many people to achieve. But it is through developing compassion for themselves that the relationship between the Hades' Angels and their inmate loves becomes transformative. Only by looking below the surface of what seems "rational" can we come to understand the deeper needs that these relationships fulfill for the Hades' Angels who have the courage to undertake them.

The story of Jamie and Darren has a happy ending. After nineteen years in prison and with Jamie's expert help, Darren was paroled. And though adjusting to life on the outside was not easy for him after the rigid controls of prison, he learned to cope with the challenges of making decisions for himself.

It is seven years now since Darren was paroled and Jamie and Darren are doing very well. Darren runs a very successful business. Jamie continues her work as a parole advocate, still a warrior in her work. "I even look forward to growing old with Darren," Jamie says, "Even though in the past I had dreaded growing old." Jamie's life has a richness that it did not have before. For Darren and Jamie, their connection is deep.

Not all the Hades' Angels have such successful outcomes when their inmate husbands are released. For some, it has had the ups and downs, twists and turns, of a roller coaster ride. There are some whose husbands leave them after being released, some who have paid a high price in money and in relationship for risking themselves with a man who has been in prison so long. But all of the Hades' Angels say that the relationship with their inmate has been worth it for the changes they have experienced within themselves.

For a father's daughter the real reward for the descent into the unknown territory of herself lies in learning to experience the richness of her internal life. With it she gains a sense of wholeness, the discovery of the passion and preciousness that was soul dead within her.

Jamie describes the relief she feels now that she is free from the need to control every aspect of life. "I know I'm a woman, but I haven't really felt feminine until now."

The work of the father's daughter is to learn to trust the strength inherent in her own femininity, to see that letting go into feeling does not mean allowing herself to get swallowed up by a vampiric energy or losing herself completely. She can still pursue her work in the world and accomplish her goals, but by "owning" the lost parts of herself she can live with much more enjoyment, a wider self, live not from a defensive "either or position"--her head or her heart--but from her core.

"I like the walking beside, instead of behind or in front," says Jamie, "that either one can take over, but that you can easily slide back beside one another. I feel totally understood and accepted. I am with a man I can trust, and it makes me feel truly feminine at last."

Chapter Five

The Demon Lover

As a psychotherapist, I often work with outwardly successful yet emotionally fragile women who find themselves caught in destructive relationships with men I call demon lovers--severely damaged and damaging men. A demon lover appears to be powerful and may even boast of his ability to control and manipulate women; he routinely devalues, objectifies and feeds off of others in order to fill his own emptiness. As a child who had to deny sadness and fear (emotions which would make him appear vulnerable), he grows up striving for positions of power and control, with an inflated false self. But his grandiose behavior, as Kernberg (1975) explains, is only a mask which conceals his dependency on others.

Nearly all of the Hades' Angels spoke of having had multiple "demon lover" relationships in the past. And though the demon lover inflicts emotional and even physical abuse on his partner, the woman and the man in such a relationship are psychologically mated-- flip sides of the same coin. Under her mask of pleasing, submissive, self-demanding behavior is a woman with her own long-held, unconscious anger, her own hidden wounds.

Jung teaches that each of us harbors a shadow--the sum total of all we refuse to acknowledge about ourselves. These rejected aspects of our psyche are repressed into the personal unconscious. The negative aspects of the shadow are the ones most often projected onto others.

It is her shadow which is a source of a woman's attraction to a demon lover. Only when she begins to know its contents—the rejected aspects of her own psyche--and learns to bring these denied qualities into her conscious personality, will she find herself able to break her attraction to the demon lover.

Olga, 36, who had just completed chemotherapy, was a client who came to understand that she needed to do this in order to save her own life. For twelve years she had stayed in a marriage "for their young daughter's sake" while her demon lover husband flaunted his drug use and his many relationships with other women. Olga's cancer diagnosis woke her up to her situation, and she asked for a divorce. Her husband cut her off financially, believing that this would force her to stay with him, but Olga felt driven to leave, even though she found herself without a home, and without insurance coverage for needed cancer treatment. Her husband's emotional dependency revealed itself when he confessed to feeling alone and abandoned without her. Still, she refused to go back. Today, she believes he was the cancer and that without him she can heal.

Many women are drawn toward their opposite only to get caught in physically and/or emotionally abusive relationships. The emotional dynamic of one partner acting out and the other acting-in is true not only for the Hades' Angels who are drawn by their own unconscious wounds to a man who is similarly wounded but who has acted out violently. This a pattern that can be useful to understand both for women who are puzzled by their painful relationship choices and for therapists treating couples in marital therapy.

I have observed the way women who learned in childhood to be the emotional caretaker of a parent unconsciously absorb the pain and anxiety of their adult partners. They believe that if they were "better" in some way, or if they only worked harder, their partners would change. These demands on the self lead them even more deeply into cycles of abuse. Many women simply don't know why these things are happening, nor do they have the tools to unlock themselves from their own inner prisons. What they do know is how to be supportive and nurturing and then hope for the strength to change and redeem their partner.

In the demon lover relationship, a woman's nurturing, empathic goodness meets its shadow self, its dark side, in relationship with a man who is driven to extract all of her nurturing juices to meet his own unmet needs. He is often persuasive, a skilled manipulator who may promise to change. She believes his empty promises because, as the perfect empathic mirror to the father-god, she can't say--has no tools to say--no. This dynamic, like the doctor-patient relationship, is, in Jungian terms, a split-archetype, meaning one cannot exist without the other. The demon lover requires a partner who is submissive and willing: a woman who will not give up trying in the hopes that the next time she will finally "get it right".

For Hades' Angel PJ, a secretary with two years of college, who has worked as a corrections officer, an alcohol counselor, and as an advocate for the mentally challenged, it was the infidelity of her demon lover husband that led her to end her first marriage after enduring ten years of abuse. PJ, who draws in chalk and pastels, describes herself as artistic and extremely sensitive. She married in her early twenties, "a violent marriage to a violent man." Her mother insisted that PJ stay with the marriage asserting that, "the women in our family don't get divorced." PJ explains that she and her husband, "had nothing in common but the bed." Why did she marry him? "He was good-looking, that may have been it. I was very young and stupid." And the marriage in many ways replicated what she had seen at home growing up—no communication, rage, frustration. It was "a real comfortable shoe, the one I was very familiar with. I may not have been happy with it, but I certainly knew how it fit." They had a little boy and then a little girl, who died at birth. When her husband had an affair with her best friend, PJ realized, "This marriage is not my lot, it's my choice. And I took myself, and my child and I left. They're currently married. I just wish them well."

When PJ left, she did so with the awareness that she did not want to recreate this situation in yet another marriage, and so she put herself "very deliberately in therapy." Her mother saw therapy as a further sign of failure, a sign that her daughter was damaged. But PJ was able to break from those restrictive beliefs. "I said something is wrong and I've got to fix it. So I did. I began to learn about me. I began to make choices for me, not for the family, not for that long list of 'shoulds'. Part of me, that precious part--my poet soul or my artistic soul--was dying. It was as if I could see a little tiny child curled in the corner in a fetal position, dying." For the first time, PJ stepped out of the emotionally submissive position and took control of her life.

In the embrace of the demon lover, it is often difficult even for a highly intelligent woman to do what PJ was able to do at the end of her ten year marriage: deliberately turn inward and learn to see the parts of herself that are crying out to be healed. Most women involved with demon lovers see them as the only ones with a dark side; they do not see their own. Their energy becomes invested in transforming his.

Another client, Betty, a professional woman with advanced degrees who had been in marital therapy with her husband, opened the mail one day to discover that he had hired a divorce lawyer and was using her credit card to pay for a divorce. This was not the first time that Betty had been caught in this way. She had had previous demon lover relationships and thought she had grown past them. Her husband, the father of her two young children, was a man who appeared to be a nice, homebound soul though he could not seem to find work that suited him. He believed that working for others was below his status. In the marriage, Betty had been trying to do it all. With two little children and a demanding profession, she was the sole financial support in the household, while her husband lived off her energy and her efforts.

How does a man like this develop, one who lacks integrity and courage, who seems to "enjoy" using women? He does so in response to a parent who withholds love and affection, offers rewards for mirroring his or her own narcissistic needs and values, is critical of the child's natural, instinctual desires--the same way that the narcissistically wounded woman develops. But when she becomes self-demanding, perfectionistic, and nurturing, he becomes entitled, manipulative, and grandiose. When the ego is too fragile and vulnerable, the damage to the developing self is very great, and what remains is an evil core that consumes and possesses the soul. A woman whose emotional make-up is submissive then "feeds" her demon lover's false image and allows herself to be manipulated and controlled, making the perfect psychological fit for the man who believes himself entitled to all that he gets.

In the wreckage of the demon lover relationship a woman is often left filled with anger and hurt. She remains puzzled; she does not transform. The demon lover is a destructive energy but it can lead to transformation if a woman turns to herself and tries to understand what it is within her that draws her to a man who acts out in ways that cause her shame, humiliation, and abuse. It takes courage to do this, to look at the shadow, for as we have seen, doing so involves uncovering the long-buried childhood wounds. That is why the Hades' Angels journeys have so much to teach us, for within their prison relationships with partners who have been convicted of violent crimes, they discover the shadow parts of themselves, and by working to recognize them through their prison relationships, the Hades' Angels are able, remarkably, to grow and transform.

PJ was working as a secretary at a maximum-security prison when she met Rob, her "man inside". He was the cute, charming cook in the prison, who had served fifteen years of a twenty-five-to life sentence for murder. Each afternoon a small group would gather in the prison kitchen for coffee and conversation. "Just regular people" she explains, "who had gotten to be friends." Sitting around the table were PJ, and Rob, a corrections officer, a couple of inmates, another secretary and some free-world kitchen staffers. Rob had a gorgeous smile, PJ remembers, which he used a lot. Even though he was dressed in prison blue, she felt no barrier between them. And there was definitely chemistry, she says, though it took PJ six months to realize it. At the time she wasn't interested in a relationship and had already dealt with other inmates who had tried to come on to her. She was simply enjoying those afternoon coffee breaks and a congenial group of friends. But with six months of comfortable talk between them on topics that included books, psychology, relationship, and a great deal of easy humor, PJ had gotten to know Rob pretty well. "Do you realize that I am in love with you?" he asked her one afternoon. PJ was surprised and immediately backed off. "You really might want to think about it because I am," he said. She knew she was attracted to him and enjoyed being in his company, but she did not think that he was the one with whom she would be able to have the kind of relationship she had envisioned in the years she had been in therapy. Years earlier, she explains, "In my prayers and in my mediation, I had consulted with the Creator or whatever name you choose to consult by—and I said 'this is what I would like to bring into my life. I want a real positive relationship with a man. It would be priceless to me. Now, if this could be arranged, I would greatly appreciate it.'"

An inmate doing twenty-five to life for murder was not the man PJ had asked the Creator to help her bring into her life. And by the time she met Rob she had become resigned to living her life alone, saying "I even thought I would die alone."

PJ had a tough exterior and a quick wit which she developed to hide the terrors and fears that still lived within her having grown up in a family in which her parents regularly and openly battled for control, and her volatile father was "busy verbally abusing us and exerting his power." PJ now recognizes her father's behavior as that of a man who, as a war veteran, was probably suffering from post-traumatic stress. But at the time she knew only that she was never certain what to expect from him or, when the next blow-up would come. Her mother did nothing to stop his rages, except defend them. In a family of three daughters, PJ was the non-conforming "oddball". Her two younger sisters enjoyed the usual feminine toys and games. She was the one her father preferred, the father's daughter who liked being out in the fields working beside him learning the lessons he taught her: about good values, hard work, and honesty. "I was the only daughter with dirt between my toes," she says. Her role in the family was "both hero and scapegoat, which can get confusing for a kid. For an adult it's not very clear either." But PJ became the family hero by asking questions when there was trouble, and then taking the heat when her questions opened up too much truth. She always felt that she was failing, always striving for praise. "No one ever said what the expectations were. I was just supposed to know." In addition she felt her sensitivities keenly. PJ was artistic, as were both of her sisters, and highly spiritual. "I was a channeling child," PJ says. Her mother's last words to PJ were to "tell me how I had never managed to meet her expectations."

PJ carried her sense of never being good enough and not knowing what to expect into her first marriage. The same emotional tone she experienced at home, she experienced with her husband. With a demon lover a woman will feel demeaned, the butt of his jokes, the target of his anger. In public he will raise his voice and "spew his venom" at her. Alone with him there will rarely be communication. She will feel his coldness and harshness, his silences. Having known all this in her first marriage, and having borne the burden of her upbringing, PJ developed a tough warrior exterior, which served her in her earlier work as an advocate. First she was a counselor for alcoholics, and with the families of alcoholics, then as an advocate for the mentally retarded and the mentally handicapped.

After her first marriage ended, PJ decided to focus on herself, too full of "war wounds" to trust herself in relationship. Nonetheless when Rob made his first advance she agreed to give him a try. Though she already felt that she knew him, what she discovered entirely surprised her. Unlike her relationship with her demon lover first husband with whom she had nothing in common "but the bed," with Rob PJ would find everything in common — except the bed.

As nearly all the Hades' Angels report, it is the depth of communication in their prison relationships that allows them the kind of love they have always imagined — a relationship of openness and equality. The demon lover cannot bear to be vulnerable or reveal his dependency on another. He does not have the ability to see the separateness in another, no less cherish it. And yet, it is with their inmate loves that the Hades' Angels discover the kind of openness and vulnerability that make for a powerful bond between a woman and a man. "Our communication is phenomenal," PJ says, "We can sit and talk about lampshades." But because all they have is talk and the hunger to connect and be known, PJ and Rob have learned everything about each other. They know each others' secrets; they talk about things they have never spoken of before.

PJ acknowledges that she carries a lot of psychological damage and that she is still "working on herself." There are times when Rob tells her he feels like he's getting "the brunt of some of my baggage. When that happens he asks, 'Is this from now or is this from the past?' He'll deal with it either way; he just needs to understand where it's coming from. He's very intuitive, very empathetic, and he knows before I do if I am fixing to go into one of my panic attacks, and we can talk about it."

This is the Rob of today. An inmate serving twenty-five years to life: a convicted of murder who has grown into the work of relationship. Obviously, he was not always "such a prince," PJ says. In fact, he has told her, "You would not have liked me before." How is it that men like Rob who have the psychological attributes of the demon lover, who have acted out violently, can engage in this level of intimacy?

"One of the things that happens in prison," PJ explains, "is either you become a person within yourself and know yourself, or your spirit is broken and you're just a walking zombie."

Rob has done a lot of soul-searching and lot of internal questioning, PJ explains, "Except he did it without benefit of the therapeutic situation. He just did it. He has read the Bible and the Koran. In his search, he found his spiritual safe-haven. He found his place, his sense of belonging with the Creator; he found forgiveness for his past." He is not the same man who entered prison fifteen years before. PJ, who has worked hard to know herself, feels safe with Rob, enjoying how well she is known and acknowledged as an individual.

When in relationship with a demon lover, most women do not recognize when they are being taken advantage of. Unaware when their emotional boundaries have been crossed or violated, they submit to the abuse that the demon lover inflicts in an assertion of his "false self", his fragile power. PJ has at last discovered that she knows her boundaries and can set them. "If I recognize that they are being stepped upon I tell

Rob, now we need to talk about this. I'm real quick to do that." As a result PJ no longer feels as if she is a victim in life.

It is common for therapists who work with couples to deal with the partner's unconscious emotional alignments and family of origin dynamics. Frequently, those dynamics manifest as splits: dominance and submission, and frequently women caught in the submissive role believe they are stuck there. The Hades' Angels who work their way past the submissive role with their inmate husbands are doing brave and bold work. For the Hades' Angels, their descent into prison also serves as a crucial descent into the self, and is a turning point in their lives. It is inside the prison that they discover the parts of themselves that have been buried - the very split off parts that have led them into repeated relationships with demon lovers.

With her prison marriage, PJ now enjoys the comfortable equality of a man whom she feels stands beside her. "I have a back-up. That's how I look at it. He makes certain that I feel special, cherished with him, even when we are disagreeing. He doesn't belittle me. He doesn't put me down. He sees the me that no one else sees."

A woman brought up to deny her own feelings because she was trained to meet her parent's emotional needs, either as a father's daughter or as a narcissistically wounded child, feels shamed and invisible. Shut down to her own anger and hurt, submissive and pleasing in relationship, she turns her rage inward where it often becomes transformed into perfectionism and workaholic behavior. The suppressed feelings that she carries in her shadow self are then expressed unconsciously in the demon lover, or in her attraction to a violent criminal, whose darkness and danger are safely contained in a six by nine cell. In such relationships she feels free to nurture what she unconsciously sees: a victimized fragile self that matches her own. But the fact that the women in this book find empathetic partners who help them to open to their own fragile selves is what makes these relationships so valuable, and so surprising.

PJ feels keenly the deep change within herself as a result of her relationship with Rob. "I feel that a lot of my old terrors and fears have been allowed to heal. I feel enhanced. I am more than I was. I guess if you could put colors on it, my ex-husband would be gray and battleship blue, my daddy would have been red, my son is green, and Rob would be pink. He's a loving man and with him I get to enjoy the kind of relationship I've waited for my whole life, one that's loving and nurturing and caring."

A born advocate, like many of the Hades' Angles, she has used her warrior energy to advocate on behalf of her inmate husband, who has yet to be released. In speaking of her advocacy work she reveals how much she has also learned about herself. "A young girl is walking along the beach picking up starfish stranded on the sand and throwing them back into the ocean," she relates, "when a man who had been watching this approached and said 'You know, you can't save the world.' The young girl answered, "No, but that one starfish I just threw back appreciates it very much."

Chapter Six

The Feminine Principle: World Soul

Marion Woodman explains that "the experience of the feminine is the psychological key to both the sickness of our time and its healing." The feminine principle is understood as the fertilizing agent for emotional life. It looks to the inner world to understand the outer world; it gives rise to a transformative energy that moves us from power to love and gives us a sense of oneness, the unity with all of life. When a culture represses the feminine, Woodman teaches, the soul of the world is denied and societies are marked by abuses of power that rape the earth threatening all life with destruction. When the feminine energy emerges in a culture, there is the acknowledgement of the community of being, of a unitary consciousness, of anima mundi, or world soul. In such a time, both men and women, and even the earth can heal.

As I traveled the country interviewing the women whose life stories you are reading, I could not help but think of the way that the feminine principle was operating in their lives. As easy as it may be for some to cast the first stone, to disparage a woman who finds her soulmate among the discards of society, to see a man society has judged as soul-less, each of the Hades' Angels is able to see more than the dangerous part of her man. She sees past the label, she sees something in her inmate love not easily seen by others. She sees the soul of the man who is before her, evoking in him, and he in her - if only for six hours a week - a capacity for deep connection and sometimes for transformative love.

Certainly these men, for whatever caused their anger and rage, or their life circumstances, committed violent crimes against fellow human beings, and now find themselves punished, condemned, doing their "life time" living out their days in six-by-nine cells. To the larger society they are at the low end of the spectrum, and have lost their humanity, but not to the Hades' Angel. As she freely enters the prison, she brings with her a sense of the feminine, the inward, of the sacredness for life. Stripping herself of ego and pride she may even carry the shadow for the larger society. In Judeo-Christian terms, through her love, she is ministering to "the least of my brethren", unlike so many of our brothers and sisters, unconsciously, doing the work of world soul.

How ironic, that in the prisons, among the obvious polarities of prisoner and guard, good and evil, among the discards of society, we see the feminine principle act as a fertilizing agent, performing its transforming work among men imprisoned for crimes of violence, the abuse of power and domination. Into settings saturated by the exercise of patriarchal power, where respect is gained through dominance and lived out in the unforgiving prison pecking order, the feminine principle emerges through the body of a woman who speaks of an instant, magnetic connection with a violent criminal, claiming that in him she has found her soul mate. Though stigmatized for her feelings and her actions she offers herself as a vessel to contain her man's pain: a mirror to a soul that the world condemns as evil, even soul-less.

"He gives my life meaning. He's entering me in a way I've never let anybody do, into my soul", so many of the Hades' Angels report. And many of the inmate's relatives declare, "She changed him. She brought him back." A special kind of energy, first romanced through correspondence, passes between the Hades' Angel and her inmate love in the prison visiting room. In psychological terms, it is understood as the subtle body, the vehicle through which the unspoken is somehow known, felt. That unconscious knowing passes silently from one person to another. To understand this depth of knowing requires that we look beyond the concrete that we see, and become conscious of both inner and outer worlds. It allows us to understand the deeper connection in the complex union of inmate and freemate.

There is a mythic element to these relationships that has parallels in the archetypal tales that describe the journey through life and the growth of soulfulness. And myths are understood as the unconscious representation of crucial life situations: the true experiences of mankind. These ancient stories tell of transformative journeys: abduction, descent, and initiation into the Underworld: about goodness transforming evil, about redemption, and about the wholeness that comes from the union of opposites. They appear in all cultures, throughout recorded history.

The myths teach us that life crises leads to suffering which can lead to the potential for transformation and heightened consciousness, a pattern which is apparent in the experiences of the Hades' Angels. The most ancient of these tales is the Sumerian poem of 3500 B.C. in which Inanna, Queen of Heaven and Earth, descends to her sister's domain in the Underworld, "the land of no return", as Perera (1981) calls it, to witness the funeral of her sister's husband. As queen of the Upperworld, Earth, Inanna is the bearer of civilized culture, but in the Underworld she becomes nothing but a single human animal, separate and alone with only her instinctual needs to guide her. While there she will learn through grueling experience the power of the instinctual feminine over the trappings of her civilized life. The laws of the Underworld demand that she be "brought naked and bowed." And so she is. Stripped and crouching, she is judged by seven merciless judges and then killed by her own sister. Then her corpse is hung on a peg where it rots; while in the upper world, her subjects mourn her abduction and her absence. Yet even the highest gods refuse to meddle in the ways of the Underworld and will not intervene on Inanna's behalf. Like Persephone in Hades, she is forced to remain there, ignored even by the gods. Only Enki, god of waters and wisdom, can secure her release by commiserating with Inanna's sister while she is enduring the agonies of childbirth (Perera, 1981).

While her subjects mourned for her, Inanna's chief consort, Dumanzi, had been enjoying himself on her throne. When she returns she looks at him with the same "eyes of death" that her sister cast upon her. Inanna's ordeal in the Underworld has given her the ability to see the naked truth; she can no longer be deceived, and so he is banished. But her descent has also given her newfound compassion for her loyal subjects. Earlier, she had ruled harshly from her head, but the tale goes on to show how she now has the ability to feel. She shows empathy, gratitude, remorse, and offers praise for her sister who has been her wise teacher.

Primary to gaining any inner awareness of self is a descent. In our lives, the descent takes us into the dark territory of the unconscious, to the unknown, hidden places of fear within us, which we must traverse in order to know our own potential, how to live fully embodied, ensouled. For all the Hades' Angels who lived, like Inanna, from the upper world, the head, it is their descent into the world of Hades, prison, that sends them into the depths of their own shadowy inner territory. Here is where, in the words of several of the Hades' Angels, "I learned to face my fears and be centered." Having done so, they emerge connected for the first time to an awakening of their own inner life and to their instinctual feminine energies that now allows them to feel fully alive, emotionally vulnerable, and opens them to love.

In the underworld of the prison, the Hades' Angel sees things that most of us prefer not to see: the injustices in the culture of the prison, the suffering of her man, and the conditions of his upbringing that have caused him such pain and served as the impetus for his destructive rage. She looks clearly at his crimes and does not dismiss them but learns to see "the person behind the act" and to love the man she believes he has become. No longer the emotionally submissive woman who served the patriarchy, she emerges from her experience with her own voice, empowered, ready to speak her truth to power.

Several of the Hades' Angels have become outspoken advocates not only for their imprisoned husbands, but on behalf of the voiceless incarcerated, and helpless victims in the general population. They are using what they have learned in their descent into the world of prison to do the work society does not or will not do: of awakening world soul.

Hades' Angel Louise, who is now in her sixties, is a nationally known advocate for prisoner rights who was born into a privileged upper middle-class family. "To whom much is given, much is expected. That was our family belief."

Louise, who had never married before meeting her inmate spouse, is perhaps the most unusual of the Hades' Angels. With no demon lovers in her past, no serious past relationships with men except casual dates, she lived the life of a celibate dedicated to serving those most in need: inner city teenagers. She began her career teaching high school French in an upper middle class school strict, but court-ordered bussing mandated the school desegregate, and overnight her classes changed. The college-bound, even Ivy-League-bound students, to whom the young Louise had taught advanced French and taken on European tours in the summers, were replaced by inner city kids who did not do their homework, tested their young teacher with catcalls and insults in class, even jostling her in the halls. What was Louise's response? "I am going to go where you live and find out why you're not doing your homework." They laughed at her. When she drove into the inner city and parked her car outside the low-income projects, and entered the center where "her kids" hung out at night, she was ignored. Pennies rolled her way—-a sign of disrespect. She was ignored. When she returned to her car it had been totaled, white latex paint covered it; the tires were slashed. Even the policeman who came to her aid, a former student, told Louise she was crazy to come into the neighborhood, that she'd better stay away because the next time it could be worse. "I'm going to find out who did this!" Louise declared.

Again she was laughed at, but Louise was undeterred. Young, naïve and passionate, she was determined to help "her kids" get a good education. No matter who turned up in her classroom, she was going to know them and find out how she could best serve their needs. Louise's work, the work of the strength of the feminine was not through power or "rules" but through love. A few days later she was back in the neighborhood, driving a rental car. A gang leader who happened to be one of her students showed her where she should park, right outside of his house. "No one will touch your car here," he said. And they didn't. It was Louise's first sign that she was on the right path. She returned to the center and a few of her students actually spoke with her, amazed that she had come back for them. This is how Louise's relationship with the at-risk kids of her city began.

In thirty years of dedicated work Louise would become a respected, familiar figure in that part of her city, teaching and advocating for several generations. Neither she nor her cars have ever received so much as a scratch. She developed longstanding close relationships with her students and their families. And when she could not help them in school, when they were incarcerated or sent to youth homes, she tutored them from the outside, corresponded with them, found out about programs within the institution, and guided them through.

Eventually her work was recognized and she ran a program for at-risk kids, advocating for their special needs. It was while she was following up on her incarcerated students that Louise met the man who would become her husband — a friendly Andy Griffith type, is the way she describes Tom, an old-timer in the prison that her "kids" had told her about who knew everything, and was helping them learn how to do the right thing: their mentor on the inside.

Louise had been single the whole of her adult life, her work-life entirely consumed her, she says. At first she and Tom had phone calls, then letters, it was all about "the kids," but gradually they began to share personal information. Both were single. They shared the same wry sense of humor. "Why don't you come for a visit," Tom said. And by the time they met they were already acting as a team, devoted to helping the young men who had been Louise's students continue their schooling and learn how to do their time in a productive way. It was another instant connection, sparked by a keen sense of humor and similar outspoken forthright personalities. Tom was a genial grandfather-type with thick white hair and a broad- shouldered dependability, Louise says. He was serving a thirty-year sentence in a maximum-security prison for a robbery he had committed in his youth. He had children and grandchildren on the outside that he adored. Louise had lived her life devoted to service with a close-knit family, a father in politics, two lawyer brothers, and a big extended "clan" who were politically active in her state. In their own ways, one on the inside and the other on the outside, Louise and Tom had spent their lives dedicated to helping the young, both doing the work of world soul.

It had never occurred to Louise to marry, but when she met Tom she changed her mind. He seemed like the perfect man for her, an upper middle class lady from a politically connected family - and a prison lifer. She just loved who he was and came alive under his patient, take-no-prisoners care. "He can give as good as he gets," Louise says, "And with me that's a lot." Louise and Tom were married by proxy, and at fifty-five, after he was released to a half-way house, she could say, "I'm no longer a nun."

Louise is a powerful force now for prisoner rights and prison reforms. Formally retired and with her husband paroled, after years of tireless advocacy on his behalf, Louise and Tom live on a quiet suburban street and though it took a little getting used to, her neighbors have come to like and trust Tom for the dependable, humorous, big-hearted, gainfully-employed man that he is. They, too, Louise says, have come to see Tom the man, not Tom the ex-con. Louise travels regularly to Washington, testifies before Congress and in her own state senate, working on behalf of a national prison advocacy group. Her life in retirement, she says, is even busier than it was when she was officially employed. She lives a full and rich life, she says, a married woman with her soulmate and life companion and the work of her life that fills her days with meaning.

Hades' Angel Lisa Heart, 49, had none of Louise's privileges. She grew up in a family where beatings were commonplace. She and her brother never went for more than week without a beating, she said. And worse, there was sexual abuse. Her stepfather was the perpetrator but her mother was sometimes involved. Her parents justified their abuse as a "demonstration that they loved us." Lisa Heart had a savior, though: her grandmother, the one who "probably kept me alive during my childhood." Sometimes she stayed with her grandparents, both of whom she was fond of. "I had the best times with my grandparents," she remembers.

The older she got the more sexual abuse she suffered. She counted the days until she was eighteen, and she could leave. Later in life she spoke with cousins who told her that they knew everything that had gone on in her family but hadn't done anything. It was the last time she saw them. "But back in those days people just didn't talk about such things," Lisa Heart says now. Her mother taught her never to get angry, never to express it. If she did she would be "beaten to death." It took her until she was thirty-eight to realize that she had been a very, very angry little girl. Her refuge as a child, her survival tool, was reading 400-500 pages a day. She excelled in school, feeling she failed if she got only 98 on a test. But she received little encouragement and praise at home. She was "only a girl," and besides, schoolwork always came easily to Lisa Heart. Her mother tried to teach her to be "the perfect little geisha girl and wait on your man and take care of him."

She married "to get out of the house" and had four children. But her step-father's sexual abuse had left its emotional mark. She was submissive, shy, scared of everything. She was cut off from her feelings in all her relationships and she married a demon lover, a man who deceived her frequently and got other women pregnant. Once, on line in a grocery store she stood behind a woman who was holding a baby who looked exactly like her own. It was her husband's child, only a few months younger than Lisa's. It took her nine years before she told him to leave. It was her second husband who encouraged her through nursing school and helped care for her children, but once she was through school, he started drinking. Years of this passed and she realized that living with an alcoholic was making her miserable. She was "doing all the stuff that I thought a man would do for me," and so she got another divorce. "I became the man I wanted to marry."

Her academic achievements won her a scholarship that put her through nursing school. She made good money, enjoying her achievements and her possessions: this way she learned she could get what she wanted through her own efforts. She traveled to China and bought a sports car.

Lisa was doing a favor for a friend, driving her to visit her husband who was in prison when the friend suggested she visit with one of her husband's friends "inside". Lisa refused, but a year later she changed her mind. "I was walking across the visiting room when I saw him - the Marlboro Man, gorgeous. I just stood there and held his hand for about ten minutes and it felt like we reached each other's souls. It was a weird experience, like finding your other half or finding something you have been looking for your entire life."

Steve had done all the right things in prison, educated himself, taken course work, and participated in self-help groups. From the start, he made it clear that his role was to encourage Lisa to be all that she could be. A regular church go-er, when Lisa told those in her congregation about Steve they only reassured her, "Christ didn't come to save the perfect. He came to save the needy." Lisa, too, sees human beings as "warty. We just have different warts."

As a woman whose childhood was marked by unrelenting abuse, she sees in the prison atmosphere "a step backward into my childhood when I had no control." The prison experience reawakens in Lisa Heart the feeling of being worthless, powerless, and less than human that she had experienced as a child. Keenly aware that prisons "are not about justice", she sees the ways they are wrong." Through her relationship, she was forced to descend into locked-off caverns of the self, into the shadows of her past, once again through those portals of dark, unwanted memories and feelings in order to be with Steve.

But it is in the prison visiting room that Lisa Heart has found the only place that she feels whole. "When I'm there, I don't see anybody else but Steve. I don't see anybody else. I don't hear anybody else. That's my time and I'm sitting there with my husband. I don't even notice the people sitting across the table from me. We don't hear their conversation."

The intensity of their connection allows a new energy to be created between them, a space in which the subtle body can do its work, unseen but felt. And even if it only happens for that moment, the Hades' Angel who is able to participate in this kind of connection has helped her man to release some of the pain of his actions and connect with the power of love instead of with anger and hate.

There was a time when Lisa was able to spend eighteen to twenty hours a week in prison visiting her husband. "A lot of married folks don't spend eighteen hours talking to each other." Now, because of prison overcrowding they have returned to a two-day visiting schedule. Still, these are hours of pure relationship. And how many couples on the outside manage that, she asks. "We are not allowed to have sex," she says, "but that does not mean we are not allowed to love."

Lisa Heart has journeyed far from the days when she was a silenced abused child. "Today I no longer swallow everything down. I can stand toe to toe with a senator and argue him right into the ground." She is a warrior, fighting for prisoners' rights and for the rights of the abused.

"My relationship has empowered me," she says, "and my husband loves me for who I am."

Hades' Angels hope not for a marriage shared of the flesh but a "death marriage". Instead, what is conceived and born of this marriage is not a human child but the birth of sacredness for life, a sense of the feminine, the inward, soul. She has emerged from the innocence of maidenhood, meaning from the imprisonment of naïve ignorance, of blind acceptance of the domination of masculine consciousness that enslaved her. Now she enjoys the capacity to bear separateness and conflict and to trust her own essence.

With her consciousness awakened, she is given a succession of impossible tasks to perform, in which survival [in the prison] is dependent upon her acute awareness. For those who choose an imprisoned Eros, such tasks include the ability to stay centered in the feminine while in the direct presence of ram (masculine) energy, without destroying either.

Joan of Arc is a historical example of this particular aspect of feminine wisdom bringing to consciousness the humanitarian spirit dormant in the human psyche. A similar humanitarian—and heroic—spirit was captured by actress Susan Sarandon in her powerful portrayal of Sister Prejean in the film Dead Man Walking, the true story of a nun whose poignant and dramatic attempt to "save the soul, if not the life, of convicted killer Robert Lee Willie, has changed our collective consciousness and paved the way for renewed debate about the death penalty" (PBSONLINE, 1999).

Like Inanna, the Hades' Angel enters the "land of no return". She can never go back fully armored. Maintaining the learned survival patterns and the internalized family myths of childhood, she had been drawn towards, vulnerable to, and kept involved in demon lover (abusive) relationships. Imprisoned internally in those previous relationships, she now seeks ways to address the unknown, split-off, wounded, isolated, stigmatized parts of the self. She learns to "rock the boat when necessary."

For here, born from empathic attunement, reciprocity, and compassion, there is revealed to her a new sense of knowing, or seeing, what was always known but cloaked in layers of adaptation —a connection with her instinctual feminine wisdom — her embodied soul.

As a society, our collective consciousness is changed by their actions, and by their love.

Now let's look at the relevance of Hades' Angels to motifs in myth and fairytale.

Chapter Seven

Redemption Motifs and Transformative Journeys in Myth and Fairytale

Myths and symbols are in the language of the soul. A myth helps us to take a situation to heart and know what we must do.

Jean Shinoda-Bolin,

Crossing to Avalon, 1995

Previous chapters (Part I) explored the Hades' Angels common threads through relationship stories that have the potential to be destructive. Instead, they prove healing and empowering for women who experienced a shift in consciousness: towards their growth, change, and transformation. Not only Hades' Angels encounter crises, turning points, destructive relationships, and shifts in consciousness; these also occur in the general population. These shifts occur in a hungry-for-life, objectified, not-taken-seriously general population of women eager for an enlivened emotional life. This chapter explores themes of descent, suffering, and redemption in myth and fairytale because, like the Hades' Angels real life journey, they describe a human journey along the path of individuation. Myths and fairytales offer guidance, a map of the soul, and a universal language to articulate this internal change as it emerges from the depths of the unconscious.

Myths and fairytales allow our experience of the sacred to be understood from a different lens. They speak of living psychological material and as such are part and parcel of what Jung calls the journey towards "individuation". Jung looked beyond pathology and the individual mind for the source and meaning of story and symbols. He believed familiarity with myths and fairytales as crucial for analytic work as a means of developing a deeper relationship with the unconscious. His ideas regarding symbols and metaphors examine the archetypal basis of fairytale motifs and the internal quest for self-realization and redemption: awakening to unconscious forces, wholeness, and a new stage of life.

Viewed from a psychological lens, fairytale plots and motifs use symbolic imagery to illuminate an inner experience, provide insight into real life experiences, and illustrate patterns [of life] that guide us along the process of transformation. Because they are written in the language of the soul, their symbols and metaphors model ways to wrestle with life's challenges, face conflicting aspects of the self, and sow the seeds of change. Through fairytale characters we encounter the wounded Angel within each of us and we relate to that wound. For my purpose, they also offer us another perspective, a different lens, from which to view Hades' Angels' journeys of descent, suffering, and shifts in consciousness.

In this chapter, I use myths and fairytales as a tool to peek down Alice's rabbit hole at redemption motifs in order to reflect on emotional patterns of functioning, learn what creates change in consciousness, and what is relevant for therapeutic intervention and healing. As a psychotherapist, listening to a patient's story means tending to the inner language, soul, which speaks through symbolism and metaphor.

An injury to the developing self occurs when the "treasured" part of the psyche is bound, gagged, buried, or held prisoner by the unmet needs of an unwelcoming emotional environment. Hades' Angels recount their own tales of imprisonment: early childhood narcissistic wounding and emotional abandonment. Such children, used by a narcissistically wounded parent, are helplessly left at the parent's disposal. The child's own developmental needs are "bewitched", or left for dead. In such unhealthy parental interactions, the child survives by becoming invisible. His/her preciousness lies curled up in a corner, dying. He/she is unseen, unheard, and trapped into mirroring the ego needs and emotional manipulations of a wounding parental environment.

Cinderella shouts out in behalf of such emotionally abandoned children: banished to the attic, and left in a state of confusion and non-communication. The magical Fairy Godmother symbolizes the wise self, the intuitive inner voice within each of us that knows our potential and pushes for transformation. Like Hades' Angels, Cinderella's childhood survival depends on masking the true self with achievement, and self-sufficiency, "working until weary" (Grimm, 1972), serving the needs of others. The telling and retelling of the soul's wound to an empathic ear awakens the deadened, wounded parts to its sleepy potential. It is in listening by "an other" with an empathic ear, hearing with the heart, telling and retelling until the wounded core feels touched, that the psyche begins healing the Self. Let your heart tune in to the richness of the underground world, the inner world, as told in myths and fairytales. It avails itself to those who can listen with the third ear. It is a timeless journey!

Psychoanalytic models of adult romantic relationships value the premise that two people feel mutually attracted by similar needs which are predicated on two main factors: the experiences of the developing child, and the child's sense of his attachment figures [parents]. Other theories expound a relationship based on the couple's wounded core, each partner expressing flip sides of a similar wounding. In other words, we tend to unconsciously search for, be drawn to what we are missing. Relationships are frequently based on an attraction of opposites. Thus, the draw of a Hades' Angels towards "my evil twin", exemplified in Beauty and the Beast, becomes most understandable in love relationships.

In *The Wizard of Oz* (Baum), our heroines Dorothy and Toto travel the yellow brick road, a metaphorical search for awareness, enhancement and further psychological development. Dorothy is not the only heroine traveling on an identity-forging series of adventures in search of the lost parts of the self, in order to seek wholeness, "home". She, like others who get hit over the head by external crisis or feel uprooted by inner turmoil, search for a cure-all, a magical wizard to make things right. Outwardly strong, achievement and goal-oriented

Hades' Angels sense a hollowness within. Though their ego's needs got satisfied with achievement and facade, the needs of the developing Self remain unmet. Thus, they begin their unconscious search for meaning. They become engaged in an inner journey, a struggle to "know thy self," to redeem from the underworld that which got "bewitched".

Myth, fairytales, and real-life human stories tell us about heroines on a journey towards psychological development, and Dorothy is unconsciously on this quest. According to storyteller Clarissa Pincola Estes (1992), what we [women] seek is redemption of the unlived, lost, split-off aspects of the self, long buried beneath layers of facade and adaptation. Presently, women face the world with their strong, good girl persona demanded by the upper world of survival. What gets hidden, banned into shadow, is the instinctual self, the embodied soul.

Hades' Angels come searching not for their own buried treasure, but for the potential within an incarcerated partner. They use a simple, unique and uncommon resource to do so: the empathic ear of their man inside, for life! An inmate-freemate relationship, and the dramatic backdrop of the prison environment become a container, a chrysalis, an ashram for inner change. For the first time, these women who have spent their lifetime being a mirror for others, get mirrored through dialogue with an empathically attuned ear. They begin looking into that reflective mirror, and find a self.

In order to move to psychological maturity, or what Jung calls individuation, one must bring consciousness into dialogue with the unconscious. Here, in a most difficult environment, a prison visiting room, that dialogue happens. Week after week, Hades' Angels are drawn to, and keep coming back to, where they feel seen, mirrored, heard, and their consciousness gets awakened. Their yellow brick road leads to descent and suffering. It is here they meet their shadow. They slay the dragons of their past. Unconsciously, they travel a road of individuation, and they are not alone. They are not the only ones who seek "home", wholeness and healing. As we shall see, fairytales and myths can be understood as metaphors for redemptive, transformative journeys.

How does a transformative journey begin? Opportunity is always knocking, often in the guise of life crisis. It can change us! Commonly, a crisis awakens consciousness, our back is pushed against the wall, and what was tolerable is no longer a comfortable shoe. Initially, it makes us feel small and helpless, small enough to squeeze right down Alice's rabbit hole. We have only to recall any number of fairytales: Snow White is cast out by a wicked stepmother, Dorothy is uprooted by a tornado, and a young King Arthur is ambushed and imprisoned by a neighboring monarch. Then, a bridge, inner self talk, or ongoing dialogue with the inner world is activated: "Mirror, mirror on the wall" speaks of a self-reflective dialogue with the not consciously accepted, darker aspects of the self. When the journey begins, the psyche is pushed towards greater awareness of the totality of the self In the shadows, it discovers what got wounded or pushed down to accommodate the parental environment.

In the classic fairytale Peter Pan (J. M. Barrie), Peter forges a special relationship with Wendy, then loses his shadow while trying to escape through her window. Metaphorically, each represents shadow aspects of the other: Peter Pan, forever a lost boy and Wendy, responsible caretaker to lost boys. In the end though, Wendy, like Hades' Angels, returns home changed from her adventurous encounter with her shadow part. Peter, however, remains developmentally stuck. Dorothy travels the yellow brick road in search of a Self, "home". Whether a Hades' Angel, or a wounded Angel in the general population, like Wendy or Dorothy, we encounter challenging tasks while on this difficult journey in search of home, a Self. We can never go back!

In any fairytale it is important to understand the depth and magnitude of the central character's traveling companions as each may represent aspects of a single psyche dialoguing with the inner world. On the road to Oz, Dorothy meets three characters she intuitively feels she knows: the scarecrow, the tin man, and the cowardly lion. She meets and dialogues with these, the unacknowledged parts of the self. The indecisive scarecrow can't make up his mind because he hasn't got a brain; the tin man who knows something in him is missing and he feels hollow; the cowardly lion, who contrary to his own nature has no courage. Focused on one common goal, they travel together to meet the magical wizard. This journey with the shadow aspects of the self represents a collective inner experience that can be understood as a metaphor for an integration of these shadow parts and psychological change.

Certain women work hard caretaking their Peter Pan-like puers, hoping to change their man, hoping to earn true intimacy and commitment, only to end up unfulfilled. *Beauty and the Beast* (Beaumont) tears at the heart and teaches us about love's power to change the other: despite his facade of anger and cursed ugliness, Beast can be changed by a woman's love. It also connects with the emotional concerns of modern life: sharing a mirror world replicated in destructive, "demon-lover", Beauty-Beast relationships of certain women today who say, "I felt beat up emotionally; I could see the patterns repeating. I was still asking myself what did I do to deserve this while I filed for divorce." When love is used to nurture the beastly aspects of the self, whether inner critic, maiden, or shadow, the hero/heroine can stop fighting a losing battle to change the other: "The only thing he wants is what he can no longer have—me." For a certain population of women, whether inside or outside prison walls, "demon lover" relationships offer a choice: to repeat old destructive patterns or confront and slay the dragons of the past. Their descent into the arms of a waiting Hades is their yellow brick road, and it opens up old wounds. If not swallowed up by the undead, vampiric energy they meet along the way, their experience of deep suffering will illuminate a new path, becoming their bath, their cleansing, their transformative journey, and their redemption.

Clarissa Pincola Estes (1992), states that, "Fairytales, myths and stories provide understandings which sharpen our sight so that we can pick out and pick up the path left by the wildish nature. The instruction found in story reassures us that the path has not run out, but still leads women deeper and more deeply still, into their own knowing."

Interpreted literally, fairytales follow a lovely linear primrose path with a beginning and ending. Understood symbolically, they offer that deeper knowing, a "heaven quake", opening portals to an inner world of Knowing that wanders along twisting, winding roads of descent, suffering, and self-discovery. Here, we meet our shadow, confront our angry wolf self, and discover the divine, buried treasure within. Listening to symbolic language gives us a way to understand the psyche: we learn how characters are cast out and unearthed from their comfort zone; are forced to strip themselves of facade and are coerced to accomplish challenging tasks; they are forever changed by their experience. Through listening to story, we learn how bewitched aspects of the self get redeemed!

What is redemption?

Redemption and salvation are not only terms associated with teachings of particular established religions. According to Jung, they are universal intra-psychic archetypal motifs, meaning redeeming the divine within, God, or the numinous from the darkness: that which has been unknown. These internal contradictions, these conflicting, opposing energies need to become integrated in the unity and wholeness of the Self.

So many women in the general population feel conflicted and bewitched: their hunger for life is deadened, objectified, and not taken seriously. They are eager for an enlivened emotional life, yet resign themselves to survive in a comfortable shoe built by "Peter, Peter, pumpkin eater". For those who choose to travel the yellow brick road, myths and fairytales offer guidance, a map of the soul, a universal language to articulate and explore this inner change, allowing our experience of the sacred to be understood. A metaphorical interpretation offers a fresh perspective. It is no longer the opposites 'God and man that are reconciled, as it was before, but rather the opposites within the God-image itself '(Jung, 1961).

In Jung's view, the New Testament's story of crucifixion, resurrection, and good and bad are flip sides of one another, polarities symbolizing the warring elements in the ego; ascension was an example of the alchemical process of death and rebirth (Miller, 1995). The "bad", the dark side, is felt as personal suffering, sometimes as evil, needing to be reconciled through integration with the Self. Understood psychologically, and in terms of psychotherapy, suffering, death and rebirth are viewed as shadow work, meaning the need to bring awareness of and redeem the golden treasure buried within.

In Fairytales

In fairytales, "redemption refers specifically to a condition where someone has been cursed, bewitched, or condemned without cause, and through certain happenings in the story, is redeemed" (von Franz, 1980). Fairytales lead us on metaphorical journeys in search of Self, for the soul that got lost, trapped, or hidden beneath layers of adaptation and facade. "It is the task of the hero/heroine to redeem the bewitched person" (von Franz, 1980), the aspects of the self that need to be built up or strengthened. Slaying the dragon or the monster really speaks about slaying the monstrous self-defeating, inner critic. Metaphorically, biting into the apple is about awareness, enlightenment, gaining self-knowledge, and pushing past social and cultural constraints. It is a redemptive experience!

Heroic Angels in Myth and Fairytale

Myths and fairytales describe universal, common themes. They act as catalysts for mirroring and reflecting about the human condition. From their interpretations, we open ourselves to benefit from many centuries of wisdom about life. We identify with them because they mirror occurring events and challenges in our own lives; yet we often lack models to guide us, or light the way, through the dark unknown. Fairytale heroes or heroines represent archetypal energies that serve as models for the developing ego. From them we are shown the "right way" (von Franz, 1980) to navigate through life stages: growing up, leaving home, going on risky adventures filled with challenges, and finally returning home, perhaps changed forever.

Like our actual lives, fairytale plots are packed with luminous and dark characters that curse and bewitch: snakes, dragons, dwarfs, heroes, gods, demons, monsters, witches, magic mirrors, magic spells, and baths. They are understood as metaphors for the polarized, warring aspects of the inner world trying to break through the unconscious. To become conscious, the hero/heroine must leave a state of dependency, maidenhood, and descend into the underworld to confront his/her shadowy dark side. Other images, such as castles, a deep sleep, glass coffins, thorns and briar bush are metaphors for protective emotional walls for childhood survival. Similarly, actual prison walls give Hades' Angels a needed protective boundary during her awakening experience. Sleeping Beauty, too, is rescued by an achetypal masculine energy, which culminates in ascension from her glassed-in, naïve one-sidedness. She is awakened to consciousness with a kiss. She is redeemed by a kiss of connection!

The hero/heroine travels the yellow brick road between the known and the unknown. Good characters possess courage, loyalty persistence and faith, while evil ones are personified by monsters, witches, and dragons. The polarities of good and bad are so often what was considered good or bad for the developing self by the parental environment. The hero/heroine's task is to overcome inertia, a state of dependency, sit in states of darkness and depression, and use it as a fertilizing agent for emotional growth. The search for that buried, golden treasure is the task of the hero/heroine. Dredging up the courage to look into the reflective mirror is not easy. The seeker of self-knowledge must see what has gone unseen, dialogue with and draw strength from its contradictory poles, and integrate it into a renewed sense of self. Ultimately, after death-defying challenges and sacrifice, the hero/heroine emerges the better for it. Redeemed!

As an example, we learn that innocent, naïve Snow White, unaware of her own beauty, is cast out of the palace by a wicked and jealous queen mother who is threatened by Snow White's youth and beauty. The huntsman drags her into a dark forest, surrounded by walls of thick trees, and Snow White is left there alone, terrified, and abandoned. Such terror and abandonment is an experience of suffering, a state of depression. The gates of the underworld open, the inner world is turned upside down bringing wave upon wave of grief and suffering. We can identify with her crisis because she portrays a real-life experience, and she acts like a human being: she is scared, helpless, abandoned, cast-out by a jealous "witch" mother, faces death, gets hurt, and we cheer for her to be rescued (von Franz, 1980). In her state of abandonment and depression, she discovers a little cottage, a safe haven, meaning a resource within where she puts herself to work, and begins a nurturing dialogue with her dwarfed, hidden aspects: Wise Doc, Dopey, Sneezy, Bashful, Sleepy, Happy, and Grumpy. As metaphors, they are understood as the conflicting, dormant, intuitive impulses that can move and guide us. As symbols, these dwarfs also provide us with insights into human behavior, moving us past the concrete world into the unfolding of a deeper layer of Knowing. When the wicked witch knocks at Snow White's safe haven with a poisoned apple, it is Snow White's opportunity to bite into newly unfolding knowledge about the self. It overwhelms her, and she falls into a deep sleep. She is forced from her innocent, maiden-like nature towards a state of emotional maturity.

Little Red Riding Hood, cloaked in the vibrant red of youth and life energy, is another naïve, maiden-like heroine. She, too, is unconscious of her own gifts. Leaving home and going into the wilderness is a symbolic move towards individuation: out of the known comfort zone and into the unknown. Carrying her basket of goodies, Red leaves the safety of home and meanders into the wilderness to meet up with Grandma, her wise, intuitive self. In the process of individuation, this is an inward journey, the royal road to consciousness, where travel is off the beaten path. Red, confronted by her shadowy counterpart, wolf, is deceived, and used by him. The sweet goodness she offers from her basket gets devoured, without appreciation. Grandma gets swallowed by the big, bad wolf, leaving Red no opportunity to learn life's lessons from her. When the woodcutter cuts open the dark-hearted wolf, the intuitive knowledge of the wise, inner world is exposed to consciousness. What was unknown about the self becomes known, and it is a transforming experience. Little Red Riding Hood is redeemed!

Beauty and the Beast guides us along a transformative process by illustrating how empathic mirroring awakens the psychological self. The tale begins with a crisis that leads to suffering, identification of the shadow, and redemption through integration of the polarized energies: dominance and submission. In one version of the tale, Beauty presents traits common to a Hades' Angel: a father's daughter who is outwardly strong, self-sufficient, and bonded to the values of the patriarchy; inwardly, emotionally naïve, and cut off from the strength of her own feminine nature. Like other fairytale characters, naive goodness feeds the emotional needs of the personal father and the patriarchy.

In the tale, Beauty's father comes upon Beast's castle, then gets caught trespassing while picking a rose for Beauty from Beast's garden. Enraged, Beast throws him into the dungeon where upon our "good father" saves his own life by exchanging it for that of his daughter! Yes! Our good father sacrifices his own daughter and Beast accepts this barter. Beauty submissively enters Beast's castle as her father's substitute. The real trespass is on Beauty's emotional boundaries when Father uses his position of authority to save his own life and seal his daughter's fate.

Every day, father's daughters live unaware of emotionally incestuous behavior by the father/patriarchy who uses her to meet his unmet emotional needs. In the fairytale, Father uses her to get himself out of his predicament with Beast. Father's top-dog position is countered by Beauty's submissiveness to him. Beast, however, is Beauty's opportunity to work through shadow problems: to grow; to stop hiding behind a facade of pleasing; to acquire the ego-strength to set boundaries with the domineering patriarchy, and to put voice to her own mind.

Beast's opportunity for redemption occurs when he stops using his ugliness and rage to mask his "bewitched", compassionate nature. By confronting the dark side of the other, each is changed. The outcome is emotional reciprocity: loving and being loved in return. Beast's compassionate nature manifests when Beauty's eyes look past Beast's ugliness, past his label, and into his soul. Beauty, redeemed from her naive one-sidedness, accepts the strength inherent in her passionate, wild woman nature.

Hades' Angel Dimples, a licensed minister, relies on the Bible as a guiding light. She faced her mirror, mirror on the wall, and came to recognize that her needs would never get met by her beastly pre-inmate spouse, "He'd talk at me and I tuned him out. He was verbally abusive and didn't work because he felt he was too good to go out and get a minimum-wage job – 'They won't hire a black man' – even though I did waitress work to support us until my feet gave out." She stayed in that marriage for twenty-three years because in "The Bible, she says, you don't get a divorce unless the other person is being unfaithful." Like her mother, Dimples was submissive to this man; like her father, she was a workaholic and totally supported him. Taking care of and being needed by others made her feel she belonged and had value. When it comes to her personal father, Dimples is openly bitter: "He never taught me anything except go to work, earn a living, financially take care of the family, talk trivia, watch TV, and wear a smile at all costs. I married my father except it was reversed in the money department -- I was the one working. A lot of churches don't tell you that if a husband is not supporting the family, there's something wrong with him. They tell you to work harder; they put it back on you." Dimples says she finally broke away from her repressive marriage after reading Melody Beattie's Co-Dependent No More. "It was an eye-opener. When I read about enabling I thought, 'That's me!' Up until then, I thought my marriage was something I just had to live with, but when I read that book I realized that it was a dysfunctional marriage and I no longer had to put up with it."

Myths use symbolic language that inform about the powers of the psyche. "Their images are reflections of the spiritual potentialities in every one of us," (Campbell, 1988). Myth, then, can be understood as literature of the spirit. In the myth Eros and Psyche, where there are gods of jealousy, passion, violence, and compassion, we get touched by such spirit images because they personify traits within us. Looking at myth in psychological terms, "it is a way of looking at oneself in relation to the world, a way of finding meaning and significance" (May, 1991). Further, through the dynamics of the gods, myth explores the numerous trials we face on the road to developing mature soul consciousness: crisis, chaos, suffering, abandonment, rebirth, and redemption. The myth of the divine Eros and the earthly Psyche illustrates a necessary differentiation of the feminine from its bondage to the masculine. It is a tale of liberation from the imprisonment of naïve innocence (maidenhood) in the soul's drive toward an autonomous feminine consciousness. Through her relationship with Eros, god of love, the developing naïve Psyche is challenged to move out of a state of unconscious maidenhood.

Eros and Psyche

According to Jean Shinoda-Bolin, "Psyche is about the growth of soul that began when Psyche decided to face the truth" (2004). She is abandoned, facing crises on her own, and is given challenging tasks beyond her ability. Initially, she is coerced into an unconscious relationship with Eros. In love, she remained in a state of illusion until she pulled back her projection. Following her sister's advice, she threw light on the truth and discovered he was a god. Paradise, her unconscious innocence, is now over. She is cast out and homeless. Death to darkness! Survival means she must perform tasks that move her from a state of dependency. In this myth, beautiful, innocent Psyche, the youngest of three daughters, is forcibly married off by her father, the king. She is led up a mountain in chains, waiting to be sacrificed to a "death marriage". Aphrodite, jealous of Psyche's beauty, sends her son Eros to shoot his bow at Psyche to inflame her with love for her beastly groom. But Eros, so awed by Psyche's beauty, pricks his own finger and is inflamed with passion for her. He rescues her but also makes her promise never to look at him. Psyche's sisters are afraid for her and instruct her to shine light on him. When she does, she loses him, and he abandons her. She is beside herself with grief and wants to take her own life. Seeing her despair, Pan convinces her to go to the goddess Aphrodite who offers redemption.

Neumann (1971) summarized the significance of Psyche's actions:

> *The knowing Psyche, who sees Eros in the full light and has broken the taboo of his invisibility, is no longer naïve and infantile in her attitude toward the masculine; she is no longer merely captivating and captivated, but is completely changed in her new womanhood that she loses and indeed must lose her lover.*
>
> *In this love situation of womanhood growing conscious through encounter, knowledge and suffering and sacrifice are identical.*

As the myth unfolds further, Psyche must perform a succession of four impossible tasks. First, she must sort seeds, meaning discern her priorities, make order out of confusion, and learn to rely on herself. Second, staying centered in the feminine while in the direct presence of ram (masculine) energy, she must gather wool from aggressive rams whose job is to assert domination. This means she must learn to overcome self-doubt, fear, and assert herself. Third, Psyche must gain an overview and observe the patterns of her life rather than be drawn to unconsciously repeat them. The fourth task is the hardest for nurturing women: she must set boundaries, stop rescuing, and impose limits on herself and others. Psyche learns to say no, learns to become fully involved with the experience of life, recognize her instinctual nature and the power of focus and determination. Focused on her tasks, psyche learns to endure pain and suffering, and from her perseverance evolves an inner sacred marriage, wholeness (Naifeh, 1997).

The human spirit, carried forward by Psyche's awakening to her own potential, is an Act of Courage. She gives birth to discerning the opposites within, to separateness, to knowing the self, and emotional intimacy, not loss of self. The potential in the true self gets redeemed!

The ancient Sumerian goddess Inanna that you read about in Part I, World Soul, also teaches us about Acts of Courage. Opening "her ear to the Great Below" informs about descent, depression, and ascension from the realm of the dead, meaning a breakthrough from the curse of ignorance. Inanna learns to see with a third eye, intuition and wisdom as we learn in the therapeutic environment. Like Inanna, we rise up renewed, aware of our potential and the strength from Knowing it. Our psyches journey to the underworld again and again to experience suffering, pain, and personal growth. Returning with the eyes of death, we, too, see and know more: we confront old beliefs; family myths get shattered; destructive, old roles must die as we give up our fundamental illusions about life. Therapeutically, we learn to welcome these descents as opportunities for growth. We focus on the totality and sacredness of life. We are redeemed, wholeness!

Hades' Angels Parallel

Such is the case with the twenty-six Hades' Angels whose real life personal stories so closely parallel those of myths and fairytales. Their stories give us a deeper understanding and appreciation for what draws them to love relationships with imprisoned men and what they continue to get out of it. Like the heroines of fairytales and myths, we learn of their deep, unconscious need to feed an emptiness, nurture the self, and heal early childhood wounds.

Kohut's (1977, 1978) self psychology claims the self needs an empathically attuned, mirroring caretaker in infancy to awaken psychological life. Hades' Angels, though a perfect mirror for others, are for the most part, needy for that same "magical mirroring".

Unconsciously, they are out to redeem the split-off aspects of the Self. So what is the payoff for living one foot in each world, for going in to rescue a prisoner, and immersing the self in a relationship that is "for life"? It is a felt sense of "attachment," mirroring, and comforting nourishment that hears with the heart. Like the walls of Jericho, what gets chipped away then comes tumbling down, are the emotional walls! About that nurturing, Dimples states, "Not only am I giving my basket of goodies to him, but he's putting some new stuff in my basket. I feel like I'm saying, here I am; this is me. I am somebody!"

Redemption In The Therapeutic Environment

Psychotherapy, analysis, "getting something off your chest", "sweating it out", is often compared to a cleansing, spiritual bath that leads to healing (von Franz, 1980). By listening to the client's story, we peek down Alice's rabbit hole to find what is relevant for therapeutic intervention and healing in their lives. In their language resides their spirit's quest for change from old patterns and beliefs that keep them "bewitched" in states of dependency. What are the client's beliefs about what he/she needs to feel redeemed? What we learn from listening to their story, the inner myth that drives them, often begins with the presenting problem -- a conflict, a crisis, a feeling of jealousy, a casting out, a curse, abandonment, or a suffering descent, followed by a state of limbo. In the therapeutic environment, the symbolic language embedded in the patient's story offers a frame of reference, a metaphor, for their healing.

Recently, a client referred herself to psychotherapy because of being frightened by a dreadful, recurring dream of being whipped and beaten while confined in a bathtub: without water, her arms rigidly strapped to her side. Here sat a vivacious, intelligent young woman, decked out in bangles and beads, and veiled in a beautiful smile that obscured an inner experience that apparently told a different story.

She felt trapped, confined, between a rock and a hard place. Though masked, like Dimples, in a smiling affect, her recurring dream exemplified her inner life as one of unbearable suffering: without the water of emotional nurturing; dry; stuck, shamed and dirty; victimized by a jealous, competitive "witch mother" who would not acknowledge the divine child within. The bath motif, "generally interpreted as the need to work through shadow problems" (von Franz, 1980), indicated this client's unconscious belief that she needed cleansing. The tub held her scared, fragile ego, serving as both her prison and safe container, and she could not escape the trap. The hazel sticks in her dream offered her hope, the potential to move from fear and concrete thinking to the wisdom of her intuitive self. This morbid dream was her wake up call! Water, baths and even beheadings are redemption motifs often found in fairytales and myths. Our lives are filled with meaningful rituals: sweat lodges, baptisms, and ritual mikvahs are about cleansing, purification, restoration, rebirth, and renewal. This client's redemption, her buried treasure, the birth of her developing psyche, required empathic nurturing "waters" found in therapeutic intervention.

In psychotherapy, not unlike fairytales, myths, and even dreams, symbols are self-reflective mirrors that bridge the contradictory, opposing aspects of the self: the conscious world above, and the unconscious world below. When understood, the psyche is awakened. Then, one thread at a time, previously unconscious psychic material is brought to life and woven into a whole tapestry, a redemptive experience. That is a numinous experience.

Redemption, then, means reclaiming a Self from the rubble, redeeming the divine aspects of the Self within.

General Population

Interestingly enough, the psychological dynamics we see in the Hades' Angels is also seen among women involved in similar kinds of love relationships in the general population, outside the prison setting. It is not just Hades' Angels who venture off the beaten path to descend into a soul-suffering hell. And it is not just Hades' Angels who are magnetically drawn to demon lovers or to men with the depth of a puddle. Even the most capable, intelligent, articulate woman, wounded at the core, may fall unconsciously into this kind of arrangement. It can happen whenever a nurturing, empathically attuned "filly" gets seduced by her shadow self, her dark side, her evil twin, whether he resides inside or outside prison walls. Here lives a Bluebearded-vampiric energy: a tragically sad, fragile ego of a man, an empty man deadened to his own soul, a man who kneads and squeezes her nurturing juices while manipulating her into believing his empty promises: I will love you always, means I will fall apart if you leave me.

The Shadow

What internalized beliefs keep certain women eating crumbs in matters of the heart? Ever the needy nurturer, and lacking awareness of her shadow side, such women are magnetically drawn into this relationship dynamic. A vampiric energy devours such hungry-for-life women, who when done being squeezed and used, get spit out. What unconscious dynamic needs to be brought to awareness? Though intelligent and articulate, such women don't know how to say no to a man who so adeptly lures his prey into believing he sees the "me" no one else sees. Book-smart, cognitive survival tools don't protect the hungry heart. Discovery of a demon lover's transgressions, calling him a snake, a coward, and a man without courage does nothing to change that dynamic. For such women, the inner world is held hostage, hungry to gain a foothold in the world of love where there is always a demon lover lying in wait. Recognizing one's unconscious role in the split-archetype is a step in the right direction. Ultimately, what needs to change is one's internalized sense of self worth.

Transforming the relationship dynamic from dominance and submission to one of reciprocity wrests in redemption of the lost, divine child within, the Self. The adult, still masked in childhood strategies of adaptation to survive and belong, must challenge childhood family of origin beliefs, lift the protective veils, discard the emotional armor, and redeem one's birthright, the true self. Hades' Angels have found a safe haven to do this inner work within the emotional environment of the prison and their inmate/freemate relationship.

As one client stated, "I was kind, loving, understanding of his faults, and never got angry with him. He walked all over me and I never understood that it was about me; I was the source of my own pain. I had to face my naivete, my shadow." After this turning point comes the curse of suffering that pushes us, often unwillingly, to proceed on a path that calls us to go within. Forced to face that "mirror, mirror on the wall", we go down and meet our evil twin, our shadow, and finally address those pushed down, repressed, intrapsychic conflicts. Here, the conscious aspects of the personality fought and won a dominant position. Now, suffering insists we bear witness to the pain of our memories. The shadow self is our "Dark Sister from Below". She is our inner figure emerging out of nightmarish windows of memory; she wants to take us sneakily from our comfort zone, out of our pond. No longer interested in protecting the facade, in purely intellectual concepts that ignore the psychic inner world, we are at the mercy of our psychic underworld, our shadow. A dormant dragon no more, we enter into a state of self-reflection, where the outcome of silent grief and suffering results in enlightenment, and connection with the repressed, cursed, unconscious parts of the self. We begin to learn to KNOW thyself! Redemption of the divine child lurks here in the shadows!

Clinical Practice

The women in my private practice, in my women's empowerment groups, and also Hades' Angels, describe their real-life fairytale-like experiences. While inwardly yearning for rescue, yearning to find someone worthy of their trust, and someone strong enough to lean on, their self-protective walls kick in to block that very possibility. Instead, they learned to stand strong and alone and supportive of others. They learned to give selflessly but are uncomfortable receiving the love and nurturing they are inwardly dying for. Childhood survival rested in the unconscious acceptance of their family role as the glue, the hub of dad's wheel. That facade level of emotional intimacy masked their fear, their deception, and their pain, and it was as good as it got. Unconsciously bewitched by the "father god" (Woodman, 1982) to whom they were intellectually and emotionally bonded, they learned to bridge, to mediate unmet parental developmental needs, and the needs of others. Cut off, beheaded, from the intuitive wisdom of the body, they had only a shallow awareness of their own strengths. Bewitched, emotionally isolated, abandoned, encased in a glass coffin, such women who keep their emotional walls up are easily hooked by the charisma of a "demon lover". Such men, wounded like the father, draw strength from these women as if it were "mother's milk". Unconsciously, these women repeat childhood patterns that haunt them in their adult relationships: attracting, and then rescuing men who use and abuse them. And they don't understand it! They must discover their inner world, become intimately acquainted with this unknown territory, their shadow.

> *Story is a medicine that greases and hoists the pulleys, shows us the way out, down, in and around, cuts for us the fine wide doors in previously blank walls, doors which lead us to our own knowing.*

> --- Clarissa Pincola Estes

Women who find themselves rotting, hung out on a peg as did Inanna, in unhealthy, thankless, one-sided relationships need to face that "mirror on the wall". As adults, they continue to function, though unconsciously, according to early childhood "either/or" survival patterns: seeking external approval rather than connecting to their internal wisdom. The strength of the instinctual feminine energy, the intuitive Knowing aspects of the self got split off and forgotten. So often these polarized patterns have a trickle-down effect that impacts multiple generations. There are many women who Know of that deep hole of which I speak. They know of their loss of passion for life, and quick willingness to sacrifice their fragile sense of self for someone else. They are craving to be loved, but unable to face their own deadness and self-destructive behaviors, so they get eaten up alive.

Angel Therapy

How do clinicians treat this population of intelligent, articulate, nurturing women, be they with inmates or partners outside prison? In treatment, competent clinicians of any theoretical orientation need awareness of the strengths and weaknesses of various modalities. Actively listening to the client's story with an empathic ear transcends all modalities. Myths and fairytales are a valuable lens to understanding the client's story, their unconscious emotional alignments and family of origin dynamics. Kohut (1977, 1978) understood that lack of aliveness and genuine life in a soul, was no doubt due to a childhood injury to the Self. At the root of the problem, was the lack of an empathic, mirroring caretaker to awaken the child's psychological life. The soul's defense against the ensuing neediness was to stay stuck at an incomplete emotional level.

What the child learned in family of origin dynamics, such as roles of dominance and submission, transfers into marital relationships where pain and anxiety of one partner is pushed into and unconsciously absorbed by the other. About such dynamics, one patient said, "I made my own bed so I guess I have to lie in it." Such women blame themselves, thinking if they work harder at their relationship they can make it work. Then they find themselves caught even more deeply in cycles of abuse and do not have the tools or the know how to unlock themselves from their inner prisons. When we observe in our clients thickened walls of self-sufficiency and inner deadness, we need to be alert to, suspicious of their unmet developing needs and the often magnetic-like attraction to its opposing energy -- *destructiveness and chaos.*

Hades' Angels and women like them are not rare. Many function like this: walking around with a wounded angel lurking inside, hungry for a relationship that offers soulful connection. Yet, what they fear, too, is that same unknown emotional attachment. Soulful women who live to fix others, yet hungry for the unlived emotional life, are anything but crazy. Many want desperately to unearth their passionate nature from layers of facade and adaptation. Often, they get shocked from a deep sleep by life crises including addictions, cancer, death of a loved one, or a husband's womanizing adventures. Then they begin their journey on the yellow brick road. In therapy, such women do work through seemingly impossible "acts of courage" towards individuation. They recognize the thrill of it as a never-ending, evolving process. Clinicians help revive the richness of their buried treasure by listening empathetically with the "third ear" and at this soulful level, the heart is touched. Such empathic attunement is empowering and transformative for listener and courageous storyteller. Psychotherapists, like certain fairytale characters, take on mentoring roles: Cinderella learns to trust her fairy godmother, her mentor, and the wisdom of her intuitive self. Hades' Angels, and those in the general population, learn to trust their KNOWING, instinctual side, see the unseen and their own potentiality. Their inner and outer worlds connect, resulting in integration of the splits (wholeness), and redemption!

Hades' Angels say they become more than they ever thought they could be, even find happiness, in their lifer/inmate relationships. How they do this may offer lessons for women in the general population, bewitched, imprisoned souls eager to reclaim an enlivened emotional life. As a psychologist, I focus on awareness and insight as the path towards deep emotional growth, wholeness, individuation and transformation. I also recognize that this process may occur independently outside the psychotherapy office. The following chapters inform about what Hades' Angels experience can offer those who remain soul-trapped in destructive relationships outside prison.

Research on emotion has shown that although attachment is largely unconscious, its proper management is critical to having a healthy, satisfying life. The soul's first opportunity for that attachment is in the mirroring, and empathic attunement from the mother — her ability to fall in love with her child awakens the child's divine potential, the blueprint in the soul. PET scans and MRIs have enabled neuroscientists to document the influence of unconscious processing in humans, providing ample empirical evidence for the value of self-knowledge (a notion advocated in ancient Greece).

Psychotherapy works on many levels: conscious and unconscious, cognitive, social, and emotional. For clients in the therapeutic process, telling his/her story offers more than relief, stress management or cognitive reframing. It offers the potential for attachment, emotional holding, intimacy, and it offers soul. The richness of the underground gets unearthed when we listen from the heart until their words drip meaning that fires up their soul. Listening empathically to the story opens the heart of the storyteller, touches heart of the listener, moving both from the limitations of the outer world to an inner world of knowing.

The common wound of certain women and their demon lovers outside prison keeps them hooked and bound for life in abusive emotional environments. Hades' Angels seek love relationships behind bars, where within this unusual arena, narcissistic healing and transformation often occur. The empathic attunement these women find in such unusual relationships awakens them. This unique population of women then transcends the limits of early childhood wounds, and previous abusive demon lover relationships.

Now let's take a look at how Hades' Angels manage to connect with their inmate spouse in the first place.

Chapter Eight

The Ways Hades' Angels Met Their Inmate Spouse

The meeting of two personalities is like the contact of two chemical substances: if there is any reaction, both are transformed.

--- C.G. Jung

Imagine, if you will, hearing the whistle from a passing train beckoning you...but to where? You've heard that blaring whistle many times and given it no further thought. Now, like a ghostly wind, it calls out your name. For months, you've been riding shotgun with a friend who visits her best kept secret, an inmate. Feeling weary, tired of going down old roads, tired of feeling alone in the world, tired of not feeling, you feel a yearning for what you can't articulate: a good love to nourish the spirit. It's screaming out inside you, silently, for a passion unknown: 'I've been in life's passenger seat long enough!' Warming up to the idea, you decide to take a step further, and follow-up on "killer letters" that bring a buried part of you to life. You decide to answer that whistling call, climb aboard a train with no final destination. Over and over, it's rhythm clanks along with your thoughts: "What am I doing? Where am I going? What am I looking for? It's okay, just keep going, break away," you say to yourself. Your passion for a wider perspective quickly overcomes initial apprehension. You want to let your hair down, want to let it blow softly in a warm breeze. Chains that gripped you loosen up. That harsh, demanding inner voice fades, releasing curiosity, excitement, fear, and a new perspective.

To one degree or another, the twenty-six women interviewed in this book felt mixed emotions about meeting an inmate: release, curiosity, excitement and fear. It was not a frivolous decision. At some point, they stepped out of their comfort zone, traveled unknown territory, and risked putting themselves in an unusual and vulnerable position by connecting with an inmate. Something within them shifted, some turning point opened them to such an unusual experience, which they say has "filled them up".

Like many women in the general population in this same age group, these women went through long periods of suffering, pain, and aloneness which encompassed divorce, widowhood, separation, loss, and deep loneliness. Unconsciously they sought meaning and they wanted connection. Some were in therapy or involved in 12-step programs. All experienced some life stage transition: one lost parents; some felt the loss of children who left for college; another was searching for her birth father. All are common life events, but for certain women they become major turning points – opportunities for life change.

So let's take a step back and see how these women met a man in prison in the first place:

Nine Ways to Meet

Generally, there are nine ways of contacting and then meeting a man in prison:

1) Personal Correspondence
2) Church Correspondence Programs
3) Outreach Groups
4) A Friend
5) Required College Coursework
6) Official Capacity
7) Working in a Prison
8) By Chance
9) Attending a High-Profile Trial

1) Personal Correspondence

Letters play a major role in prison life. Letters are encounters between two human beings, but in this case one of them is locked in a 6x9 cell. Incarcerated, isolated, cut off from female contact and the outside world, inmates place ads for pen pals to initiate relationships. Women answer them! Correspondence may be merely an avenue for friendship, but often becomes the basis for courtship and romantic love. "Being kind of scared of men," says Hades' Angel Betty Jo, "correspondence seemed like a relatively safe way to connect. I was looking to alleviate loneliness, not a love relationship, and I made a good friend." Letters, the power of the pen, cannot be underestimated. Resonating to something inside, they link writer and reader in an ongoing connection to self and other.

Before they met, Bridget Kinsella (not a Hades' Angel), a vivacious, upbeat career girl, fell in love with a prisoner's prose: she never suspected he would help heal the wounds of her divorce, (Benson, July 1, 2007). They first shared correspondence, which gradually deepened their trust and intimacy. Bridget exchanged letters with her inmate for nearly a year before she felt compelled to see him face-to-face. It was a revelation that she describes very simply: "I met him in prison and we fell in love, even though I tried not to."

Hades' Angel Lady Honeybear, a counselor for runaways, was enticed to shed her protective skin after reading an inmate's 21-page letter. She said, "I was held by his up-front style of telling about himself and his tales of life on the streets. I felt as though I was almost inside his skin."

Inmates advertise for "pen pals" in newspapers or on the Internet, seek correspondence so he can lessen isolation, connect with the outside world and talk about himself, his ideas, his thoughts and feelings. Women answering such ads address responses to the inmate's serial number, such as H56789. Below is an example of an ad taken from the classified section of a major California newspaper; they can be found in papers all over the country, any day of the week:

*Incarcerated SWM 31, handsome, love sports/outdoors,
slim figure. Attentive, seeks attractive SF 20-40. Race
unimportant for correspondence.
Sylvester _____ K12345, PO Box 5002, Calipatria, CA*

By engaging the writer in states of self-reflection, letters bear witness to one's internal experience and pave the road towards self-awareness. Letter writing, like journal writing, is a medium that bridges the writer's thoughts and feeling. Correspondence actively creates a safe "holding environment," (Winnicott, 1958) to dialogue with feelings and make sense of difficult internal emotional states: confusion, tension and anxiety. When read, the writer's powerful internal experience gets validated.

For certain inmates, correspondence, which uses symbolic imagery, is a tool that initiates connection with previously split-off fragments of the self. Through correspondence and meditation, some inmates learn to bear internal tension and conflict rather than react to or be controlled by it. "An unawakened person is seeking pleasure and trying to avoid pain. A conscious being is working both with their pleasure and pain in order to be more conscious," says Ram Das, a spiritual teacher and psychologist, who created and financed the Prison Ashram Project in 1973.

Since that time, Bo Lozoff (1985) has directed the Ashram Project. It teaches spiritual renewal through meditation, and uses correspondence as part of a program towards self-awareness so inmates learn "to use their prison cells as ashrams and do their time as prison monks, rather than as convicts," (Lozoff, p. xvii). Further, Lozoff encourages inmates to correspond with him and, in turn, teaches them to move towards states of self-reflection. Says an inmate in a letter to Bo: "I've learned a lot about myself and others. Society has given me a gift I would never have given to myself, a chance to find my true self."

The Prison Lionheart Foundation is another project that teaches inmates emotional awareness, emotional healing, and psychology of self.

"After teaching in the prisons for more than seven years, I have seen that more and more people want the guidance and direction to help them use their incarceration productively," says Robin Casarjian (Houses of Healing, 1995). One inmate, who validates this reluctant embrace of guidance and direction, wrote, "I never had time to get to know me until I was locked away, alone with myself."

The Dark Side of the Correspondence

However, not every woman has a healthy experience corresponding with an inmate. Some inmates use letter writing as a tool to seduce and manipulate their "pen pals" to keep themselves from falling apart [inside]. A Florida inmate, states, "Some inmates cultivate pen pals and manipulate them into becoming emotionally involved. Their goal is to get money, postage stamps, packages and, if possible, personal visits." Reader and writer have a choice: to seduce, manipulate, and project one's fragmented self onto the correspondence, or begin an effort to "know thyself".

From the perspective of inmates for whom aloneness is very frightening, the pen is a powerful tool to project the more socialized, attractive part of the self. Seeking to alleviate anxiety, the rejected, lonely part uses correspondence to defend against that loneliness. Phoebe Ellsworth, who teaches in a law school as well as in the psychology department at the University of Michigan, has corresponded with a number of "dead-men-walking".

Ellsworth discusses her correspondence with Arizona death-row inmate, Paris Carriger. "Two or three letters is about par for the course. Then they get into how I'm going to be their own personal mother and bank. Paris was much cleverer. Paris told me he was interested in doing research and that he was uniquely positioned to do studies on the mind of the murderer. There were layers and layers of scam that only gradually dropped away," (Trillin, April 19, 1999).

Joyce Maynard (Vogue Magazine, February 2007), seduced and manipulated by an inmate during her time of emotional vulnerability, thought he "read her" correctly. Here she writes about her on-going correspondence with Lucky, an inmate:

One day, a letter dropped through my mail slot.

I will tell you now one thing about men in prison: As much time as the rest of us spend going to jobs, taking care of our houses and meals, our children, our pets, carrying on relationships and breakups, paying bills --having sex perhaps, if we are lucky -- that is time men in prison have for writing letters. Not surprisingly, they get good at it.

So when I wrote a sentence to Lucky, as I did that first time, he wrote back five pages. When I wrote back a paragraph, he sent 10 pages. When I wrote back a full-page letter, the envelope that arrived back, in record time, contained 50 pencil-written pages, with writing on both sides.

The relationship with Lucky, whatever it was, continued to develop. When I wrote back, now -- as I did, at greater length than before -- I didn't simply respond to his stories. I told him mine. I told him about my life, and about my children. I described a terrible argument with my son Willy, then age seven, who had ignored my request to do his chores. I had stormed into my son's room then. I had taken his CD player away, I told Lucky. My son called me a terrible name. I slapped him. He picked up the phone and called his father, who was now charging me with child abuse.

In all those fifty pages, there was nothing of romance or sex, only the deepest kind of respect and affection, and something else too: From what Lucky wrote, I got the sense that he understood me in some strange way, as nobody had for many years.

And here I was, at eleven o'clock on a Friday night, pouring out my story to a man I'd never met, in the Calipatria Correctional Facility. I had begun to consider the possibility that maybe -- by some odd corollary -- I had actually located the one truly good, honest man on the planet. Someone who was -- as he himself reminded me every time he signed off -- "for real."

When he informed her about his release date, she became fearful and called the prison. "Your friend will not be released on parole any time soon. Considering the fact that he is serving two consecutive 80-year sentences, he will not be eligible for parole until sometime after the year 2150.

After I'd gotten the news about Lucky and ceased writing to him, I opened one of the letters that continued to arrive. When I did, the words I read hit me like a blast of some noxious gas: toxic and putrid as decaying flesh. The same hand that once filled the pages with words of loyalty, compassion, and understanding -- and undying love -- now formed accusations of wrath and contempt beyond any I had encountered in my life. I used to say of Lucky, that although he was a man who was unable to make love to a woman in flesh, he had developed the ability to make love solely with words, more powerfully than I would have known to be possible. Now I discovered the power of words on paper as a force of unspeakable violence. His words did everything but draw blood.

Correspondence offers opportunity for a heart-to-heart connection leading to self-awareness and even emotional intimacy. Opening up, putting one's history, thoughts and feelings on paper, does involve a risk of being enticed and manipulated by a writer's seductive, socially appealing false image. Hades' Angel and their inmates, driven by a deepening need for connection, use correspondence to tap into their inner world because each feel "held" and "heard" by the other.

2) Church Correspondence Programs

Correspondence is also carried on by church pen pal clubs and prison advocacy groups rather than on an individual basis. These church programs reach out to save souls. Church members set time aside, sit down together to write to -- and often mentor – men who request to be saved. Eve's prisoner wrote her church "because it was the only church in the phone book that advertised meditation. And meditation was the way that he could calm down, look at things in a different way, and begin to detach his identity from his emotions." It is not uncommon for church members to become part of such programs, of which there are many across the country. Often, they also encourage church members to make prison visits. As a result, members may become more involved than originally intended. Hades' Angel Dimples, a licensed minister, met her current prisoner husband while ministering to someone in prison: "It occurred when I was going through a trial process, spiritually supporting another person. We'd pray over the phone."

3) Outreach Groups

Outreach and advocacy groups are another way of creating an inmate, "freemate" connection. If loneliness and desire for connection are what drives participation in prison outreach groups, then some type of more intimate inmate relationship is likely to occur.

Sarah James, a Long Beach, California tax consultant, visited a prisoner under the auspices of an outreach group. His name was Jack Kirschke, a former deputy district attorney, sentenced to life for the slaying of his first wife and her lover. Sarah was smitten immediately: "It was the most passionate and most dangerous relationship I have ever had," she said in an article in the Los Angeles Times (Warrick, January 23, 1997). Sarah and Jack began a courtship of monitored visits and censored love letters. They married in 1976, and are now divorced. Kirschke's life sentence was commuted after ten years and when released, James stated, "He turned into this tyrannical, cold-hearted stranger… and when I stood up to him, he left me for one of my best friends."

4) A Friend

Commonly, women meet an inmate through a friend's matchmaking introduction after she requests a ride to visit a spouse, a son, or a friend in prison. She is then encouraged to fill out paperwork in order to visit an inmate inside who may ask permission to write to her.

Hades' Angel Beth, 42, a database administrator met her lifer husband while accompanying a friend who was visiting her husband in prison. Beth says, "The first time I met my current husband I was immediately and intensely interested. Nobody had ever caught my attention that quickly. The biggest thing was his smile. I just felt strength coming from him." Prior to meeting him, she describes her life and her relationships "like a box of chocolates, I never knew what I was going to get."

Typist Cheryl (not a Hades' Angel) describes her friend's matchmaking. Cheryl met her husband, Paul, incarcerated for murder, when a friend showed her a photograph of her brother (Paul), then housed at a State Prison, east of San Francisco. "Cheryl began to correspond with Paul, then visited him, and began driving the one hundred or so miles between San Francisco and Folsom when he was transferred there. They exchanged vows in a prison chapel wedding, kissed, then walked into an adjacent room and sat side by side in plastic chairs bolted together, chatting with the best man and with Paul's mother. Afterwards, Cheryl returned to her home in San Francisco and Paul returned to his cell" (Hurst, April 17, 1983).

5) Required College Coursework

To fulfill requirements for a sociology class, such as one at Valley College in Los Angeles, students are required to visit the local jail. Students may choose to continue visiting on a volunteer basis; many do. Some university programs require internships for graduation, such as facilitating a prison support group. Continuing to volunteer time and energy may lead to personal involvement with an inmate. Asha

Bandele (mentioned in another chapter) describes her initial involvement (Bandele, 1999):

> *The first time I went into a prison, it was for a class I was taking on the relationship between black people and incarceration in the United States. Months later, long after final exams had been taken and grades received, my former professor called me and asked if I would come with him and a few other people to a place called Eastern Correctional Facility in upstate New York. It was just about eighty miles from Brooklyn, New York. He said he wanted me to participate in a black history month program. I agreed and we all went to do the program, and this was how we met.*

6) Official Capacity

Other women got involved with inmates while in an official capacity such as a social worker, courtroom artist, court reporter, or even defense attorney.

Such is the story of Jane Burleson, 48, (not a Hades' Angel) a Solano County, California public defender, as reported in the San Francisco Chronicle (Goodyear, April 15, 1999). Jane met her now ex-husband, Gaylin Burleson, in 1985 while she was a defense attorney and he was in custody on a 1971 murder conviction and robbery charges at California State Prison-Solano in Vacaville. Jane, a defense attorney in private practice, was assigned to investigate a suicide at the Shasta county jail in a case where Burleson was a witness. They struck up a friendship, began a correspondence, and she fell in love and married him in 1987. After he was paroled in July 1993, he stalked, attacked and threatened to kill her. Burleson says, "I spent my whole life trying to keep people out of prison. I didn't want him to go back to prison. I just wanted him to get away from me." Though already released on parole, because of the three strikes law, her testimony revoked his parole and sent him back for life. In 1995, Jane was told that her ex-husband put out a contract on her life from his prison cell, so she was whisked off to a secret hiding place while an investigator tracked down Burleson's hit man. If a sentence has the possibility of parole, an inmate may be released on parole after serving his minimum time. If Burleson is found guilty he could be sentenced to thirty-five years to life, but that won't necessarily help Jane who still lives in fear for her life.

In another instance, Tennessee attorney Mary Pentecost Evans was to represent William Timothy Kirk on charges of murder when she became involved with him.

> *"They met in the attorney's room at Brushey Mountain Prison in Tennessee. Already serving a life sentence for armed robbery and other felonies when he was brought up on this new charge, murder, there was little hope that Kirk, 36, would ever get out of prison. Mary Evens was blond, beautiful, bright, and from a wealthy family. Both Kirk and Evans, 26, had been married and divorced before. But the day they met, it was as if no-one else in the world had ever existed,"* (Isenberg, 1991).

7). Working in the Prison

Prison is a big business and like other big businesses, has a huge support staff: correctional officers, doctors, teachers, secretaries, ministers, psychologists, social workers, legal personnel, and administrators. With such a huge support staff, it is easy to understand that inmate-staff relationships might occur.

Physical proximity and emotional vulnerability are two major factors that can trigger relationships, and although unpublicized, inmate and Department of Corrections relationships do occur: Hades' Angel PJ was a prison secretary, Michelle was a prison therapist intern, and Maria was a very reputable corrections officer. "All the years as a corrections officer, I felt like I was bridging the gap between those people who were in prison and the outside, and I loved my job," says Maria.

8). By Chance

Typically, Hades' Angels and other good women have lived life according to society's rules and are unconsciously drawn to men who don't.

Before Hades' Angel C.C. saw the benefit of adhering to the rules, she says she was the girl your mother warned you about. "I walked a different mile. I still walk right up to the edge, and sometimes I'll step over it if I want to." There were repercussions, however; it got her into trouble and at one point she ended up in jail. Her assignment led to meeting someone special: C.C. and her "friend" started their friendship in 1976 while she was in jail and he was incarcerated in a penitentiary for murder. He worked as a clerk in a prison woodshop making desks, chairs and credenzas for state offices and nonprofit organizations within the state system. She worked outside in connection with a state correctional enterprise.

The system began a pilot program for prisoners who wanted to travel from the prison to the central offices and do paperwork. Angel C.C. knew she needed to learn some skills, so she took advantage of what was being offered. She took a typing course and some college courses, and worked in the bakery for a while. "Part of my job was to make sure shipments arrived at their destinations on time. I had to talk to all of the clerks in the different shops. One day the woodshop clerk asked me if I would write him and I said I would. What I liked about him was his straightforward personality and I thought it would be worth investing time and becoming friends."

Hades' Angel Ann "chalks up" meeting her current husband "to fate." They became acquainted while attending a doctoral program together. "I met this man in class. He was a lifer who got hooked into education." She found it difficult to look at this man and imagine that he'd killed somebody. "I wouldn't judge a person because he was incarcerated, but I wouldn't intentionally seek him out either." For the majority of Hades' Angels, connection with a lifer comes as a surprise: not sought, not particularly wanted, and certainly not something that could have been predicted. For those Hades' Angels who took a chance, who let go of the known, it became a transforming experience. These women "began to follow the lure into the unknown," (Campbell, 1988). In myths, heroes and heroines set out intentionally in quest of a task or a deed whereas these Hades' Angels were drawn in, captivated by a certain look or a feeling, then followed their sense of having "found my soul mate."

9) Attending a High-Profile Trial

A less common and more dramatic way of meeting an inmate is by catching the inmate's eye while attending his trial or witnessing it on television, hoping for some sort of connection. A woman almost wills him to look at her. Once she feels that connection, she gets his inmate location number and writes to him. During the high profile trial of brothers Erik and Lyle Menendez, accused of murdering their parents, Tammi Menendez (not a Hades' Angel) felt a connection with Erik. After watching his first trial on television, she began a correspondence with him and later married him.

For Doreen Lioy (not a Hades' Angel), a magazine editor that "moment of connection" with the Night Stalker Richard Ramirez, first occurred via television: "The police broke into a television show I was watching to broadcast his picture…and I saw something in his eyes, something that captivated me. It wasn't as if I knew him, but there was…maybe vulnerability. I don't really know." Lioy and Ramirez later married in a prison ceremony, where 'Till death do us part' is an ever-present reality.

The Magnetic Draw

Many women have no intention of becoming involved with an inmate; however, they say they feel emotionally pulled in once they do meet following correspondence. They cannot fully explain it even to themselves, especially because, unlike themselves these men are socially stigmatized lifers who live life at the bottom of the social spectrum.

Many describe this "felt sense" as magnetic. Hades' Angel Betty Jo says, "There is this magnetic field that draws us together, but neither one of us has ever been able to figure out what it was. From the start, I felt a tremendous pulling, an intense pressure, like I know this person and I need to know him better." Hades' Angel PJ doesn't understand this relationship: "It is a blessing, and it is an unbelievable fit that I would never have thought could be there with two total strangers coming from totally different backgrounds." She has searched psychology books trying to figure out what created this dynamic experience between them. The unlikelihood of their deep connection confirms what she has read: "When your soul mate comes into your life, he is going to know the core of you and you will be totally accepted."

Similarly, other women in this unique population describe an immediate surging energy at first meeting that far surpasses friendship or shared interests. Their original intention may have been to reach out and selflessly nurture the "least of my brethren". However, upon meeting him in the flesh, these women say they experienced "instant recognition", a "kindred spirit", a "soul mate", or someone the woman feels she has "known all my life". They say that, "the pieces just fell together". Although all these men who are lifers live in the Belly of the Beast (prison), Hades' Angels say they "feel at home with him in his home", believing they "have everything in common but the bed".

Kissed by Connection

Hades' Angel, Michele, 45, a psychotherapist, says: "It wasn't love at first sight, it was comfort at first sight -- it was knowing at first sight." While she interned in a correctional facility, "the psychologist asked me to sit in a group therapy session that the inmate had been asked to co-facilitate." Michele was emotionally and spiritually drawn to him because "his poetry and songs touched a soft place in my heart." She explains, "It's like when you're swimming, the water's not inside you but all around you, and it's supporting you and you feel free within that support. I was an intern and I didn't want to ruin my schooling or my career." Michele, however, left her internship but not her relationship.

Why Do They Do It?

"We marry men on the inside for the same reasons people on the outside marry each other – people with their own particular set of problems," says Lori Girshick, (not a Hades' Angel), a sociologist and the wife of an inmate. She is an attractive, professional woman who doesn't fit the image of a prisoner's wife. She writes to help other women like herself: "People believe wives of prisoners are stigmatized because prisoners are seen as very lowly, and are not sympathetic to the wives or their families. It is a very uncomfortable way to live. Sometimes it can be a tough way to go." (Girshick, 1996).

A woman who enters freely into these men's lives, unconsciously carries a sense of the feminine when she descends into the prison underworld. Previously romanced through correspondence, she enters the "belly of the beast" with its repressed chaos and underlying tension, to minister to an inmate's lost soul and, instead, finds love among society's discards, and that she "gets fed, nurtured, and filled-up."

Here, she connects with a man who cannot possibly "hold" her, physically. How ironic: imprisoned for crimes of power, domination, and aggression—these men find themselves imprisoned by those who exercise power, where respect is gained through dominance and manifested in the pecking order among men. Here, at the crossroads of death, the feminine principle, understood as world soul, enters through the body of a woman who claims to have found "love" among those whom society has judged as "soul-less". Though stigmatized for her feelings and her actions, she offers herself as a vessel: to contain his pain, and as a mirror for a soul the world knows as "evil", a lifer or a convicted murderer. Hades' Angels hope not for a marriage of the flesh but reprieve from a "death marriage", in this case meaning marriage until death. Psychologist Richard Tarnas describes such relationships as "the reconciliation of two polarities, a union of opposites: a hieros gamos (sacred marriage) between the long dominant, but now alienated masculine and the long-suppressed but now ascending feminine," (Tarnas, 1991).

What is conceived and born from their relationship is not a human child but the birth of a sacredness for life, a sense of the feminine, the inward, soul. Conscious of their man's inner world, Hades' Angels see something in these men not seen by the rest of the world. They see beyond their label of inmate, lifer, murderer, -- they see the man who lies deep within.

Who are these women, these beauties, these Hades' Angels, who strip themselves of ego and pride to enter, like Inanna into the depths of hell? What is the experience of women who find their "soul mate" in the belly of the beast? Are they kissed -- or cursed -- by what they describe as a powerful, instant, magnetic connection?

Many find their love put to the test when they encounter the exacting prison protocol placed upon visitors of men behind bars.

TWO STORIES: Ann and Maria
Portrait: Ann

Hades' Angel Ann, 41, a public school administrator with two children from two previous marriages, condenses her early years as having a very happy childhood, although she says something was missing, meaning, she wanted "attention from a stay-at-home mom who was also a room mother wasn't there." Ann continues, "My parents were soul mates who found each other the first time, and I applaud them."

Neither Ann nor her sister had such easy-going relationships. Theirs seemed flip sides of the same coin: while Ann had two divorces, her sister got involved with drugs. "My parents, though caring, don't rescue anybody. They don't offer to pick my sister up and dust her off. Their approach is: 'We're here if you need us. Call if you want help. If you don't want our help, that's your decision.' Of the two of us, my sister is the one who was always more likely to take risks."

Ann recognizes the value of different, which she sees in her two children. She says, "My son is wonderful, passive, artistic, and musical, and my daughter is athletic, academic, dynamic, and real argumentative."

Early Relationships

During her young adult years, Ann says she was a fairly sexual person who felt needy for loving: "I was so needy I loved more strongly than I was loved in return." Her first husband was a popular high school jock. "I think I walked all over him. He was a very passive person and I'd say 'the bills are here and you don't want to pay them, so I'll do it. Give me the checkbook.' It was like I didn't have respect for him. I didn't realize that until later. He also didn't know how to handle his anger." After a while he became physically abusive, and I refused to accept it. My second husband was brilliant and the antithesis of my first husband. He spoke five languages, knew history, was a classicist and a storyteller -- but he was all in his head, noncommittal and unavailable for me emotionally. He had an affair; then left me two weeks after our son was born. That's harsh!" Still, Ann has only kind things to say about her ex-husbands as a father: "The relationships didn't work out. But they are good dads."

Meeting Her Lifer Love

Oddly enough, when Ann met her present lifer husband, she had no idea he was a prisoner. He was attending class outside the prison, working on his doctorate, and she was in the same doctoral program class. Ann had no clue what his circumstances were. He wasn't physically restrained in the classroom. She enjoyed talking with him. "He had little education or training prior to being incarcerated, so when he got there he took advantage of what was offered. He got hooked on education, working his way up through the prison system. He got his G.E.D., then an associate's degree, and bachelor's and master's degrees. I think he gained a lot of respect from the Department of Corrections employees who came to trust that he truly was trying to improve himself, so he was allowed to go into a doctoral program outside the prison."

Unfortunately, politics changed within the Department of Corrections. Ann continues, "A new warden came on board and said there's no way he's going to let a lifer convicted of first-degree murder leave the facility, so my husband had to drop out of his doctoral program. When I first found out he was an inmate, I felt very guarded, wondering if I was being manipulated or if he was going to use me or ask me to do something illegal. I went and asked the prison director of education about him: 'Do you think I will be used?' He told me, "Absolutely not. This is a man of integrity." At 42, he has now been in prison for as long as he was outside -- twenty-one years.

What She Sees in Him

Unmet historical needs play a role in their relationship. Even with no sex in their marriage, Ann still feels she found the right man: "He is loving, kind and encouraging. When I tell him about how my studies are making me nuts, he tells me how proud he is of me. He feeds the emotional side of me that never got supported before."

He seems to understand what she needs. "When we first met, he appeared distant, but when he starts to talk, he is a warm, funny, engaging, bright man. He lifts me up. He completes me. His smile can light up the room. He makes me laugh and he makes me think. He is the most supportive person I have ever known. He loves me unconditionally and even though we have had some nasty fights, I have never ever doubted that he is my soul mate. We both have our light side and our dark side and he has allowed me to explore the shadow part of me; he's like my evil twin."

Ann was very cautious about going deeper into this relationship. "I wouldn't judge a person because he was incarcerated, but I wouldn't intentionally seek him out either. He had pled guilty, so there's not any doubt he did it. There's no trying to make excuses or saying, 'I didn't do that, I'm falsely accused,' none of that at all. I could never set myself or my children up to be in danger from some maniac, so I grilled him about his crime: 'Why did you do it? What gives you the right to take somebody's life?' I gave him a hard time. I also went to the county court house and read his files. I pulled up articles about the murder that were in the newspaper, and read those. I really did my research. And I see such a huge difference in the man he is now and the man he was then."

Family values and fear of stigma have prevented Ann from rocking the boat. She chose not to tell her parents about their marriage: "I think they would hyper-analyze it," she says. "I trust them not to make judgments, but this would be a real hard one for them. They are in their late seventies. I know they would be shocked if I said I'm married to a man serving a twenty-to-life sentence for murder. We'd talk about it and work through it, and eventually we'd all be okay. I know that, but I don't want to subject them to that. They will think of themselves as the in-laws of an inmate, and I think it would be tough for them."

"I'm a believer in fate," Ann goes on. "I'm not really sure we have a whole lot of choice about who drops into our lives. I'm a professional person. I don't go seeking my thrills with high-risk people and life-threatening situations. But I met this man in class and he seduced me intellectually. I saw that under this hard exterior was a warm, wonderful, fascinating person. I'm still learning about him."

About Shame and Stigma

Ann's is aware of the stigma attached to people involved with prisoners. "I feel it when some people look at me like, 'This woman must be so desperate for affection that she sunk to this level.' The irony is that this relationship has pulled me up. Still, I know there's prejudice. I'm a good, honest person. I don't lie. I don't do drugs. I don't drink. But the very fact that I am the wife of a lifer sends a lot of prejudice my way. The truth is nobody can shame you without your permission. When my husband and I were first married, I tried to set up a joint savings account with him. The bank wanted him to come in and sign, so I braved the stigma and was up front with them: 'My husband's incarcerated so he's not going to be able to come in and sign, so what do I need to do?' I got turned away by three banks! Finally, I went to a bank where the woman said, 'Oh, not a problem. Does he have a picture ID?" I said, "I think so." She said, 'Well, if he does, send in a Xerox copy and we'll send the signature card to him.' It was just not a problem."

As a professional, the stigma shows up in other ways that force her to live in two worlds. "Probably the hardest thing about being married to him is that I have to live this double life. I'm an assistant principal, so I have this exterior about being the disciplinarian. I love my students, they are great kids, and I can usually get them to comply and understand and accept consequences, but boy, for so long that was all there was in my life -- work and school. That's challenging enough for a person. Then when I made this really strong connection with another human being, it took me to another level. I have two worlds: in my professional life people see me in one light there, but then I get to explore this whole other piece where I can be honest and real."

The Visits

When visiting, Ann gets a lot of what she felt missing in her childhood: time to just be. Even the problems in visiting don't deter her: "It's where I'm whole and peaceful and the world is right and I'm not stressed," she says. "It's not work for me; it's not living a double life. It's just being who I am. My husband and I talk more than I ever did with my children's fathers. I know talking is more important to women than to men, but we'll sit there and talk about whatever comes up whether it's important or not. I went to visit him today and sat with him for four hours. Sometimes we talk, sometimes we don't. Sometimes we just sit and hold hands."

Ann was brought up to not tolerate abuse and injustice. Witnessing what she considers abuse of the prisoners or their visitors upsets her. "One November day I visited with my children. It was very cold outside, but the guards wouldn't let my husband into the visiting room as long as my kids were present; they rudely made them stand outside for an hour in the cold. I'm even a state employee, for God's sake. It was a horrible experience. It frustrates me that some other person has control over my husband's life and thereby over my life -- and worse, that that person is accountable to no-one, and has to answer to no-one. There's no-one I can complain to or say, 'I wish you would review this case,' or, 'I'd like to speak with you and tell you about my husband because I know him better than anybody else.' They don't care. Their response is, 'It's discretionary.'"

What could possibly be amusing about a prison visit! "They allow you to bring change for the vending machines, so on my first-ever visit I brought fifteen dollars worth of quarters. I put them down on the table. When we were going to go outside, I started to scoop up my quarters. My husband said, 'Just leave them there.' I said, 'I'm not going to leave my money just sitting there in front of everybody,' and he said, 'Nobody's going to take it,' -- and he was absolutely right."

Ann gets serious when describing an abuse incident that happened to her husband. A guard pushed a prisoner really hard and her husband stepped in and, in doing so, put his hand on the guard. "My guess is it was probably pretty forceful, like he was trying to break up a fight but wasn't interested in engaging in a fight. Because of that, the guards stripped him naked, tied him down and beat him and kicked him until he lost control of his bodily functions, and then left him there. So if anybody ever tells you that prisoners aren't abused in prison, don't believe it. That's only one example of the kind of thing that occurs behind the walls. When I asked why he didn't report what happened, he said it's not worth it because of 'reciprocity' and 'retribution.' He'd pay for it ten-fold. When I asked why the guards would do such a thing, he answered: 'Because they can.' I know he feels hopeless and helpless in prison in terms of their control over him." Many prisoners, Ann says, don't survive prison. "People lose their lives for stupid reasons. They die over cigarettes."

Parole Hearing Wars

Ann has become a strong advocate for her husband. Ann's entire life has been vested in helping others, so hearing her anger about the unfair parole system comes as no surprise: "There are unfair things that go on in prisons. My husband worked very hard and he has done everything expected of him including meeting the standards and criteria set for him. He started off as an illiterate, angry young man incarcerated for a crime but he educated himself, got involved in rehabilitating young offenders, and then the parole board members come in and shoot him down. They never ask what he's done in the past twenty-one years. All they want to know is, 'What kind of gun did you use?' and 'What did you think about when you were doing it?' His answer to these questions is, 'I don't know,' so he gets turned down for parole."

Ann takes his parole denial very personally. "It's like I'm denied parole. It's tough and it feels like the whole world is crumbling around you. As an adult, I have control over my life. But when it comes to the parole board, it's totally out of my control. Parole games make me crazy. Aside from taking care of my kids, getting my husband home so we can have a healthy family life is my greatest priority. If somebody would just tell me what I need to do for my husband's release,' but that's not what happens." When her husband gets turned down, it stirs up his fear that Ann will leave him but she thinks they have gotten past that now.

The parole board has a huge responsibility when it comes to release, but Ann doesn't appreciate the unfairness of it all. "If they let somebody out who is convicted of first degree murder, and he reoffends, they don't look good. I understand that piece, but here's where another huge political piece comes in. We recently elected a conservative governor elected on the tough-on-crime stance. His version of 'tough on crime' is to keep criminals off the streets -- which means no parole. Typically, when the parole board has twenty-to-lifers actually eligible for parole, they'll wait until they are a year from their mandatory release date -- when they're going to be released anyway -- and then they'll parole them." These men get no reward for working hard and getting all that education -- other than the education itself. "If a child does the right thing we say, 'I'm proud of you,' or 'You get a scholarship to college,' or something. I get real frustrated with that."

Prison Advocacy Work

As an advocate for prison reform, Ann has volunteered for a reading program within the prison system. "One of the reasons is to gain some kind of understanding of my husband's world -- see what a cell looks like, see the hallway he walks down, see what the chow hall looks like, and interact with some of the other prisoners through the reading program." She'd like to be even more active, but they are afraid that his case could be hurt because of it. "Besides, I really don't have the time until I finish my doctorate, and I don't want to subject my family to any embarrassment." Has advocacy work changed her or made her wiser? "I'm trying to learn. I've certainly had my biases challenged. And I no longer take for granted my freedom, my right to vote, my right to get in my car to drive to the store and buy groceries."

The Future

Ann never tires singing her husband's praises. "I am extremely proud of him. I think he has overcome more obstacles than any other human being I know. I don't want people to think of me as irrational because I married this man. I want people to understand I married a good man. It has been a very long journey, and hopefully it's a journey we'll be able to continue -- but there are no guarantees."

Ann's Update

After four and a half years of marriage, Ann's husband was released from prison. She mortgaged her house to pay for the costly legal work. She saw herself as the catalyst for his release: his prison advocate, his emotional resource, and his financial support. Things went very well for a couple of months. He attended paralegal school, had a successful paralegal internship, and began work for an attorney. He seemed to have an excellent relationship with everyone in his life, even his parole officer. "He was awesome," Ann says. "He was the love of my life. He was a survivor." They were mutually supportive, and a special "aliveness" existed between them.

As time went on, however, Ann began to notice a side of him she'd not seen before. She had never experienced the dangerous part of him; it was the part that simply cut her off without notice! He had his own agenda and he walked out without even giving his forwarding number. "I got pregnant, lost the baby, then filed for bankruptcy, and he said, 'I'm done!' He just cut me off." Still, Ann defends him, believing he was overwhelmed with stress. "He was inside for twenty-five years. As long as he was on the inside, there was hope. But on the outside, he couldn't handle stress, death, loss, anxiety-- or a relationship." Today, Ann says, he shows no desire to work things out or have a sense of responsibility after all that was given to him. He has no remorse, and shows no grief for the loss she feels.

Ann's Transformation

Being abandoned, this time by her inmate husband, forced Ann to become aware of her own destructive relationship patterns, and how she gets drawn to the same type of man who walks away when things get difficult. "At first I felt stupid and naïve. I didn't get it," she says. "But the experience taught me something new about myself: I identify with the wounded, lonely, and hungry-for-love part in a man." Now, she recognizes that is what she needs. "I tried so hard to give him what he needed that I ignored my needs." When she saw that her inmate spouse could not fight for himself, she fought for him, leaving herself and her family vulnerable and unprotected. Today, she is also aware of creating dependency situations by rescuing and doing for others, robbing them of their chance to learn to be self-sufficient and independent.

Her husband's emerging independence "outside" appeared to leave no room for Ann: "I didn't count. When he was inside, he understood my stress, listened to my feelings, and his need for attention got met as well. Outside, he was not interested in working things out. He cut me off as if I were dead." Drained financially and emotionally, Ann says: "It was an up-and-down roller coaster ride. Would I do it again? Absolutely! He enriched my life. It was exciting. I met amazing people and saw a part of life I never would have known. I have good memories that I wouldn't give up for anything. He was such an intense partner, a protector, and well respected in the prison culture. We are so much alike but, unlike him, I don't walk away."

Ann learned the hard way. She has the inner strength to put herself "out there" again, on the forefront this time. "I no longer need to live any part of my life vicariously through someone else." She has also learned that she has a right to expect more from a partner than she previously thought -- love, not abandonment.

###

Portrait: Maria

Hades' Angel Maria, 61, is now a realtor although she worked as a corrections officer for the Department of Corrections for sixteen years. "During all those years, I felt like I was bridging the gap between those people who were in prison and the outside, and I loved my job."

Family history played a big role in Maria's decision to care for and protect others. Maria became familiar with being needed and with the fear of living with anger, rage, and the effects of alcohol on the family. Her mother was only fifteen when Maria was born. She is the oldest of four children, and the only girl. Her father was 35, a bricklayer and "Jack of all trades." He was also an alcoholic. Small in stature and usually gentle and quiet when sober, he changed when he drank, "It was like this little man got big and mean, although he was never mean to us children, only to my mother. He was always threatening to kill her with a knife. I can remember gathering up the knives and the scissors and sleeping on them at night, not knowing that the knife he was going to use was in the closet."

Her father never went through with his threats, but her parents divorced. Her mother went to work so, at age 9, Maria became the caretaker of her three brothers. Her father never came around after that. Maria downplays the impact this had on her, admitting only to her feeling unloved and abandoned when he went away and there was no contact for the eight years before his death. She relates, "The night he died, he told his boss he was going to look up his children to see if he had any grandchildren or anything. But he died in his sleep that night."

Maria's mother remarried and had more children – ten altogether. "She really didn't have time to give a lot of special attention to any of her kids, so I was pretty self-sufficient. I thought I could take care of the world." Most members of Maria's family, including Maria, ended up in law enforcement. "One brother was a deputy sheriff and then in the highway patrol. One was a chief of police, and another brother was a wildlife game warden. Still another was a policeman in New Mexico. Mom was a jailer and a matron in the women's county jail and her brother and three of her cousins were all sheriffs. So it's kind of in the blood." Time is a precious commodity in Maria's family. Having received so little personal attention, Maria had no expectation that somebody could be there to share her burdens, or try to make her happy; "My first husband had to be taken care of. We were married eleven years and parented three girls." One is theirs, one is adopted (and happens to be blind), and Maria is the guardian of another she raised as her own birth daughter.

She says this was a difficult marriage: "He was not a companion for me emotionally. We were like two ships passing in the night. I met his needs. I think I was there just trying to prove that all women weren't like his mom. He wanted me to cook and clean, but he didn't want me to demand any relationship. We divorced because I figured if I had to be lonely, I might as well be alone. I am alone now and I am not lonely." Deep inside, Maria wanted more control over her own life. "I was involved in a good Bible-based church. I wanted to find out who I was and become different than I had been." That's about the time she asked God's help to shed her old caretaker ways. "This time, I just wanted to have a relationship that was a partnership."

How They Met

Maria believes her prayers get answered. Sitting around a warden's conference table at a maximum-security penitentiary is hardly the place to meet a husband. Secretly, Maria hoped for a very special person to enter her life, one who possessed six important qualities: "Godly; respected by others; strong-willed; intelligent; encourages me to be all I can be; and not feel threatened by me. I wrote these down and prayed about it to God: 'If that person is out there, bring him into my life. You will have to hit me over the head so that I know beyond a shadow of a doubt this is the person.'"

About a year later, her hopes were realized when meeting her husband-to-be. "I thought, 'He is a really good man; everyone respects him and wants to talk to him.' And he was an inmate! At first he was kind of stand-offish because he had nothing to do with either staff or inmates. He was very much of a loner, did his own time, and did it his own way."

With her family history, one can assume Maria was resistant to any relationship with an inmate: "I was a very credible professional correctional officer and had a big ego. Plus he was Hispanic and I certainly was not looking for a Mexican inmate for a husband." Over the course of the next few months, Maria got to know him a little better:

"I thought, 'Yes, this man is a very respected person by staff and inmates. He is intelligent. He is strong-willed.' She began considering he was the man God had promised her: "I spoke to God, 'Well, your sense of humor is not even funny. I mean, I am a professional corrections officer and this would be disgraceful.' But I knew that this was the person."

All For Love

Realizing this was the man for her, she quit her job and went to work as a private investigator. During that time the inmate's attorney contacted her to help work on his case. The whole case was being reinvestigated so she had to go into the prison and talk with him as a professional and get acquainted. She says he never tried to manipulate her or take advantage of this situation.

Things progressed. Maria and her inmate have now been married for nine years. "I have never sent him money. He pays for all of his phone calls. He has a job inside. He is thrifty and disciplined. He has never demanded anything of me or tried to control my life. I guess now I can say I kind of know what the word cherish means."

The Stigma Issue

Maria has felt no stigma about being married to an inmate. "There has been no retribution towards me. No one has been disrespectful in all the years that I have been married to this man and visiting him." The staff, she says, who knew her as a corrections officer, has been surprisingly supportive -- as have been her relatives, many of whom also visit him in prison. She feels and appreciates their validation. She lets her real estate customers know about the relationship if the topic of family comes up.

What's the Appeal?

Maria accepts that separateness is a built-in feature of being married to a man behind bars. "I am okay without him. I don't need him to be happy. I have had more peace, more joy, and more spiritual and emotional intimacy than I have ever had. Our relationship is warm and wonderful. He is proud of me and understanding of my activities on the outside." They have much in common. "We are both patriotic and we both served our time in the armed forces. We are proud we did that. I think going into the service is where he got his first taste of dignity."

Having worked in corrections for so many years, Hades' Angel Maria is acutely aware of what can happen to prison relationships. "I saw how the guys control, manipulate, and use the women in their lives. Having worked in a prison has made it easier for both of us. I know what he experiences in prison. He has never had any reason not to trust me; he is very grateful and thankful for me."

Fears

They've had their rough moments, especially when he feels insecure about not getting released or gets afraid she won't remain committed. But when her back is up against the wall, Maria shows how strong she can be. "Once, he even asked me about getting an annulment, because it looked as though he'd never get out. I simply told him that's not the way it is going to be and I picked up and left. I said, 'I'm leaving. You can consider whatever you want to consider, but when you get your head on, you know where I am at.'"

Maria says commitment is the very reason she married this man in the first place: "I wanted some commitment, more than just a friendship. I think we need a commitment to each other." Being religious, Maria puts her husband's release in God's hands. "When we got married, we were acting upon the faith we had as if the release would happen. It hasn't happened yet, and I believe that's because we have waxed and waned in our commitment to keeping our eyes on the Lord. But I believe one hundred percent that it could happen any day."

The Dangerous Part of Him

Though convicted of first degree murder, Maria says, "I think my husband was unfairly convicted of a first degree murder. He was guilty of being there and there was a struggle over a weapon and someone did die. But there was nothing deliberate."

Personally, she has no fear of him. She comments, "Now, you have to remember that I have been in law enforcement and corrections for twenty-three years. I should be smart enough to know what I am dealing with. I can't believe that there is any danger and that the relationship God brought to me is going to go sour in any way, shape or form -- as we keep our eyes focused. I think the judge knew the conviction was not right. Currently, we are in the process of trying to hire an ex-judge who is now practicing law to take his case."

Those All-Important Visits

On weekend prison visits we sit across the table from each other and we're allowed to embrace and kiss when greeting each other, and again when it's time to leave. "It is fulfilling to me. Not draining. I look forward to the visits. We can put our arms around each other and walk in the yard and hold hands and talk and laugh. We don't even pay any attention to anybody else. The visits seems short -- three or four hours go by without even realizing it and then it is time to go. We don't do any lingering or kissing because that would only make it more difficult."

As Maria says, there's a downside to visiting: "Lots of waiting; lots of disappointments. Sometimes you think the visit is all worked out, and then it doesn't happen. But I try to develop that gift of patience." As to how her husband spends his time, she says, "He spends a lot of his time studying and teaching and counseling the guys inside. He is a teacher, something he wasn't when sent to prison. But today he is thoughtful and very concerned about other people, not just about me, but about the rest of my family too."

Changes

Chemistry and friendship are two major factors in any relationship. There is chemistry in their relationship even though there's no sexual intimacy between them. "I try not to spend a lot of time day dreaming about the intimate part. I think that side of it is going to be okay." More than wondering if they will be compatible sexually, she wonders matching up daily routines. "I have my morning routine and he has his. I get up first thing and go to the bathroom and then I come back to bed and read for a while. Then I do my quiet time, and then I get up and make the bed. At night I like to get ready for bed and read. Maybe those seem like funny things to be worried about, but how we are going to do that? I don't even know where we are going to put his clothes in the closet. He may have to sleep in the other room. It's kind of amusing to me that these are the things that I think about."

She wants her husband's release, yet she also really enjoys being alone: "I can work as late as I want. I can choose not to come home if I don't want to. And now, I can take whatever invitations I want and I realize that I won't be able to do that."

The Future

Having been a caretaker all her life, Maria looks forward to being taken care of someday. "I want to be in a partnership where he takes care of me; where he looks after the bills and the insurance and the car and stuff like that." Being in charge of everything is pretty overwhelming at times. She has a lot on her plate: "I've got a home; I've got a business; I've got a ministry."

Still caretaking, Maria makes hospital visits five days a week to a good friend who is dying. "I am trying to be in three different towns at the same time and I would really like to have somebody here to help me." Unlike her father, she believes her inmate husband takes care of her as best he can: "He is always there emotionally. Sometimes, he sends money to me, if he can, and if he thinks I need it. I have a small check that comes to me from his retirement. We discuss how he is going to take care of me when he gets out. I love my husband and I am proud of him and I look forward to the time he gets out and we can start our life together. And I know God will give us some time together."

Maria believes her marriage to this inmate has changed her for the better: "In many ways, I am pretty much the same as I was before we met, but I also think that I have mellowed. Before, I ran everything and I was probably the dictator. Now I think I am not quite as controlling."

When Maria chose to take off her guard's uniform to be with her inmate husband, she discovered who she could be without it. On the other hand, when he was put in a prisoner's uniform, he became more than he thought he was.

Hades' Angel Maria chose to step away from her position of power, her role, and her persona, and knows she is no longer hiding behind anything. "I had pride in my job. I had credibility, and it took a while to not miss it, but back then I didn't have the freedom of expression I have now to be the person that I am today."

Maria has always been the stable factor in the lives of friends and family. Whether family caretaker, in a guard's uniform, or running her ministry, Maria has touched the wounded part of others many times over. As far as her daughters go, she sees herself as "the one stable thing in their lives." Now she asks for reciprocity of that stability for herself.

Doing for others is easy, but issues of emotional intimacy such as "matching up routines and closeness" is something different. "I am willing and I might have to work at it." She sums up her life to date: "It's been a good ride."

Maria's Update

Maria's husband was sentenced to twenty years to life for murder; he did the twenty. He took a personality test (MMPI) that supported his emotional stability enough to be released. When he went up for parole, however, none of that mattered. He was told that he had not done enough time. She was disappointed but not surprised. Angel Maria's not the type of person to put all her eggs in one basket. Major players in the system do believe in him. His case manager is preparing a commute-the-sentence package for him and the prior prison warden is supportive as well. She believes the delay is political and fear-based on the part of the current governor who doesn't want to release him. In the meantime, Maria waits, applies her legal skills to his case, and works her ministry and her job. She has had health problems (one knee replaced and another yet to be done) that cause her physical pain and cause him much distress because, as she says, "He's not there to take care of me. He feels he owes me the rest of his life."

Maria's Transformation

Hades' Angel Maria has spent her life-time doing for others, expecting nothing in return. Family, friends and colleagues have always respected Maria and viewed her as an emotionally strong woman. However, what others saw and the way she felt inside were often quite different. For Maria, the inside and the outside didn't match. She felt emotionally guarded, controlling, and lonely living inside a guard's uniform. Today, she has a man in her life she trusts and respects, and whom she doesn't need to coddle or control. He does not feed off her perceived strength; instead she feels he takes care of her emotionally. Leaning on anybody is new for Maria and she can lean on him. His support and his love have changed her. She says, "He believes in me and that makes me feel fulfilled." Like Maria, her inmate husband used to be a dictatorial person. She concludes, "I have learned to talk about things. I've learned I don't have to be in charge. God is the head of our house. I've learned that things happen in God's time, not in my time. I've learned to let go, to sit and wait. I can help him only so much, the rest is up to him and God. We have a commitment to a three-way deal: we have each other and we have God to share. My way or the highway has changed to working it through."

Now that we know how Hades' Angels met their inmate spouse, let's find out what it's like visiting in Hades.

# # #

Chapter Nine

A Visitor in Hades

*"Once you have visited an inmate, you become an extension
of that inmate. Half the time, when I think of the days that
I don't visit, they seem like time off from my life; they are
what I do in between the times that I have my life. Those
whom God has joined together, only the CDC [California
Department of Corrections] will separate!"*

--- Hades' Angel Lisa Heart

In this chapter we'll learn about what happens when visiting
prison: the arrival; the visiting room experience; and learn the facts,
rules and regulations and woes of inmate visiting. This chapter also
addresses the stigma of visiting a prisoner, meaning "stigma by
association". We explore the impact of visiting on recidivism; guard and
inmate dynamics; read about a prison wedding, and get to know a
Hades' Angel through her life portrait.

What is visiting like? Let's find out why Hades' Angels say
visiting is such a difficult and unpleasant experience and how they deal
with it.

Arrival and Pat Down

Inmates know that once incarcerated, they are dependents of
the state; therefore, they are subject to their rules and regulations. What
families do not understand is why they are treated as though they, too,
are incarcerated. "Having been a good corporate wife in my first
marriage really pays off when I visit and some of the guards look down
their noses or treat me like I'm the one who committed a crime. "I get

angry, but I don't dare let it show," says Hades' Angel Cretia. Nothing prepared her for the intimidating, restrictive environment of a "super max" (maximum security institution). "It was scary. If the huge, double entry razor wire gates weren't foreboding enough, then the little room where you were searched thoroughly certainly was. Here they patted me down and ran their hands down between my legs. Sometimes I'd have to take off my shoes and lift up my feet, which was very embarrassing and humiliating. Then I was led to another room where I'd have to take off my shoes, belt, and jewelry in order to go through a metal detector that is so powerful that the wires and fasteners underneath your bra, even the most ordinary bra, would set it off."

Such emotionally demanding and often-painful prison visits provoke a lot of soul searching "to understand why God sent me someone like this," says Hades' Angel Sabrina. She endures the prison procedures, the searches and the pat-downs, because as she says, "I know he will be in there waiting for me. I see that people outside prison take their relationships for granted, and here we are -- we can't even be together."

The Visiting Room Experience

Hades' Angel BJ, 55, edits technical magazines. Her inmate/freemate relationship began when he wrote the publisher for journals to "take his mind out of his environment." BJ sent him the journals and received an appreciative response. This started a "tremendous pulling," an "intense pressure," like "I know this person and I need to know him better." Says BJ, "I'm glad I grabbed at it when I had the opportunity but visiting is trying. It sucks me dry. I have no clue if or when I'll be allowed in to visit. During one visit I was taken by surprise when an officer came up to me and said, 'Oh, your visit is terminated.' They gave me no reason. They aren't required to give reasons or let you know in advance. The worst came after relocating across country: When I went to visit last week, I was shocked to discover they moved him 300 miles away. Now, he is kept behind glass; I can't even touch him."

At one time, visiting was playful and friendly, says Hades' Angel Jo Anne, an office manager who met her lifer husband through her daughter. "He'd just squeeze me or hug me. Sometimes he'd give me a short kiss. Then hidden cameras were installed in the room and we were no longer able to have our stolen hug. Then they brought down a whole bunch of guards. Instead of having one guard, there were five in the visiting area. They came to our table and sort of hovered, and were really intimidating. They'd say, 'All right, that's enough. Out, out, everybody out. Visiting is over.' I call it cow-herding because that's the way I felt."

Sometimes issues in line cause problems inside prison. Hades' Angel Beth just wants to visit, but she describes fights over spots in line. "My street personality used to come out when I went into the prison. My attitude came first; the explanation came later. Once, a woman started telling me, 'You are prejudiced and you are this and that...' Well, she went in and told her husband; I didn't tell my husband anything. Her husband went to my husband and my husband came out and said, 'If you ever, ever have a reason for somebody to come and talk to me about you again, don't come back.' He didn't give me a chance to explain. Somebody next to us happened to overhear and knew what it was about and they talked to my husband afterwards and he apologized to me. He told me that when I come to that prison, I'm   reflection on him – the way I carry myself, the way I act, it's all a reflection on him."

For Eve, the visiting environment is ancient history. "It reminds me of Catholic school because they have a way of making you always feel guilty about nothing. 'Quit touching her face. Hands on the table.'" Childhood survival skills help Angel Betty Jo create her own little visiting world. "I can block out the noise of the myriad of families and the verbal abuse of the guards." The strain has gotten to her and she is tired of the whole experience, especially what she has to go through just getting to the visiting room. It all occurs in a very cold environment where you can't show any love or affection."

Somehow, in the middle of all the frenetic energy and restrictions, visiting can unintentionally foster emotional intimacy. Says Jamie, "When we're visiting, that's all we have: no diversion, no movies, no dinners, and we don't have other couples. We have six hours every Saturday and six hours every Sunday, and in some ways it forces you to deal with issues that you don't have to focus on outside. I am conscious of an empty piece of me I wasn't aware of before because I threw myself into my work." The silence when he can't call takes her back to her childhood anxiety. Ann relates that, "I learned to endure that deafening silence, but it reminds me of a family tactic of cutting me off when I didn't fulfill my dad's expectations."

Leaving

Parting is such sweet sorrow, that I shall say Good-bye until it is tomorrow

--- William Shakespeare

Shakespeare wrote eloquently about the pain of saying goodbye. It rings a sorrowful bell for Hades' Angels who know the hardest part of visiting is leaving him. "After the anticipation and excitement of going to visit, leaving is a double-edged sword," says Callie. Joy suddenly gets shut off. "You go in and come out, but he stays in there. I don't regret marrying my husband; I regret marrying someone in prison because it's so hard, and so painful and stressful, like leading two lives, and just getting to the prison means you're on the road half your life. But the preparation for leaving, and the emotional withdrawal, is the hardest to deal with." Hades' Angel PJ also struggles with the pangs of leaving: "I would gladly sacrifice this outside world to be with him inside, and just walk back through those doors with him, and we would spend the afternoon. Our world is together, even when we are apart."

VISITING ROOM FACTS

Procedures

Visiting a prisoner does not occur without preparation. This is an official process that requires prior approval (Visiting Questionnaire, CDC 106), whereby visitors are checked out for any previous criminal record. Once approved, visitors arrive early, and stand in line outside for hours before they are processed for that day's visit. Visiting is not guaranteed, and is subject to events at the prison (i.e. lockdowns), time limits, and termination due to overcrowding. The journey tends to be difficult, time-consuming and costly. Because most prison facilities are located in rural areas. Once through the metal detector, visitors are escorted and seated, and wait in the visiting room for the inmate to be called, searched and brought in.

Hades' Angel Bianca can deal with these procedures but she says, "It's all nerve-wracking; I have to put on my armor before I go in there. If I go in feeling vulnerable and weak, I have to shift personas."

Hades' Angel Bonnie, 67, a widow, met her lifer husband through a friend who was visiting an inmate. She found the visiting room experience hard to get used to and very intrusive of her personal space. While talking about it, she tried to retain a pensive dignity. She says, "First, you have to fill out a paper with your name and address and license number and give that to the guard. They run it through a computer to verify approval, and then they locate the inmate and send for him. No jewelry except a wedding ring or a religious medallion is allowed. You go through the metal detector and if nothing goes off, the guards start the personal search. The guard looked behind my ears, ran his fingers around the neck of my shirt, and his fingers around the band of my pants. You have to open your mouth and wiggle your tongue. Then they pat you down starting at your shoulders, down your arms, and down your legs. Then you can go in."

Contact visits are in the visiting room and visiting patio areas. Noncontact visits are in noncontact monitored booths. Family conjugal visits are not allowed to lifers; they are for eligible inmates and their approved immediate family members. All visitors and vehicles on prison grounds are subject to search if cause arises. All visitors must go through a metal detector that may lead to a body search.

Visiting and Recidivism

For those not familiar with the prison situation, here are a few sobering facts: prisons are big business with two objectives, incarceration and rehabilitation. In the late 1970's, however, rehabilitation was dropped from the mission statement of most departments of corrections. In the last decade the American prison population has doubled, increasing to over 1.3 million with a corresponding economic and social impact. Ninety-three percent (93%) of those behind bars are men, most of whom have committed a violent crime. In 2005, about 1 out of every 136 U.S. residents was incarcerated either in prison or jail(White, 2006). Yet, scant attention is paid to rehabilitation.

There are problems of high rates of recidivism and in California, two- thirds of state convicts return to prison within eighteen months. Successful completion of parole is significantly related to the maintenance of family ties during incarceration (Kupers, 1999). "The evidence is pretty overwhelming: The fewer quality visits a prisoner receives, the less chance he has to turn things around. If a prisoner has no contact with family, it's almost inevitable the prisoner will fail once he gets out," states Terry Kupers, an Oakland, California psychiatrist who works with inmates and the effects of prison visitation.

Family support and family visits are high predictors of lower rates of recidivism, lessen the number of people who commit new crimes, decrease prison overcrowding, and those add up to taxpayer savings. Yet, in a shortsighted attempt to save money, California's Department of Corrections officials have reduced the number of visiting days from three or four to two, Saturdays and Sundays, hoping to shave off more than $11 million in personnel costs. "What people forgot, is that 97 percent of the nation's inmates eventually get released and have to go somewhere," said Senator Brownback, (Butterfield, 2004).

Rules and Regulations

The reception room is manned by a day commander who oversees procedures outlined in *Prison Visiting Room Rules and Regulations*, California's bible of rules and regulations (www.cdc.state.ca.us). All states have similar booklets and websites. The inmate and visitor may embrace and kiss once at the beginning and at the end of their visit. Holding hands on top of the table in plain view is permitted. Kissing, rubbing, or sitting close together is interpreted as excessive contact, which may result in termination, restriction, or denial of future visits, and disciplinary charges may be filed against the inmate.

The application of the visiting rules and regulations is subject to change, and may differ from prison to prison depending upon events such as lockdowns, meaning when inmates are confined to their cells. Changes and fluctuations may also be at the will of the guard on shift or influenced by a visitor's attitude.

Hades' Angel Bianca, a stickler for following the rules, says "I have even earned myself a reputation as a "book girl", meaning she knows the rules and when in doubt refers to Title 15, The California Department of Corrections (CDC) Visiting Rules. "If I feel I've done nothing wrong and if someone is giving me grief, then I'm going to challenge it." She has taken action on behalf of herself and others. "I recently spoke at a hearing on the issue of recorded telephonic interruptions and the rates charged families of inmates in California. It was a big deal for me to go in front of a large group of people, stand at a podium with a microphone and camera and talk about the injustices of their exorbitant rates, but I did it."

Changeable Rules

Hades' Angel Bianca, and other visitors, say they are convinced that some guards go out of their way just to mess with people, just to make their day lousy: "Dealing with the guards makes visiting difficult, especially because of the inconsistent ways they apply the rules." The rules may change with each visit, leaving visitors confused, discouraged, angry, and at a loss for how to cope. Knowing the following visiting facts and rules relieves some stress and anxiety: having proper identification, colors and patterns that don't resemble state-issued inmate or guard clothing; dressing conservatively so skin is not exposed; wearing no underwire bras and no jewelry other than a plain wedding band; and bringing a clear plastic coin purse with up to $30 in coins or dollar bills to purchase food from vending machines in the visiting room. Cameras, books, food, purses, gum, cell phones, pagers and medications are not permitted.

The worst part for most visitors is the waiting -- waiting in line outside, waiting for your name to be called, and then waiting for the guards to bring out the inmate. Usually it takes from fifteen minutes to an hour, but it can take up to six hours just to have a fifteen-minute visit. Hades' Angel Beth's unfortunate visiting experiences have hardened her. "Being a hard-ass is tough on me. I don't like to be like that. It shouldn't have to be that way," she says. Her visits feel like she's fighting a battle after she has already gone through a lot just to get there -- the drive, the expense of staying somewhere, and getting up at 2 a.m. to be outside the prison at 3 a.m. "The guards make me wait; treat me like crap in the processing center, cheat me out of hours I should have for visiting, and make it necessary to stand my ground."

Although the tension is evident, it's different for PJ, who speaks as though she's fought many battles defending her territory: "Visiting is my time with him and nothing, not electrified razor wire, guards, gates, noise, none of it is allowed to interfere. The guards pretty much ignore us. I give the message, 'Do not come over here and mess with me. Go pick on somebody else. I am a warrior.'" She and her husband use that warrior energy for one another like a protective shield.

The Rule in Title 15

It took Hades' Angel Stephanie years, slowly allowing herself to trust enough to rely on her husband's input in making decisions. Then the state up and moved him 700 miles. Stunned, she says, "I was visiting him four or five days a week. It hurt because he was like a drug to me at the time. I had to have him. He was like heroin. So when they took it away, I went crazy."

Stephanie is convinced that the authorities separated them deliberately: "They didn't want us together. They found a little-known rule in the Title 15 California Code that if you don't know the person prior to his incarceration, you can't see him. " She tracked down and explains this rule: if he's at place, A, and I met him through a newspaper ad at place A, then I couldn't meet him. I'd have to wait until he got transferred, then apply and say, okay, I know him from place A. Denial was because they said I had no prior knowledge of him. I had to produce the letter and show the proof I knew him prior to him coming here." It's simple: if you can prove you visited the prisoner in another prison, you can apply to visit in the new one.

Support Organizations

The dress code applies to all visitors and wearing the wrong colors or an outfit considered inappropriate violates that code. Hades' Angel Stephanie's huge apprehension about visiting stems from prior visits: "I never know what games they might play. Either they're not going to like the way I dress or something else triggers them, so they see me as their target. I wore a pair of purple velvet pants one day and was told it looked too much like inmate attire. I said, please show me an inmate in this system that wears purple velvet pants and I will agree with you. The guard points to a guy in blue denim jeans and I said, 'You must be colorblind.'"

Friends Outside, a supportive, nonprofit organization specializing in addressing social services needs of prisoners and their families provides a change of clothes if that violation occurs. "Friends Outside, founded in 1955, is a California-based non-profit organization to address familial issues associated with incarceration. It links providers of direct services to inmates, former inmates, their families and their children. Organizations working with this population have varying approaches to treatment; including anger management; domestic violence; substance abuse; sex offenders. Their goal is to reduce the inadvertent affects of incarceration upon all members of our communities," explains executive director Mary Weaver.

Visiting Woes

Hades' Angels echo their frustrations and their anxious, uneasy feelings about prisons: they are about power, not justice.

Hades' Angel Lisa Heart cringes when she talks about the attitude of the guards and the environment. They are stark reminders of ugly childhood injustices that come right up close and smack her in the face. Visiting brings back ghostly memories of childhood shame, worthlessness, and powerlessness. "Prisons are not about justice; they are about power and its abuse. It's like a step backwards into my childhood. A guard once asked me, 'What kind of slut are you that you would come in here and marry a *blankety-blank* inmate?'" She relates a revealing incident involving, of all the mundane things, a doorstop: "For years guards would prop open one of the visiting-room doors with a rock. So, one of the women decided to bring in a new rubber stopper to use instead. The guard wouldn't take it. He said, 'You're only an inmate's wife.' A $1.98 doorstop and they wouldn't take it because 'You are only an inmate's wife.' Like it's a dirty word!"

It's no secret that abuse happens within the prison; abuse known about by visiting families has been going on for years. These widespread abuses are frequently revealed in the media and news stories. In a previous chapter, Hades' Angel Ann vividly described what happened to her husband when he stepped in to protect an inmate from being roughed up by a guard. Hades' Angel Eve also bears witness to some of these horrors: "The state prison system is a gruesome entity. Apart from the abject filth and overcrowding; the sadistic practice of putting nonviolent offenders in with violent ones to be raped and otherwise abused; the lack of decent food and adequate medical care; the system takes all hope away from anyone seeking to better themselves. Rehabilitation is given lip service only."

Stigma by Association

Generally, though visiting a prisoner is not expected to be a pleasant experience, more often than not, it is humiliating and shaming. Because of association with the prisoner, the visitor carries his mark, his stigma by association, "The fact that I am the wife of a lifer sends a lot of prejudice my way," says Ann.

Commonly, visitors complain that correction officers treat them as if they were the inmate even though they've done nothing wrong. Shelly (not a Hades' Angel), the wife of an inmate and founder of a support group called WAIT (Wives Are Incarcerated Too), comments: "Most people think all prisoners' wives are low-income, strung out on drugs, barefoot and pregnant. My own mother wanted me to tell people my husband was in the service, not prison. I said, 'In the service they come home,'" (Steese, 1988).

A 1994 study examined the unique difficulties of families of incarcerated men: "Stigma was immediately present for all the 35 wives in the study,"). Kepford summarizes:

> *The official labeling process is accompanied by informal labeling process that internalizes the blame and the responsibility. This informal labeling is seen in the prison system and the criminal justice system, which is involved in identifying both the prisoner and his family as social deviants. (Kepford, 1994 p. 67)*

Although stigmatizing and humiliating encounters are not representative of all visiting experiences, 29 wives in Fishman's (1988), study recalled unpleasant experiences while visiting their husbands in prison, such as being strip-searched. Here is one woman's humiliating account:

> *"When you walk into a room there are two women in the room with you. They ask you to remove all your clothes and*

place them on the floor. Then they take a flashlight and shine it in your eyes, up your nose, and in your opened mouth. Then they ask you to let your hair hang loose, then you're supposed to hold it up so that they can shine the flashlight into your hair around your neck. Then they shine the flashlight under your armpits. Then they ask you to lift one breast at a time and they shine the flashlight under your breast. Then they ask you to run your fingers around your belly button in such a way that you place pressure on the skin in that area. Then they run the flashlight through your pubic hair. After that they ask you to bend over with your hands touching the ground. They ask you to 'crack a smile' and they bend over with the flashlight and they look at your vagina with the flashlight. After this, they make you stand for 15-20 minutes while they check your clothes. The two female officers like to make sarcastic comments, like, 'It's time to buy a new bra, don't you think?' If you have your period, then you have to stand there with blood flowing down your legs." (p.188)

History Repeats

The rawness, tension, and attitudes of guards and family alike, stir up unwanted, masked, or denied childhood feelings of humiliation and shame. What happened in the early lives of some of these women loops around and gets revisited here; it can also get changed with new choices: sometimes, backward into the past, leads forward to the future.

Humiliation and shame dealt a heavy blow in the lives of some Hades' Angels like Bianca, who firmly denies feeling it from her inmate partner: "It [shame] doesn't come from my relationship. It developed while growing up in a Catholic community where my mother was the only divorced parent in church. I'm so used to feeling different from everyone around me that at some point I embraced my differentness and looked at it with humor." "Shame," echoes Lady Honeybear, "is what I felt in other relationships in my life because I was afraid of putting the real me out in front, fearing it would be laughed at or overlooked."

Hades' Angel Jo Anne survived being the butt of neighborhood, school, and even family bullies because of being born nearly deaf, as well as her unusual coloring: her red-colored hair, prominent freckles and nearly translucent skin. The emotional trauma about feeling ugly and unaccepted led her to social and emotional isolation. Her sister could be her best friend or her worst enemy. Her mother was in and out of depressive cycles, and when Jo Anne became pregnant and was unmarried, her mother couldn't handle the shame and told Jo Anne to get out of the house. Jo Anne recollects, "It was easier to shut up than to stand up for myself or express what I felt." So, it is no surprise that the attraction to her inmate spouse was his sense of humor and the part of him that grew up learning to smile at all costs.

Such early childhood feelings of shame get emotionally revisited, and acted out in repeated encounters with prison authorities. Once again, outwardly armored, Hades' Angels know how to hold their anger, humiliation and shame inside rather than risk denial of a visit. What they want and cannot hold is him. Stigma by association causes many Angels to keep their relationships a secret and it impacts family members as well.

Secret Love

"I was a licensed minister, and when I married this husband, the church I belonged to told me they would have to revoke my license. People I thought were my friends were not," says Hades' Angel Dimples. Rather than bear that stigma or be ostracized by family, friends, and co-workers, other Hades' Angels keep their prison relationship hush-hush, and that secretiveness ends up isolating them. "Even my sister didn't know about my prison marriage until five years ago," says Hades' Angel Sherry, 62. She's afraid if people know about him she will be stigmatized and cut off by her church. So her relationship is pretty much a "secret love" she conceals by staying to herself, and doesn't talk about.

Others deal with this stigma differently. Callie guards her privacy in a humorous way and keeps insisting her marriage confidential rather than secret. Callie laughs out loud now when she talks about her husband. "Friends and family know about it, but when outsiders ask questions, I just tell them he works for the government and I can't talk about it. After all, it's the truth!"

Hades' Angel Louise recognizes the stigma but copes with it by toughening herself to any remarks: "I wouldn't wish this being married to an inmate on my best friend. When I married him, I found out really fast who my friends were. I am not taking all the raised eyebrows and comments that I did before, such as, 'Oh, you married some lifer and you've never seen him out here on the streets.'"

Lori Girshick (not a Hades' Angel), a D.A. married to an inmate, writes about that stigma. She states:

> *I shared the issue of secrecy with the other wives. This was a very uncomfortable way to live. I told some family and some friends, but not employers or acquaintances. I did have some rejection from family and friends, and that was painful. There's no question that wives of prisoners are stigmatized. People believe prisoners are very lowly, and are not sympathetic to them or their families. (Girshick, 1996)*

"People think I'm nuts," says Hades' Angel Danielle. "I get, 'aren't you afraid of him? What if they let him out?' I wish they would let him out. I don't care what other people think. They are not the ones that have to deal with him. Everybody at work knew that when I went on vacation in July, that's where I was going, that's who I was going to see."

When a woman falls in love with a prisoner, stigma by association spills over into everyday life outside the prison environment. It is a "shared stigma"—a mark or stain that spreads out. Though not fair, this societal stigma exists in a variety of ways and it has driven some wives and families of prisoners to take social action. In Sacramento, California, for example, one such group voiced to their concerns about being stigmatized:

> *"The mail we receive is branded [State Prison Generated Mail] which stigmatizes us and embarrasses us. Further… phone access is severely limited. Collect calls are incessantly interrupted with a recorded message reminding the recipient that 'This call is from an inmate at a California prison,' and suggesting that the recipient 'Push 1' to never receive another call from this institution again We are forced to pay more than other members of the public for the phone calls we do receive because the State profits from our hardship." (Centerforce, 1999)*

Hades' Angel Lynn learned to speak out and defend against the felt stigma, ignorance and the stupidity thrown at her: "When I asked some acquaintances to sign a petition for an inmates' Bill of Rights, some of them looked at me and asked, 'Can you vote?' They thought my husband's losing his voting rights extends to me."

Hades' Angel Lady Honeybear, 61, works as a counselor for runaways…from her wheelchair. Stigma is something she knows firsthand. What she has difficulty swallowing is the stigma by association when visiting her husband. Here, she recounts her demeaning interplay with the guards and the system:

> *She says, "The guards don't show any courtesy whatsoever. I don't think I have ever run across a single guard at any institution who was even nice enough to call me Miss. Visiting is just like the army. Hurry up and wait. Once, I went to visit him only to learn that he'd been called to another part of the state for a court hearing. It was my*

birthday. We had arranged with the prison to have a weekend visit. Not together as a conjugal visit, but to see him three days in a row. I had just traveled 1400 miles to see this man, and all I got was a hello kiss and a good-bye kiss all in one. The officer put him in the van and drove off. I called the county jail where he was held temporarily, explained the circumstances, and said I wanted to see him.

Here I was, in a wheelchair at the bottom of 329 steps, and there were a couple of officers milling around, and I said, 'Don't just stand there like a couple of stumps. Help me up these steps.' "When he came to the window, he had a look of surprise on his face. I said, 'Well, I told you I'd see you.' He couldn't believe it. To talk to him I had to stand up and talk through this little hole in the window and then sit back down. When I asked him why he had tears in his eyes, he said, 'Because, I feel so blessed that you are here. And look what you're going through to be here.' The officer took pity on me, unhooked his chains and said, 'Give her a birthday kiss.' Lord Honeybear fell to his knees in front of my wheelchair and gave me a kiss. It was the most loving, tender, sweet birthday kiss in my entire life. But just then some other officers that were coming out of the building at their shift change looked at me and pointed to him, the inmate, walking away from me in chains, and laughed."

GUARD AND INMATE: Top-dog and Under-dog

The Emotional Environment

Power, control, structure, and order, not conduits for rehabilitation, go hand-in-hand in prison reality. The interactions between inmates and guards, and among the guards themselves, are tightly controlled. Underneath, yet always close to the surface, pulses an undercurrent of anxiety, tension, and rage not necessarily held at bay by confinement, lockdowns, or silent threats of retribution.

Here, unspoken rules determine survival. Polarities of dominance and submission are the underpinnings of relationships based on power: guard over prisoner, and prisoner over prisoner. Here, where might triumphs over right, it is the survivor who earns respect! Few of us on the outside ever confront the kind of tensions that inmates experience daily in this unrelentingly threatening environment.

The prison world is divided into pairs of opposites: Top-dog/under-dog; good guy/bad guy; victim/victimizer. These splits are everywhere. Here, the "good guys" (guards) wear green, and the "bad guys" (inmates) wear blue denim. The "good guys" carry guns and nightsticks, and the "bad guys" carry homemade weapons: their suppressed rage. Here, power, force, retribution, and authority is the morality used to control, contain, and suppress an outbreak among the "bad guys" – men who ironically are inside for causing bodily harm or exerting force and control over those outside. Inside, however, the "bad guys" impose their own top-dog/under-dog, good guy/bad guy divisions by sometimes using insider information about crimes, thereby ultimately perpetuating polarities within the topsy-turvy brokenness of the rigidly controlled underworld of prison.

Into this emotional environment, into this underbelly world of tension, with its twists and bends, descends a visiting Hades' Angel.

A Prison Wedding: Rose

Correspondence leads to phone calls and visits and sometimes, to a prison wedding. Hades' Angel Rose did not enter armed and clanging prison gates to find a husband. She was searching for her biological father in order to get a medical history for her daughter. Her search ended in prison where she also met her current husband. "Believe me, I wasn't looking for any man"-- in fact, she was married to her second husband at the time -- "but he caught my eye because he was so big. He's 6' 5". His prison job is taking family photos. He came over to where I was sitting with my father to take our picture. We spent the next three days visiting: my birth father, my brother, and this man who is my now husband." He had a way of engaging her with his eyes that created an immediate connection. "He's not this beautiful GQ- looking man. Other than his eyes, if you saw him walking down the street, you wouldn't look twice, but there was a spark from the beginning, a sense of electricity. He is warm, sensitive, sincere, my knight."

When they began corresponding, her husband didn't mind. "I wrote him for about a year and a half." But it turned out to be a big factor; in fact the whole relationship occurred as an outgrowth of correspondence. "After two years into the relationship I started having feelings for him. Since I didn't have an emotional connection with my husband, this man was kind of my surrogate husband. My husband wasn't interested in hearing about what was going on in my life, but this man gave me feedback; he was able to really hear me. I felt close to him, like with my dad. That felt special."

Rose turned from a prisoner's pen pal into a prisoner's wife after she found out her husband had been unfaithful. They divorced and a year and a half later, she married her "pen pal".

For Rose, like other wives of lifers, a prison wedding does not result in a conjugal visit, not even a bite of cake. Still, says Rose: "I can't tell you how wonderful he is! He had never been married before and when he asked me to marry him I said, 'I'd never been married in prison so this ought to be an experience.' Our wedding was the biggest wedding they'd ever had there. He really tried to make that day special despite the fact that we had an hour in the visiting room, with guards around us. It was as if nobody else was there but our friends and family. This was our special moment: he asked me to get a wedding dress, send out announcements, and I got our rings engraved. Basically, we did everything as if we were doing it at home, including family. He got donuts from a vending machine and fed them to me like it was wedding cake. Then he sang a song so that we could dance together. I told him that when he comes home if he doesn't behave like this, he's going back!"

When Rose attended a wedding of a relative who didn't know her husband is in prison, "She asked, 'Where's your husband?' and I said, 'He's in prison.' And she said, 'Oh, that's a good one. Can I use that? Next time my husband doesn't want to go to one of these functions, I'll tell people he's in prison. She wouldn't believe that he really *is* in prison.'"s

Ups and Downs

Rose weighs her difficult reality. "A prison marriage," she says, "is not like a real marriage; we don't have a marriage. There are no conjugal visits. We have never been intimate. But we are each other's best friends, and I think at our age, it's the way to be anyway. He's a gentle spirit. He's very calming. I am at peace."

"When visiting, I'm in his home. It's our chance to sit and have a hamburger from the vending machine together, and we can hold each other for a moment," she says. Oddly enough, behind these walls with her husband is where she feels safe and secure. "Prison is the only place I've ever been with him."

What's the downside to her prison marriage? Living in two worlds is difficult. "I think about him every time I go out. Today, when I had to buy a refrigerator I said to the guy, 'I wish my husband could be here, because I don't know what I'm doing. I don't know what's what.' I think about him every time I have to call the plumber. I think about him when I go to a wedding alone." These things upset her husband, but he helps her out when he can. Rose adds, "When his father died he received an inheritance, and he gave me money to help with my expenses coming to see him."

Another downside is the physical distance, which makes getting there a big trip. "I hate to fly, but I get on an airplane to see him. It scares me to death, but I've been doing it for seven years and I will do it until he gets out. They say absence makes the heart grow fonder. I guess it does for us. I think it gets better every year." They visit every three months. "When we do, it's like this big honeymoon. I get all excited to see him; I get hives. Talking on the phone is very expensive, so we talk only once a week for an hour. He can only talk for fifteen minutes at a time, then he has to call me back and it costs $10 for fifteen minutes."

On the upside, this relationship has changed her. "I'm not sitting at home going, 'Oh, I miss my husband.' I belong to support groups, work with a homeless shelter, and am very involved in the community. Advocacy means writing to senators and district attorneys and bettering the world through fighting for issues I believe in." Today, Rose sits on the board for the New York State Families of Inmates. Perhaps her prison marriage gives Angel Rose the best of both worlds: her need for connection and separateness.

Rose has become acutely aware of patterns of distancing and abandonment in her relationships. Through no fault of her own, she got the short end of the stick on fatherly love from her biological father. She was short-changed again in love and marriage the first time around through her young husband's untimely death. She felt close to her stepfather, but the price she paid was her mother's emotional distancing. The second time, she chose friendship and a loveless marriage, and got wounded by his unfaithfulness. Rose survived, worked through early grief and loss, and adapted to the unfortunate circumstances in her life. A smile covered her "pain tape" (Loomis, 1995) of grief and loss. Though she never seemed to have it all, she prioritizes what's important: love, respect, and emotional intimacy over the physical. Today, Angel Rose says she enjoys the love and friendship of her inmate spouse without fearing the abandonment she knew the first and second time around. "Home and security is not a place, it's a feeling and wonderful things can come out of a loving relationship."

ONE STORY: Hades' Angels Cretia
Portrait: Cretia

Cretia, 54, who owns and operates a beauty salon, comes from a well-respected, influential, and politically active family. She states, "My father is a critical, demanding man used to getting his own way and we usually give him it because it's the easiest path." She was introduced to the prison experience through her son. Being recently divorced after a 25-year marriage, Cretia was in touch with a deep loneliness for herself and her son. She says, "My son was serving a few months for something real minor. Prior to this, I would never have thought of, or considered what went on in a prison. At the time, I had a good job, I would date, but I felt lonely. I realized how important it was for inmates to receive letters and have communication."

Mrs. Three-Piece Corporate God

Prior to marrying her inmate-spouse, "I was the trophy wife of a three-piece corporate god. At the time I married him, I was madly in love with him. My husband, like my father, was a very handsome, successful businessman. Money was not ever an issue. In that marriage, my main function was to be a dutiful wife and do what was expected. The problem was that all the women liked him and he liked all of them. Finally, I became fed up with being the third girlfriend of the night, and I divorced him."

Staying with her critical, controlling first husband until their son left home was a conscious choice. She and her mother differed on the marriage issue. Her mother would do anything rather than make waves. Cretia's parents have been married sixty-five years. "I made a commitment that I would stay put until my son was out of school. He went into the navy and that's when I left." To stay put in the marriage and in the home, she was outwardly submissive while, as she says, "Inside, I fumed and burned with a mean-spirited rebellion every time I submitted to his weekly weigh-in. Because I had to look real good, every week I had to weigh 103 pounds or he deemed me not loveable. For 20 years I was hungry—but I'm not hungry now." She now "feels loved for me" by her current husband. "He tells me his love for me is not measured by numbers on the bathroom scale."

Hades' Angel Cretia feels a common pain in the fact that "no-one had ever really loved him. He'd had a real disastrous home life, and I think we just felt love for each other." She says, "I always felt loved and accepted by my mother, but not from my father. Deep down I felt unwanted by him. I knew he didn't love me. I knew he didn't even want me. My father finally admitted this was true. He told me: 'I never wanted to adopt you; your mother wanted to, so I let her.'" That lack of acceptance spread from Cretia's father to other relatives as well. Around them, she always felt as though she didn't belong. "With my mother's side, it was the exact opposite. I always felt loved and wanted by my aunties and my grandparents on my mother's side."

Angel Cretia recognizes that earlier part of her life was all about appearances and realizes how superficial it was. From her mother, "who would do anything rather than rock the boat," she learned to be a good girl, a good daughter, and a very dutiful wife. "I see the similarities between my father and my first husband; they just wore a different suit of clothes." Cretia has certainly rocked the boat with this relationship; it is not like any other relationship she's ever had. It has evoked a radical transformation of her self: It's not about facade, and she doesn't have to be a "superwoman". She says, "My current marriage has more depth and intimacy than the first one. When it's not about looks or sex you really get to learn a lot about someone. Now, I have found a man I can believe." She feels valued by him and also knows where he is every night.

Meeting Her Prison Love

A lonely reality crept in after Cretia's divorce and her son's imprisonment. She used pen pal correspondence to reach out to the lonely part of another human; it touched a cord in her. She had no idea what he looked like, but very much enjoyed his attitude: his sense of humor, lack of blame, and his honesty about the reasons for his incarceration. Cautious about being manipulated or lied to, she checked out his trial transcript prior to considering greater involvement. Further investigation through his classification officer—a guard who later played matchmaker—encouraged her to pursue their relationship. "I called his classification officer who said 'I don't recognize his name, so he must not be a troublemaker.' Then the officer checked on how many women were visiting him or sending him money. It turned out that since my husband was incarcerated, he had never had even one person visit him. The officer then told me that 'the only money on his books was five dollars a year at Christmas, and it's the state that puts it in. This was not a man who was scamming or just trying to get someone to send him money." After six months of writing, Cretia decided to make the cross-country trip to visit.

Face-To-Face Visit

As mentioned previously, visiting her son at a minimum-security prison did not prepare Cretia for the intimidating, restrictive environment of face-to-face visit at a maximum, "super-max," security institution. "It was scary," she says. "If the huge, double-entry razor wire gates weren't foreboding, then the second razor wire gate and the search room certainly were." Then the guard finally escorted her to the visiting room where she waited for him. "I was sitting in this big room. Several guys walked in and with each I'd wonder, 'Is that him?' It almost didn't matter what he looked like because I was already in love with him because of his smart and witty letters. Finally, when he appeared I was not at all prepared for him to look as handsome and as good as he did."

Guard plays Cupid

"It's highly unusual for anyone in the Department of Corrections to take an interest in a particular inmate. But he was one of the good guys. He made an impact on my life that I will not ever forget." After visiting, Cretia continued writing and checking on him through his classification officer who told me 'he had come to life.' He said, 'Had you not come into his life when you did, I feel he would have been one of those quiet ones we'd find hanging in his cell.' One day he said to Cretia, 'You know, if you all were married, he might get transferred to the state where you live.' "He really played Cupid with us!"

Not An Easy Life

Hades' Angel Cretia and her inmate were married inside prison and eventually he was indeed transferred to the state where she lives where prisoners were allowed to visit in a courtyard. She says, "We could sit down on the grass and hold hands and talk and almost pretend like it was a Sunday afternoon in the park."

This situation remained stable for "five years and three days," then due to overcrowding, riots and upheavals in the prison in Cretia's state, her husband was shipped back to his original state. She says, "It has been devastating because it's so hard to visit. You don't have much of a life while they're in prison. I go to work, come home, play with the grandkids. I fill in the time the best I can, but it's not like having the spouse in the house." She has faith. "I cannot believe God has allowed us to find each other if he didn't mean for us to be together."

Cretia worries about her husband's safety in prison. "They're not at summer camp, you know. It's a rough place for them to be because there are some inside who are really bad. If they see anyone having any kind of happiness, out of jealousy or whatever, they create problems. If someone tried to create trouble for her husband and he defended himself, he could get a write-up, so he's always walking a tightrope."

The prison experience informed her about life's tragedies she never knew about as the daughter of an influential family: the use and abuse of power, the inadequacies and injustices, and the unfairness that goes on below facades of normalcy in the home, in the prisons, and in society at large. "This is a big lesson for a daughter coming from a political background: that if I had bucks to go plop down in someone's campaign fund, I could probably get my husband released from prison. It's not fair. I grew up believing in mom, apple pie, the flag, and I believed that the political system would do the right thing, but it doesn't." Through this relationship, Cretia's inner rebel has been released, she is questioning old values and changing the status quo.

A newly found core value includes discovering her self worth, and fighting for her husband's rehabilitation. She states, "I still have little aunties that say, 'Couldn't you just visit him? You didn't have to marry him.' They don't get it that there can be people in prison who are worthwhile and at some point in time can be productive members of society if they're given a chance."

She is particularly bothered by the stigma stemming from associating—and marrying—a prisoner. She knows that a bad attitude on her part can backfire and end up hurting her husband. She says, "Having been a good corporate wife in my first marriage pays off when I visit him and some of the guards look down their noses or treat me like I'm the one who committed a crime. I get angry but I don't let it show." Inside prison she holds in her anger, puts up with the frustrations, and prays for his release. Outside, however, she speaks her mind with the women who come into her salon. Cretia says at work, "I'm around a lot of ladies, and one day when a prison situation aired on the news, one my customers began making really snide comments about prisoners. So, I said, 'Maybe you should know that my husband is in prison.' Well, she no longer comes into the shop." All Cretia's customers are not so harsh. "You'd be amazed at how supportive some of them are to me," she adds.

Warrior of Reform

This relationship taught her about going inside more than the prison; it taught her about going inside herself. It encouraged her to make doing life-time more worthwhile: finding out who she is, and becoming acutely aware of other men who act from a sense of jealousy, emptiness, and entitlement.

Cretia believes strongly that her husband was unjustly accused and tried for a murder in an incident that was clearly self-defense. "He lashed out at a man who tried to rape him, who turned out to be HIV positive and the man died as a result", she says. Cretia became her husband's advocate: "I sent his entire trial transcript to an attorney I know who told me he had never seen such an incredible travesty of justice in his entire life. He said my husband should never have been charged with anything but manslaughter. With no prior record, he should never have spent one day in prison, let alone receive a sentence of twenty-five years. My husband's parole date will be worth the wait."

Cretia says, "My goal is to be an activist and help educate other people to take action to improve the prison system." She has become a kind of warrior of reform. "There's right and there's wrong and what is happening in prisons right now: lack of rehabilitation, vocational training, violence, humiliation, and mistreatment by guards, is not right."

Cretia used to focus on appearances. This experience has awakened the silent rebel from a deep submissive sleep, empowering her to create change and live from the inside out. "I see a tremendously inhumane injustice about the way inmates are treated, whether they deserve to get out or not." The quiet rebel has found her voice, her mission, and her purpose. Her goal is to advocate for human treatment, justice, and educate and empower prison families to call and complain about violations of prisoners' rights.

Cretia says she is grateful for the love and respect of a marriage that seems to have so much more depth and intimacy than she ever experienced in her unhappy first marriage as third woman of the night. She sought connection and found meaning. Through this relationship, she has found her voice, her mission, and she does not feel lonely.

Now let's find out a lot more about Hades' Angels seven common threads.

Chapter Ten

The Anatomy of the Hades' Angel: Common Threads

With my father, there were rules, "You do as I say or else.
My mother did tranquilizers; she taught me to lie down
and play dead."

--- Hades' Angel Danielle

If mutual attraction to a partner has its basis in similar needs and fears, then what is it that both binds and blinds a Hades' Angel to her imprisoned love? Is it something she brings with her from her childhood? Does her inmate husband/partner sense it?

Different as they appear on the outside, the twenty-six Hades' Angels interviewed share seven characteristics which run like threads throughout their lives that help explain why they are drawn – and held – in committed relationships with men behind bars, men who are held there because they have acted out violently. Many women, not just those involved with prisoners, have these traits in common. Not surprisingly, they unconsciously impact the choice of a mate on the outside. We will look again at some of these choices in this chapter in a section on "Demon Lovers".

Seven Common Threads

The twenty-six Hades' Angels are linked by seven common threads:

1. Early Childhood Narcissistic Injury

2. A Controlling/Submissive Family Marital Dynamic

3. Role as "Family Caretaker/Nurturer"

4. Identification as a "A Father's Daughter"

5. Emotional/Intellectual Split

6. True Self/False Self Split

7. Previous Demon Lover Relationships

1. Early Childhood Narcissistic Injury

I was always being told that I couldn't do things, that I wasn't smart enough; I didn't have enough sense.

---Hades' Angel Danielle

My parents argued bitterly. The house was filled with their tension. While Dad was at work at night, Mother, an alcoholic, had other men over. I was abused physically, sexually, verbally, spiritually and emotionally by my mother as well as by her secret boyfriends. I was terrified of being abandoned by my father -- the only possible protector I had -- even though he was a distant, emotionally walled-off man who was unaware of the amount of abuse taking place in the household.

--- Hades' Angel Betty Jo

The child's deepest emotional need is to be genuinely loved by the parents. Such parental nurturing builds a sense of healthy narcissism, which fosters development of a strong sense of Self.

When that love and caring is absent, discounted, or shame is attached to it, a "narcissistic wound" develops. Such narcissistic wounds are present in some form in most Hades' Angels who commit to men convicted of crimes of violence and aggression (assault with a deadly weapon, armed robbery, and murder). Kohut's self psychology provides a framework to understand the dual expressions of narcissistic injury: narcissistic rage and shamefaced withdrawal. For Hades' Angels, their narcissistic wound resulted in closing down to protect and hide the self. Such closing down provides a perfect fit with a man who reacts to a similar wounding by violently lashing out. In summary, they share a common wound.

> *We had a similar upbringing. I felt like a worthless piece of shit.*
>
> --- Hades' Angel Stephanie

The wounded child, totally dependent upon parents or caretakers, desperately searches for ways to survive: creative, adaptive or self-protective. Such defenses include denying feelings that make them appear vulnerable, such as anger, sadness and fear, or by striving for positions of power and control. Three ways a child finds not to feel this hurt are: *acting in* (shutting down, withdrawing, internalizing to avoid vulnerability); *acting out* (anger, rage, and aggression against others); or compensatory pleasing to achieve a sense of belonging and inclusion in the family.

This narcissistic wound is quite different from "healthy narcissism," (Kohut, H. 1977), which occurs when parents respond to the child with empathy, understanding and connection, thus encouraging the child's ability to stand up in behalf of the self.

Denied that healthy interplay, learning to disown anger and other feelings in their early emotional environment, Hades' Angels, and many women in the general population, get unconsciously set up for similar wounding in adult relationships. Hoping for, yet never really expecting one's needs to be met, is part of that set-up. Hades' Angel Michele says, "I never expected to win." When that old bell rang, Hades' Angels responded with old survival tools, hiding part of the self to meet the other's needs, and giving away what she needed and didn't get: understanding, mirroring, and empathic attunement. This disaster story becomes a foot in the door, drawing her like a magnet, pulling her into relationships that again foster isolation, withdrawal, neglect, shame, and even violence. This early childhood wounding resulted in her acting-in – her closing down to protect and hide the true self – and this dynamic provides the "perfect fit" for a narcissistically injured man who responds to a similar wounding by *acting out* with rage.

Inner Prison

Among the general population, early narcissistic wounding doesn't always lead to uncontrollable rage that results in murder, but (discussed in the chapter on Demon Lover), it often results in a destructive dynamic: one partner exerting power and control, while the other shuts down and withdraws. This pattern is evident in many emotionally and physically abusive relationships where the woman's longed for connection is through soothing the "rager's" insatiable hunger. This method of a hoped-for connection maintains old, learned survival patterns that attract women in the general population as well as a Hades' Angels and keep them as imprisoned as her spouse.

In relationships between two people suffering from early narcissistic injury, their common wound draws them like a magnet: each unconsciously hopes to get early childhood needs met by the other.

Trauma

Mutual attraction of partners is further based on similar needs and fears, meaning each attempts to overcome past trauma and conflict through their relationship dynamics, including using the guise of pleasing behaviors. Chronic rejection by a parent on whom the child depends for physical and emotional survival has a devastating impact over time. Trauma shuts us down in body, mind and spirit.

Betty Jo graphically describes her early trauma:

> *I was never wanted. I never knew if my mother would beat me or hug me. She would pound my head into the wall, then turn around and just start hugging me and kissing me and telling me she was sorry. Once, when I was 2½, my mother grabbed my hands and broke my two baby*

fingers. That was the moment when I swore I would never cry again. After that I tried not to feel anything because I was tired of being hurt.

Chronic narcissistic injury develops along a spectrum from humiliation and shame to narcissistic rage and mindless aggression which, when vengefully perpetrated, results in imprisonment, a life sentence, or death. Life, for the externally inflated narcissistic personality, cannot be lived alone in a vacuum, or in a cell. It reaches out, not in, to get its needs meet by another. The self, for the narcissist, is experienced only when needs get met by an "other," not in relationship with an "other". The injured part of the personality seeks nourishment—from a tender-hearted soul, in this case, a Hades' Angel, who defends against her own narcissistic injuries by feeding those needs in her inmate spouse and soothing his internal states of tension.

When the Self gets lost, rejected, or used to feed an emotionally hungry or needy parent, it gets internalized in the child's sense of identity: "I was invisible", said Hades' Angel Sabrina. The wounded core is but a jumping off place from which other destructive dynamics evolve. When the "I" is invisible, the child learns early on that what he/she wants is never as important as what others want. To protect the self from further hurt, she learns to relegate her own feelings to shadow territory, hiding them away in the deepest recesses of the self. The heart remains hungry when the self is shamed over normal but unmet needs; this shame gets internalized and survival depends on pleasing and learning to "walk on egg shells". A description of this common dysfunctional relationship dynamic evident in the general population is submissively playing into the "cycle of abuse": honeymoon, tension building, and explosion.

2. Controlling/Submissive Family Dynamic

My early life was all about appearances and I realize how superficial that was. Dad was a big, powerful man. He was a political man, well respected, and a leader in the community. Mother was submissive. She would do anything rather than rock the boat. From her I learned to be a good girl, a good daughter, and a very dutiful wife.

--- Hades' Angel Cretia

Chaotic and traumatic events in the lives of these women often stem from historical multigenerational family patterns of dominance and emotional submission. Problems such as developmental deficits, feeling objectified, and learned helplessness are likely to develop. Where mothers modeled "laying down and playing dead," daughters learned to be submissive and that women are worthless in relationships.

I learned to be a co-dependent at the sacrifice of the self.

--- Hades' Angel Michele

Family belief systems are powerful nonverbal, silent messages that become the foundation of family functioning. They are unconsciously passed down through multiple generations. Dominance and submission are learned, modeled, felt, witnessed, and expected behaviors within the family. The child's survival depends on learning these unspoken messages: don't speak up; smile at all costs; I'll only love you if you do as I expect; don't show your emotions; peace at all costs, and so on. Some are related to anger: don't show anger; anger is bad. Some family belief systems are gender related: men rule; women don't count. Some, like Hades' Angel Michele's, focus on the spiritual: If I'm not loving and doing for someone else, I'm not a good Christian.

"The women in our family don't get divorced" is a belief intended to hold the family together. However, when a woman gets abused because she must submit to a spouse who feels entitled to rule the family with murderous rage, the marriage is not bound by love. It is noosed by fear, control, and retribution. Family members learn to respect control and fear, not love. Belief systems, meant as moral guidelines, either serve their true purpose, or exact a toll over multiple generations, generating fear, anxiety and distorting the lives they are meant to support.

The roots of early narcissistic injury lie buried in such twisted, polarized family dynamics. With few exceptions, Hades' Angels perceived their father as dominant, critical, and controlling, while mother was his emotionally submissive and passive partner. Exceptions were a reversal of this polarized position: a very domineering mother who used verbal and emotional abuse to control the family. The wounded child, the future Hades' Angel got triangled, caught between these two parental energies, or put in "a special" position, attuned to the father's *emotional* neediness (see *Father's Daughter*) that were not met by the wife.

Old, multi-generational belief systems, internalized family myths that often disregarded emotional boundaries, and childhood family alignments colored Hades' Angels' actions and behaviors, becoming the lens through which they viewed their world. Family communication patterns made room for small talk only. Being "heard", or understood, was a foreign language. Words confused and controlled; they did not soothe. It was a growing-up world of *shoulds* and *should nots*, where being different was not acceptable.

Belonging meant fitting the mold and going along with the perceived strong end of the pole. Where the parents major concern was "What will the neighbors think?", Hades' Angels learned to stuff their doubts, their anger, their questions, and shut up to survive. They rebelled inside, seethed inside, or outside by marrying a black man when it was not the societal norm.

I want to go out and save the world.

---Hades' Angel Ann

In these dominant/submissive parental marital dynamics, the message was clear: women don't count. Women, considered emotionally weak, were therefore worthless, which paved their fall into submissive roles in destructive adult relationships ---and led to additional narcissistic wounding.

> *I grew up in a field of roses with thorns.*
>
> --- Hades' Angel PJ

These factors, at least potentially, blocked self-awareness. They kept Hades' Angels invisibly armored to protect the Self from further emotional injury and from developing their own true potential. Devalued and unaware of their strength and their worth, they gave it away to manifest the potential in someone else. When that potential in another did not develop, it was internalized as their shame, becoming part of the self: "I failed." BJ says, "I wasn't good enough to love or be loved." This twisted family dynamic offered a bleak outlook and perpetuated additional self-defeating and abusive relationship patterns, widening the gap between sense of self based on external achievement, and a *sense of self* based on knowing who one is.

3. The Role as Family Caretaker/Nurturer

> *I was put in this world to fix people.*
>
> --- Hades' Angels Beth

As a child, Hades' Angels took on the role of the super-responsible caretaker, peacemaker and nurturer. Otherwise shamed, criticized, objectified or devalued, this role is a clever adaptive strategy, an unconscious survival tool to address unmet dependency needs. It earned importance and offered a sense of belonging. A Hades' Angels was the go-between who served the needs of the parent, and they came to heavily rely on her for that. In a chaotic, confused family, she was the one stable factor, the dependable one who kept a sinking boat afloat. It translates in adult relationships to an emotionally submissive, nurturing caretaker with no voice of her own. What these women don't see, can't see at the time, is the destructive aspects of their role in regards to adult relationships!

> *I'm the glue. My role has been to hold everything together. If someone's got a problem, anybody, it's me they come to.*
>
> --- Hades' Angel Lynn

Insight about their learned family roles can become transforming: "I was a caretaker my whole life"; "I was the peacemaker"; "I was the go-between"; "I was the mother when I needed a mother."

Angel Bonnie was put in the role of "mini-mother"—a familiar role to her—when her mother, diagnosed with tuberculosis, went into a sanitarium. Three years later, she died there. "I'm 12 years old, I'm the oldest, so I have to do the household stuff, but I needed a mother myself." Then, in her previous marriage, she was discounted and emotionally abused. She didn't have much in common with her first husband, who had been closed-mouthed and secretive. "I didn't know until years later that he was cheating on me. With others he was a sociable man, while I stayed at home and raised the kids." After he had a stroke, Bonnie became the breadwinner and the caretaker.

False Self

In families where a parent is narcissistically injured, mirroring roles are reversed and the child, acting as an extension of the parent, learns to mirror or meet the parent's needs. It causes a split in one's core. The split-off true self, rejected and repressed, lies dormant within, and a false self is presented to the world. Hades' Angels created an internally demanding "false self" package filled with nurturing, achievement and perfectionism that got them what they needed: praise, love, or recognition.

For the Hades' Angels, that nurturing, internally demanding "false self" role becomes her *modus operandi*, and she identifies herself by how well she fulfills that it. Hungry for approval, she unconsciously now puts herself in a position of having to please and nurture others. A creative "false self" evolved from needing to mirror a narcissistically wounded parent, fit in, and feel a belonging in the family. But the "true self" paid a price; it got lost in this destructive process.

> *I had to hide a part of myself.*
>
> --- Hades' Angel Sherry

This early family role is fertile training ground for adult relationships -- a school for how to adapt, how to be an empathic listener, and meet the needs of others -- but the true Self remains hidden, dependent, vulnerable, and even stigmatized or gets sacrificed in the process. The "caretaker false self" becomes the new identity, who one is. Hades' Angels, separated from seeing their preciousness, didn't know they were giving it away. This achievement-oriented, nurturing caretaker becomes a doormat with no voice of her own. And like the mother, it is in relationship to a dominant, critical, controlling partner.

Sabrina says, "I married a man like my dad—a rager. I felt like I was in prison because he was just never there and when he was, everyone needed to make him happy, not mad."

> *Women who fall into this doormat pattern wonder how they got there. "I'd go after the same kind of man over and over again, people with excess baggage. I'd do that to distract myself from my own discontent and sadness. I'd want to fix the world.*
>
> --- Hades' Angel Beth

The majority of Hades' Angels interviewed shared this caretaker/nurturer pattern, either in connection to their current prison relationships or in previous "demon lover" relationships. However, because of the nature of these prison relationships, the Hades' Angels could see their part in such destructive dynamics and take action to change things. Looking back on previous demon lovers, Hades' Angel Beth recognized that every time she submissively turned her back on her own needs, she was abused. Survival means more than learning to take it; awareness protects her against it reoccurring. Such insights into the self are crucial.

4. A "Father's Daughter"

> *I was the only one Father wanted. I was the only daughter with dirt under my nails. He would let me ride a cow and I'd feed them salt blocks. I was the most popular kid in the pasture. He was an upstanding honest citizen who would sit and talk with me about his experience in World War II with General Patton, about the wind, walking in the snow, and seeing bloody footprints. My only complaint is that he had control over my life. My mother was a loving woman; she just didn't understand her child.*
>
> --- Hades' Angel PJ

"Father's Daughter" refers to a daughter who is unconsciously aligned with the values of the patriarchy and the masculine principle (Woodman, 1982), and the values of the personal father. While her achievement gains paternal approval, it also polarizes her against the mother, the feminine, and her own emotional side. Unconsciously, her feminine aspects of the self get sacrificed to meet the father's emotional needs. Unlike *Daddy's Girl*, who can generally do no wrong in the eyes of the father, a father's daughter is emotionally controlled by a hunger for the "father god", who pours his woundedness into her and she then mirrors that pain, often in another, throughout life.

Hades' Angel BJ, triangled in by her father, believes her mother was jealous of their close relationship. She constantly tried to interfere, telling BJ she was upsetting him and "making him crazy." She says:

> *When I was a kid, I was able to sit down with him all the time, and he'd listen to me, and it seemed to me like I could communicate with him. He was of the old school—he believed in telling my mom what to do. There was always conflict between my mom and me. I never felt comfortable giving her a hug. She blamed everything on me, but she got along great with my brother.*

The closeness BJ felt to her father ended as she reached puberty. When she began to like boys, he suddenly became very strict with her: "He didn't know how to relate to me anymore and I was afraid of disappointing him." She got cut off and found it hard not being able to relate to either of her parents.

A father's daughter receives praise and validation from an often critical father through her successes in the world of the masculine. Generally, she becomes achievement and goal oriented in order to obtain his approval. Her father is her rock, her mentor, her hero, her "father-god".

> *The men in my life have been variations of my father.*
>
> --- Hades' Angel Eve

To meet his emotional needs, her own developmental needs get sacrificed. Empathically attuned to his needs, she is his perfect mirror. Unfortunately, she unconsciously carries his wounds inside, and later into adult relationships: "I was choosing men like my dad, emotionally unavailable", says Hades' Angel Sabrina. Still further, she denies her own emotional side, thinking the feminine as soft, weak and submissive. Angel BJ explains, "I didn't go into teaching because it was something that my mom wanted me to do, and I wasn't going to do it. It was too much of a woman's profession. I was very rebellious. I wasn't going to do what women should do -- get a teaching job so you could have summers off and get married and raise kids and that was it, that was your life." Father's daughters get sacrificed by their "father-god". Starting out young, self-esteem, praise and validation are earned by pleasing this oftentimes controlling, domineering, critical father figure in arenas of academic achievement and, later on, worldly success.

> *I was a good girl who graduated seventh in my class with awards and honors for just about everything. I wanted to please him [Dad] but that wasn't easy. He thought I should do a little bit better. I learned to model mother's submissive behaviors. Her philosophy was: Her husband came first, then her children, then herself.*
>
> --- Hades' Angel Sara

For most Hades' Angels, the inside and the outside don't match. Sacrificing her wants and needs to help someone else became a relationship pattern– outwardly driven towards success and achievement, but inwardly hungry for the love they so generously gave away.

The real sacrifice of taking on the role of emotional and intellectual partner to the father is a lack of connection to her own true core. The inner world, born from states of self-reflection that emerges from a feminine consciousness, remains hidden in the shadows. Also sacrificed is her sense of attachment and connection to the mother, the feminine, because it is considered weak. The daughter's allegiance is to the father, the patriarchy, not the mother/feminine. It is for him, for his perceived strength, his world, that she has empathy, admiration, and respect. Desiring to please the father, she mirrors and selflessly serves the very hand that only occasionally validates her. She learns to live for crumbs!

This "emotionally incestuous" special connection to the father, and the values of the patriarchy is detrimental to the daughter in many ways. It causes even greater separation between the daughter and her mother, and cuts her off further from her own feminine nature. Without her own voice, she serves him, his values, achieves his goals, and lives primarily from the consciousness of the upper world -- her head. She is clueless about her identity apart from what she can accomplish in the name of the father (the masculine). Feeling disregarded, cut-off or rejected by an emotionally unavailable mother (the feminine), she is an eager student, nurtured and mentored intellectually by the father. In the outer world, she continues to meet patriarchal demands. In the blood of the inner world, her creative, intuitive nature is repressed, drained by her drive for perfectionism and achievement. It goes on and on.

Father's daughters learn about surviving in a man's world, but not as a woman fully aware of the strengths that lie dormant in her repressed, instinctual feminine nature. States BJ, "Instead of talking to me about sex, I got a newspaper or magazine articles to read." She becomes intellectually armed against the seductions of sensuality and unconsciously cut off from her instincts, her intuitive nature, and the wisdom of her body. The cognitive is validated while the feminine remains hungry for praise and affirmation. Thus, early childhood patterns repeat. She is vulnerable to a man who mirrors her woundedness. She is easy prey for a narcissistically wounded man who needs to harness her strengths, and her strong facade to fill his own emptiness. Often, that someone is just like the father. Outwardly, she is in control just like the father; inwardly she is emotionally empty and submissive, just like her mother.

5. Intellectual/Emotional Split

I became an overachiever, a perfectionist, to compensate for feeling worthless and for having no value because I was female. I learned to do everything the hard way, on my own.

--- Hades' Angel Lisa Heart

The fragile and defenseless part of the self is protected by the woman's over-intellectualized sense of identity. Intelligent and articulate, Hades' Angels survived their narcissistic injuries by becoming grounded in the cognitive, becoming academic stars or "golden girls", book-wise, not streetwise. Cut off from their feminine essence that values emotional intimacy, what these women need and want, and fear, is attachment and intimacy. Attachment has been to the perceived strength of the cognitive pole, not the emotional one.

I learned to justify, not feel from the heart.

--- Hades' Angel Callie

Healthy babies thrive from attachment and loving parental touch. The lack of this healthy touch has been found to be associated with delays in growth. Without healthy emotional nurturing, these women often end up searching for a different kind of touch in the form of an intellectual communion essential for her emotional and psychological survival. Her narcissistically wounded, emotionally passive mother does not provide a healthy model of how to relate to men emotionally. Mother and father live on two different planets intellectually. Like Angels PJ and Sabrina, Hades' Angels wanted the mother to know them; but, for the most part, she didn't. Mother lacks either the ability or the desire to meet the father's or the daughter's emotional, developmental, and intellectual needs. The daughter, already cut off from her own feminine nature, turns to the father and later to other men for intellectual relating, substituting it for attachment and emotional intimacy.

> *All the way through college, I was still trying to do what*
> *Dad wanted.*
>
> --- Hades' Angel Cretia

Repeated rejection, retribution or psychological abuse cause a vicious cycle that repeats throughout one's life. The child subjected to such repeated rejection splits off the pain of shame or humiliation, and then defends against remembering it. Knowing that the parent is unavailable to offer empathy or mediate that pain, the child pushes it outside of the conscious mind. This is a survival tool. When the coping capacities are overwhelmed, the impact of the pain doesn't just disappear, it simply exists outside of time, frozen, separated from affect, pushed down and split off from awareness -- and later relived in relationships.

As a father's daughter matures and goes out into the world, her relationships with men reflect her intellectual/emotional split. Her inner world of self-reflection and feminine consciousness remains in the shadows, waiting, hungry for nurturing and affirmation. Outwardly, she appears to "have it all together" and certain men who need to harness that strength for themselves are attracted to it.

These Hades' Angels, intelligent and articulate, are caught between the devil and the deep blue sea. They survive their narcissistic injuries by becoming the father's daughter -- his "golden girl" or his "academic star", becoming book-wise not streetwise - while down deep they pay a heavy price for not getting what they really need and want: attachment and closeness based on who they really are. Unconsciously, they choose one over the other. Their strong bond with the world of the masculine, the intellect, and patriarchal values recognizes her for what she can do, accomplish, not for who she is. Beth felt sucked in like a vacuum. Seduced by her perception of her inmate spouse as a respected survivor, she bonded with him intellectually, and became his support in the world of the patriarchy: writing letters to his family, his attorney, and even the warden. When she asked for his unconditional love and acceptance, he shut down verbally and emotionally. Beth got pushed away, distanced, and then cut off.

6. True Self / False Self Split

I was very shy and very much a loner. I spent my life emotionally walled-off in my own protective prison.

--- Hades' Angel Betty Jo

I think I learned very early that you do what you've got to do to survive. If that means shut your mouth, you shut your mouth.

--- Hades' Angel Lynn

Hades' Angels are articulate, hard-working, productive members of society who live by the rules, even though inside they tend to feel different, isolated and alone. Masking one's true feelings to mirror the unmet emotional needs of a narcissistically injured parent gets praise and validation but it "forms the foundation of an entire false-self system" (Kalshed, 1980). The parent, intolerant of the child's normal dependency needs, makes the child feel shame and humiliation for even having these normal needs. The child responds to this emotional depravation by concealing the true self, replacing it with what she thinks others want her to be. Thus, a false self is created. For Hades' Angels at this point, their own self-protective wall kicks in and they become intolerant of their own neediness. Like other victims of an early emotional environment whose basic dependency needs were chronically thwarted, they do not generally have an awareness of -- or are afraid to state -- their own wants and needs.

To defend against such early narcissistic injuries, Hades' Angels develop a *true self / false self* split. A pretty "false-self" package is presented to the world, characterized by a facade of normality, self-sufficiency, perfectionism and reliance on achievement. All the while, the true self remains wounded, powerless, dormant, and walled off. The overly self-sufficient false self, caretaker of the wounded true self, kicks in at the expense of age-appropriate emotional development. As a reaction to the choice between a life of feeling worthless and having a sense of identity through a man, Lisa Heart says, "I identified myself by my job (a registered nurse), by my possessions, and what I could achieve on my own." Like overachiever Lisa Heart, Angels are driven, unconsciously perhaps, to deny their sadness and fear, to mask their anger, and to fill up the emptiness they feel inside with things, with goals, and achievements -- while the precious true self remains hidden in the shadows.

Masks, or emotional cover-ups, are also used to hide shame about dysfunctional family beliefs. If how the family appears to the outside world is more important than who it really is, the child gets a clear message about shame which he/she internalizes as his or her *own*. When family shame is being compounded with personal shame, the true self gets masked beneath layers of invisible walls. True feelings get hidden when deemed not acceptable, becoming a basic rule of survival: Hide the precious part of the self; internalize the rage, shame and humiliation; look good, be good, follow the rules, find a way to make peace at all costs, and find a way to survive. Over time, the masked self actually begins to feel like the true self. But the real true self has not disappeared. Like Sleeping Beauty, it simply lies dormant, curled up in a fetal position waiting to be coaxed into the open, waiting to be kissed into the light of consciousness:

> *I can't remember a time I felt comfortable with me or worthwhile.*
>
> --- Hades' Angel Michele

7. Previous Demon Lover Relationships

> *My first husband was 15 years older than I, had a doctorate degree, and worked as a professional jazz musician. He was also an alcoholic who physically and emotionally abused me. I was one of those emotionally and physically abused wives that just kept coming back because I had to prove that I could do it.*
>
> --- Hades' Angel Sara

> *In my family the men got away with doing whatever they wanted. My first husband was a womanizer who had children by other women. For 18 years I believed that I couldn't do anything about this situation, that I was helpless.*
>
> --- Hades' Angel Sabrina

What has historically been viewed as pathological behavior on the part of women drawn towards an impossible prison love is a positive move, a step up for many Hades' Angels. Prior to her prison relationship she had been involved in a pattern of destructive, abusive relationships with the kind of man I refer to as a "demon lover".

Here, the demon lover is understood as a well-packaged, manipulative trickster, himself narcissistically wounded in childhood, who swallows women up to feed the hungry caverns of the self. His controlling, grandiose way of relating masks the enormity of his true dependency, and his fear of falling apart. His relationship with a self-sufficient, nurturing, empathic woman, such as a Hades' Angel, is the very glue that holds his internally fragile self together. A perfect match for a hungry heart!

I was supposed to have walked two steps behind.

--- Hades' Angel C.C.

In these demon lover relationships many Hades' Angels found themselves nurturing men who easily took advantage of their goodness and acted as though he were entitled to it. Yet these women kept on nurturing them, paying the bills, and coming back to them again and again, replaying earlier family roles and learned survival patterns. They choked back angry feelings, and became emotionally submissive to critical, domineering, controlling partners, all the while pleasantly presenting themselves to the outside world as intelligent, articulate, assertive, goal-oriented, high-achieving, and financially stable. In their naiveté, these women keep hoping for reciprocity to their goodness, but never get it. Instead, early patterns get repeated: used, abused, manipulated, swallowed up and spit out.

The concept of a demon lover is consistent with self-psychology's notion of narcissistic pathology (Kohut, 1971). The term presents a softer, more tragic image of the devouring, vampiric energy inherent in the pathological narcissistic character disorder. For the narcissist, grandiosity masks the extent of the dependency needs to maintain self-cohesion.

He wouldn't leave. I paid all the bills.

--- Hades' Angel BJ

The demon lover has a desperate, even parasitic need to hook onto the strength of another because inside he is inadequate and desperately fragile and needy. He hides his true self behind his attractively packaged "false-self", a facade of bravado, strength, attentiveness, loving generosity, and even financial success. The emotionally hungry woman gets manipulated -- seduced emotionally and intellectually. She is deliberately led to believe she will get more from him than she'll actually get. She gets "hooked" into his elusive potential. The vicious cycle in her historical family pattern repeats: "If I give more of myself, he will love me more."

The reality is that this is as good as it gets. The demon lover cannot give more because the facade is all there is. Such men "read" the innermost needs of a strong-minded female because he desperately needs that strength which is lacking in the self. Unbeknownst to her, he is literally falling apart and she holds him up. Without her he is nothing.

The demon lover feeds the needs of an inner demon and cannot be ignored here. According to Woodman, the negative aspect of experiencing herself as the father's beloved not only prevents the adult daughter from seeing her own shadow and fully embracing life, it encourages her to see the demon lover as the only one with a dark side:

> *Her love is split-off from her sexuality. She tends to fall helplessly in love with a man who cannot marry her and around whom she creates an ideal world in which she is either adored or dramatically rejected. Having been filled with her father all her life, she has learned how to mirror a man, but remains a reflector. (Woodman, 1982, p. 135)*

As long as early childhood narcissistic wounds remain hidden from awareness, buried in the shadows or locked up behind emotional walls, the woman's unconscious choice controls her and keeps her from finding her own preciousness, her true self. Rather than acknowledge the demonic wolf energy that is devouring her, she gets eaten up alive, spinning her wheels trying to transform his potential instead of looking at the darker aspects of the self.

Hitting bottom in her demon lover relationship is often a trigger for change. For many Hades' Angels, and women in the general population, there comes a point when "enough is finally enough", the last straw! Now, energy previously channeled into such destructive relationships can get used to light a new path that brings about internal change, recognition of old, destructive patterns, awareness and integration of one's shadow parts. By opening up to kiss the toad within, to accept and embrace the unknown "shadow" aspects of the self, transformation takes place.

In conclusion, reaching out, extending to meet a man in prison is not the *cause* of her relationship problems, it becomes the Hades' Angel's unique, though unconscious, solution to her relationship problems.

Getting this point across to outsiders, Hades' Angels agree, is difficult. Many complain that people don't want to see their prison relationships in this different light; they hope that a book such as this helps shed light on their truth: certain prison relationships can be healing.

These women fell in love with men in prison, and in the end, freed themselves.

Portrait - Dimples

> *Growing up I felt a huge emptiness -- like I'm a nobody screaming, Somebody love me; somebody tell me who I am; tell me that I'm somebody important.*

> --- Hades' Angel Dimples

Hades' Angel Dimples, 49, a customer service representative, uses her life time for her grandkids and heavy church involvement, in addition to her inmate spouse, a lifer. She met her current prisoner husband, twenty years her junior, as the result of being a licensed minister. Her initial contacts with him were for the purpose of prayer while he awaited trial. "What drew me to him, and still draws me, is the Christ in him. He looked kind of innocent and sweet, and yet I knew that he had done something terrible." Their personal relationship came later. A bright, curious woman, Dimples is openly interested in the psychological dynamics behind her choice of a prison inmate as a husband. Searching for meaning in her life, she believes her choice was no accident. Rather, she sees it as an opportunity, although an unconscious one, to "learn more about me."

Devotion to her religion guides her and frames her present marriage as a job that God wants her to do. After her first marriage, she used to joke about her inability to pick a good husband: "Okay, if I get married again, God's going to have to tell me 'This is who I want you to marry and that's what I want you to do,' because otherwise I wouldn't be able to do it. The Lord put this relationship on my heart, and to me this is more than a job, more than a marriage -- this is my whole life. We're building a marriage on the eight or nine hours that we spend together."

Like other Hades' Angels, Dimples bears the pain of her childhood "narcissistic wounds". Her life was without a felt connection or any ability to complain about it. The silent, but powerful childhood admonition was to wear a smile at all costs. That's why the name Dimples appealed to her. "I always feared authority; now I recognize how that fear programmed me to be submissive, just like my mother who taught me to wear that smile." Her mother, a homemaker, was weak and submissive, and her father, a high school principal, was a prejudiced, controlling, workaholic who was rarely home and as she says, "He didn't teach me a damn thing." As a child, she felt no sense of direction from her family, no sense of identity, no mentoring, and no structure. Outside she adhered to the rules of the house like a good girl. But inside she felt differently: "Inside I felt like a nobody. I was a rebel inside. I had an inner rebellion that manifested by marrying a black man when it just wasn't acceptable." She also rebelled against her father's prejudice.

Her home was cold, without any loving or a felt connection. It's easy to see the similarities in terms of hours actually spent together between her relationship with her "there but not there" father and her husband: little time spent together. It's also easy to feel the similarities in terms of the coldness and underlying tension between her childhood home and the prison visits.

When it comes to her father, Dimples is openly bitter: "He never taught me anything except go to work, earn a living, financially take care of your family, come home, talk trivia, and watch TV. Today, long-distance phone calls are all the closeness I want from my father because there's too much emptiness." When Dimples tries to talk or to get close to her mother, now in her 70's, "it's like she's saying 'don't get too close'. It's the same old thing – just superficial talk; no feelings: 'How's work? Did you take your vitamins?'"

Not getting the emotional nourishment she needed at home, Dimples put her energies into her work: "That was my Dad's model and it was where I got the praise and affirmation that made me feel good enough," she says. Dimple's first marriage was to a black man who used and manipulated her to meet his own need not to work. She stayed in that abusive marriage for twenty-three years because "The Bible says you don't get a divorce unless the other person is being unfaithful." Like her mother, Dimples was submissive to this man and, like her father, she became a workaholic and ended up totally supporting him. For somebody who used to feel like she was "a nobody", taking care of others and being needed by others was what gave her a sense of value. "I married my father except it was reversed in the money department, I was the one working. A lot of churches don't tell you that if a husband is not supporting the family, there's something wrong with him. They tell you to work harder; they put it back on you," she says.

Dimple's turning point came after reading Melody Beattie's *Co-Dependent No More*. "It was an eye-opener. When I read about codependency I thought, 'That's me!' and I realized mine was a dysfunctional marriage and I no longer had to put up with it." That's when she broke away from it.

Her life, though stressful, is now manageable, and she has more control in this marriage than in her first one. Even though her inmate husband is "inside" for being violent, she has no fear of him. She feels safe because she can read him. "I can tell when he gets angry because his lip quivers and he gets this look on his face. It's like he goes inside, and I know that something's really upset him." But he doesn't throw blame and his anger is never directed at her. Glass walls and protective bars guarantee her safety. "In the beginning, we always visited behind glass, and we got married behind glass. Unlike my first marriage, in this one, I don't have somebody spending money that I earned. Now it's my choice how I spend my money. I still have control over pretty much everything in my life."

As a couple they are trying to create a relationship of trust and respect, "things we haven't had before", she says. Like her first husband, this man, too, is black. Unlike Dimple's first husband, she says, "He is always very appreciative of my efforts and my time, and we are learning to give and take. We're trying to build a marriage on the eight or nine hours a week that we spend together."

Creativity and time to play is something she never experienced growing up in her home. Dimples is "held" and intrigued by his creative imagination. She listens eagerly, loving that with him she gets the opportunity to play with thoughts and ideas. "He writes poetry and tells stories for hours and I enjoy just listening to him. One day he told me a story that lasted for hours. He says he always wanted to be a writer, but he doesn't have any kind of formal training, so I don't know what will ever come of it. But it's incredible to see somebody with such an imagination. He needs me to listen and I am a good listener– but I also get heard by him." It's the polar opposite from the conversations she used to have with her first husband who would talk at me. "I finally learned to protect myself by tuning him out." This proved good practice for turning out the noise and the stressful visiting room environment when she visits him.

Thanks to his encouragement, she believes this marriage has helped her grow. By reading, questioning, and sharing her thoughts and feelings with him, she has a sounding board she never had that helps her make decisions that benefit her. "I'm closer to my husband in these five years without ever having sex than I was with my ex-husband after twenty-three years." In his company, she is building a sense of self-worth and acceptance. "It's almost like I'm trying to re-parent myself, and in the process I'm also being a parent to my husband." She is no longer programmed to shut down. Dimples handled many life stresses alone, such as the drive-by shooting of her son who- luckily survived. But all this has strengthened her emotionally: "My voice used to shake because I had so much fear. He's taught me how to stand up and fight for what's right, even when I'm scared." Angel Dimples has also developed a budding sense of her power and is aware of what she unknowingly gave away in her first marriage. She stopped blaming herself for the failure of that marriage. She says, "I learned to discern the Bible's view of marriage differently, less concretely and more deeply. This deeper view holds both parties responsible, and informs me that a man who does not care for his family is 'worse than an infidel.'" Angrily referring to her first husband, she says: "If a man does not work, he shouldn't eat!"

There was a high price and a stigma attached to her prison marriage. "I paid a high price for my prison marriage. As soon as my church found out, they revoked my minister's license." Many friends have fallen away. "I found out who my real friends were. Some of the people I thought were my friends weren't." What she gets from her inmate husband is something she never had before: a felt connection, love, acceptance, and nourishment. "Not only am I giving my basket of goodies to him, but he's putting some new stuff in my basket. Now I feel like I'm saying, here I am; this is me. I am somebody!"

Knowing she has a right to speak her mind, she works openly for prison reform: "I finally feel like I have some power."

Dimples Update

Dimples is still with her husband, but spends less time visiting now. It was important to her and "it kept him calm, but a problem with one guard, who probably doesn't approve of mixed-race marriages has kept me at arm's length. We were given 5 seconds for a hug and time for a very brief kiss. The guard said things to me about kissing too long." Because of this too lengthy kiss, her husband was put behind glass. She was never notified as required by Title 15 rules. Dimples got upset seeing her husband behind glass but did not show it. She held herself together in the visiting room. As later reported in the local newspaper, she says, after she left, her husband shouted at the guard about it, then he was then handcuffed, shackled at the ankles, beaten with a baton and kicked in the head and face. This brutality, witnessed by 25 inmates, rendered her speechless because she feared retribution for her husband, she states.

Dimples Transformation

Dimples learned a lot about herself through her current relationship, and it has continuously fueled her movement towards that self-awareness. She never knew how to play, but she plays now though listening to his stories. She recognizes, too, the major themes in her own life story. She grew up believing in duty but never knew about love. In fact, duty and responsibility were equated as "love". Whatever attention she got as a child, whether from good grades in school or negative attention by dating and marrying black men, came from her deep desire to fill the emptiness felt in her childhood family and home. Love and duty were polarized aspects of her lonely existence. These two opposing aspects, like beauty and beast, have come together from her current relationship. Love, caring and even play, occur in a cold and repressive environment, not unlike the one in which she grew up. She has always cared for others yet never been cared about as she so needed to be, either by her parents or her previous husband. In her current relationship, she has learned what her parents never taught her: reciprocity. Dimples gives generously of her time, her understanding, and her love to others, and she acknowledges that it feels good to get the same back. "It has empowered me to believe in myself."

Chapter Eleven

Turning Points and Transformations

Genuine beginnings begin within us, even when they are brought to our attention by external opportunities.

--- William Bridges

I went in to help him and found me.

--- Hades' Angel C.C.

The repressed tension of a prison setting seems an unlikely environment to work on unfinished family-of-origin issues, yet here many Hades' Angels have experienced a transformative healing journey, a "corrective, emotional experience"(Alexander, 1961) they clearly feel has changed them for the better, empowering the way they live their lives. Against the nonclinical backdrop of the prison, the Hades' Angels find they have recovered from early childhood narcissistic wounding and the destructiveness of past relationships.

For many Hades' Angels, their journey along the yellow brick road got jump-started by a particularly significant and specific external event that they can point to -- a turning point.

Turning Points

He kept pushing me so after nine years I finally said, "Pack your clothes and leave."

--- Hades' Angel Lisa Heart

A turning point, either an external event or internal life crisis can create opportunity to transform "fate" into a deep life change. For Hades' Angels, a "last straw," a separation or divorce, a trauma, an illness, a death – pushed their back up against the wall—beyond the comfort zone – and there was no turning back. It led to an acute awareness of something missing within, an emptiness inside, and a felt need for change that sent them searching, along the yellow brick road, into the unknown.

The lack of awareness of essential, emotional boundaries, and the resulting emotional and mental mergers, exists in the general population of women involved in destructive relationship patterns. Growing up, Danielle says she was never allowed to think for herself. "I was always told that I couldn't do or say whatever it was I wanted to do. All that changed after my mother got sick with cancer and I learned the importance of speaking up and asking questions. Her mother's illness and death caused an internal shift away from the family's emotionally enmeshed "my way or the high way thinking" to having a right to her own thinking identity. "Until then, I was always afraid somebody might get mad at me. I never used to stick up for myself,"she says.

Angel Eve's turning point was in the assessment of her own life after the death of her mother. She set her intention to walk through life without fear, to break away from the submissiveness inherent in her cultural and family belief system. She says, "I sent a spiritual message to the universe. To prepare if Jesus came today, I would find people in prison open to what we are teaching in church." When the pastor handed her an inmate's marvelous letter of introduction, she felt her prayers were answered, and her journey began.

Turning points also occurred in the context of destructive demon lover relationships, draining them of their aliveness and their sense of self.

Angel PJ talks about her shift out of the comfort zone:

Up to a point, I was perfectly comfortable with relationships that replicated the lack of communication, the rage, and the frustration that I'd witnessed in my family growing up. It was a real comfortable old shoe. But then one day I realized, "No, that's not comfortable at all. No more!"

Lady Honeybear suffered a painful, long-term marriage prior to meeting and marrying her inmate partner:

I was married before and I don't know why-- except it got me out of the house. He tested me too many times so I left him, preferring that God alone, not man, be the one to test my strength.

Prior to the birth of her children, Hades' Angel Sara took her first husband's abuse. It built up to the point of no return.

I allowed a lot of stuff to happen when it was just him and me, when it was all directed at me. The straw that broke the camel's back was he came home one night and we started arguing and he ripped the phone off the wall. That was it. That was when I knew. I'm done; it was all it took. When he didn't drink, we were perfect, we got along, we shared everything, and we liked everything. In fact, the best times we had together was when he had no money because then he couldn't get drunk. It was good times —except when he drank and then it was hell. It was truly hell.

Angel Dimples is a religious woman who ended up supporting a controlling, demanding, verbally abusive, nonworking alcoholic spouse.

She reached her turning point after reading a book on co-dependency. She began to discern the Bible's view of marriage with new eyes and that did it.

> *It informed me that a man who does not care for his family is worse than an infidel and that if a man doesn't work, he shouldn't eat. A lot of churches don't tell you that if a husband is not supporting the family, there's something wrong with that. They tell you to work harder; they put it back on you.*

A mysterious depression kept Angel C.C. locked into medication for ten years straight. Her turning point got jump-started with the internal revelation that she needed to take action. "I needed to work towards getting my friend out of prison. That's what I've be doing the last six or seven years, being his advocate." She stopped the pills cold turkey.

Angel Beth's first husband was murdered; it led to a downward spiral. Without him, she no longer had a desire to live. While trying to recover from her depression, she got involved in a very destructive relationship:

> *I was in self-destruct mode. It pretty much destroyed me as a human being. I was in my own prison. I didn't want to be in reality anymore. I didn't want to feel what I felt. I didn't want to accept what was happening to me, so I felt it was better to be numb.*

An internal decision that 'You are not going to do this to me' was her turning point. It led her into counseling, which she says, "was the best thing that I ever could have done. It helped me work through feelings of guilt, of being judged, and of loss. I no longer felt so alone."

History Repeats

Women involved in destructive relationships unconsciously seek a resolution of that early wounding through a revolving door of destructive relationships. Learned behavior patterns evolved from fear of abandonment, aloneness and lack of boundaries; the upshot is further danger and abuse in relationships that replicate early emotional environments.

Angel Bianca compares visiting her boyfriend to scenes from her childhood. As a child, she emotionally armored herself in order to be insulated from her mother's mood swings, and from her father's criticism and rigid control. Today, she again stuffs her emotions inside and walls herself off from the guard's criticism and rejection just like she did to protect herself from the nun's slights and abuse.

The prison has stirred up the pain and helplessness BJ felt as a child when she shut down and turned the anger inward. The prison situation feels just like when her mother tried to keep her away from her father. She says she has a hard time controlling her anger and frustration.

> *Once again, I feel pushed around by external forces that I have no control over. I get consumed with frustration, and rage because it's arbitrary and capricious, and there's no reason for it. I can't explain it. I'm consumed with it. I can't accept it. It was like everybody was putting me off and just shining me on. It was like I was being shut out, like a nonentity.*

She has since been able to make the obvious connection to her childhood.

Survival Tools

What fears hold them? What brings insight into self-destructive relationship patterns? Conscious awareness alone about a painful or emotionally unfulfilling or destructive situation does not always translate to needed change. Oftentimes, it only brings more being stuck and depressed.

An internalized protector-critic is an adaptive childhood survival tool that allows the developing child to protect a chronically wounded core (Kalshed, 1996). Unfortunately, it often remains in adulthood, preventing the fundamental emotional intimacy so essential in healthy relationships. The empathic attunement felt in their prison relationships slowly chipped away their protective armor.

Angel Bonnie recognizes her nurturer/pleaser part as a needed protective shell that later got used echoing a needy, controlling, womanizing husband. She has a closer relationship with her inmate spouse than she did with her first husband—who, she says, "called me a damn dummy. You know, if you're told something often enough, you wind up believing it. The damn dummy no longer feels dumb about how important I really am, especially in his life. He lets me know," she says.

By the time Hades' Angels meet their prisoner love, a transformation is lurking around the bend. The catalyst that leads to this deeper level change is the inmate's empathic attunement. It may not necessarily be an end in itself but it often is the guiding light, the compass along the Hades' Angel's path of individuation.

Abandonment

Abandonment, isolation, and nurturing others are key issues that keep one stuck in that old protective pumpkin shell. When you can say: 'I don't deserve to be treated like this' and you recognize you are allowing yourself to be short-changed, then it's time to turn the corner and put that nurturing into the self. When getting "small change" is no longer good enough, you can make change happen: the need to nurture takes on a new twist, the fear of traveling life's road alone is no longer an invisible string that draws you in to abusive or co-dependent relationships. Finding a self inside is a draw for healthy relationships.

The feared loneliness and abandonment of speaking your own mind lessens its hold or becomes a non-issue. Hades' Angels looked within, owned their shadow, and reinvested their nurturing energy to manifest their own buried gold.

Hades' Angel Beth woke to the realization that she was giving love to someone [her lifer spouse] who just didn't want it. She was starving and his crumbs were no longer enough. This was another turning point:

> *This last year has been holy hell for us. There used to be some affection – I'm a very affectionate person. I say, 'What happened to the kiss on the cheek? What happened to the pat on the butt? What happened to telling me you love me?' When I tell him I love him, he'll just say, 'That's good. That's a good thing.' Well, that's not good enough for me! It's not working. I am getting nothing out of this relationship. Zero.*

Abandonment issues play a big role in hanging on to an unhealthy relationship. After Angel Bianca's father left, which she perceived as abandonment, she rarely saw him and it was one of the most traumatic events of her life. Making things worse was the fact that her mother went back to work after the divorce, so Bianca was left in charge of the house, to clean up and watch her younger brother after school. "I think my mother was somewhat dependent on me because I was the oldest one home at the time." It is not surprising that she was drawn to her inmate because of his willingness to make a commitment, something no one else, starting with her father, had ever done. "He wants to marry me. In other relationships, I've always been the one who cares more about the other person. In this case, I think he cares more."

The fear of being alone, and a life time of feeling emotionally isolated, drew BJ into a long-term relationship with an alcoholic with whom she didn't feel close enough to say, "I love you." He took advantage of her: "I paid all the bills. I guess maybe I wanted to be in control, but I would have been very grateful if he had contributed. When I finally asked him to leave, he threatened me with palimony," she says. BJ started dating anyway, going out dancing -- and that's when she met the man who fathered her son, now twelve years old. Even though she loved him and knew he cared about her, she ended up being the one who left. She adds, "I just didn't feel good enough about myself and I thought he could do better."

Angel Rose enjoys the security of her inmate spouse's love and friendship without the fear of abandonment she knew first and second time around. Though scared from the storm of those relationships, Rose comes alive on the drug of a nurturing love. "Home and security is not a place, it's a feeling and wonderful things come out of a loving relationship," she says.

Adaptive Tools

The protective armor of adaptive childhood survival tools transfers into adult relationships, often preventing one from "turning the page." For Hades' Angels, the empathic attunement they get from their prison relationships becomes a key impetus, a secondary turning point, that unblocks the road to change, deepening their self-knowledge and insights about old relationships patterns. Moving out of the shadows into the light brings a new clarity in how the woman sees herself.

Danielle's real eye-opener is her awareness of what she's been doing wrong in relationships, and with herself in general. "I recognize that I've always done what someone else wanted, always put myself out for others, always made them feel better." Recognizing this behavior as having built up over a lifetime is also an insight. Danielle learned her childhood lessons well, carried them into present and past relationships, and fell right into the trap of giving sympathy to someone who never gave love or compassion in return. "I felt guilty. I let other people do that. I'm not responsible for what others feel about something but I thought I was. I'm going on a vacation and I feel guilty about that." What jolted her to this personal realization was the time she told him about some difficulties she was having with her adolescent daughter. "What I wanted was for him to listen. I got a deaf ear and I got no support. I got blamed." The guilt and lack of support hit pretty close to home, so she decided to develop boundaries to protect herself rather than give of the self.

Turning points enabled Hades' Angels to break old patterns of seeking external achievement and perfectionism, and begin a quest for the gold within, meaning accepting and embracing her uniqueness. Through the experience of non-judgmental acceptance they learn to appreciate, even love, in another what they disown in themselves. Danielle says, "What makes him so special to me is that I can say anything I want to him and he's not going to be judgmental."

Being released from pejorative statements gives fresh breath to the imprisoned soul; new life energy to soar; to smile from the heart; to feel high as a kite. What kind of love is this? The label it wears and where it's housed become unimportant. Her maturity is unleashed and so are her fears. Hades' Angels insist they are happy in their relationships in spite of all the problems surrounding the prison setting:

> *Out of all the relationships I've had, this one is far better and there's more communication than I ever knew was possible with a man. With him, I'm learning how to be myself, knowing he's still going to love me. I'm happier than I have been in twenty-five or thirty years.*
>
> --- Hades' Angel Callie

By identifying that empty, split-off, disowned shadow part of the self, the Hades' Angel begins the process of integrating them into her personality. Masculine and feminine energies, Logos and Eros intellectual and emotional splits, are each recognized and valued rather than polarized. Out of this is born a sense of wholeness.

What Gets Transformed

Continuously reaching for a loving connection that never comes back, reinforces the inner message: "I'm not good enough; I don't count." Until finding her own distinctive turning point, Hades' Angels choose love relationships that set them up for repeated wounding, re-creating earlier childhood pain.

Fearing the usual rejection and aloneness, Angel Betty Jo lived anxiously in fear of abandonment, particularly by her father, the only possible protector from her mother's abusive clutches. Deep loneliness drove Betty Jo to respond to a letter in a Friendship Booklet for pen pals. Being "kind of scared of men", correspondence seemed like a relatively safe way to connect with a man. She was looking for a connection to alleviate her loneliness, not a love relationship. She was drawn to her friend like a magnet, first by his handwriting, and a certain warmth that radiated through his words.

> *Before, I knew I was hollow. I had very hard feelings, very cold feelings. When I see him, I get this warm feeling all over. When leaving him, the emptiness creeps in again.*

Walls are very much a part of Betty Jo's story. The "wall with my father is an invisible wall, emotionally and probably spiritually. He created that wall. The wall between my husband and me is a physical wall." Her husband breaks down those walls and fills an empty void. Just holding his hand in the controlled environment of the visiting room completely "fills her up," she says.

Reaching out to someone, in this case an inmate, who says he wants her, initially gratifies a need for belonging so she takes a chance. Her own neediness and her caretaker role lead her to accept the prison love. Unconsciously, it becomes the vehicle that helps her work through lifelong pain, and heal from it. What draws her is his pain, and she reaches out to fix him—but this time, she ends up "fixing" herself. No more blaming; no more being victim, solely a commitment to the self.

Once I needed to be needed. Now I just need to be loved.

--- Hades' Angel Lynn

Sacred Space

The continual process of coming together, followed by separation, like the ebb and flow of the tides, is an important and valuable movement in Hades' Angels transformative journey. The containing prison walls serve as invisible emotional boundaries, allowing for a "space between". Separateness, not jumping into the soup of physical or sexual merger, gives time to define emotional boundaries: you from me. Whatever "I" there is, is not swallowed up by a "you". That space between is sacred; it prevents falling into the emotional merger that tends to happen so easily to these women. Two minds, two thoughts, two opposing views, and two lenses from which to view the same situation – this takes precedence over a comfortable merger. For Bonnie 'you are me' is no longer her internalized language. The pleaser and striver part of her that was starving for emotional intimacy, affection, and conversation, is getting those needs met, giving her a sense of dignity, a kind of security—of being loved just for being herself.

Ten Transformations

As the result of their inmate relationships, Hades' Angels begin to experience the following basic transformations to varying degrees:

#1   Healing of Early Childhood Narcissistic Injury

#2   Shedding of "Assigned" Family Role

#3   Discarding of Dysfunctional Beliefs

#4   Creating Relationships of Reciprocity

#5   Integration of Psychological Splits

#6   Owning of the Shadow

#7   Awakening of the Feminine

#1 Healing of the Early Childhood Narcissistic Injury

He feeds the emotional side of me that no one has ever supported.

--- Hades' Angel Ann

When the developing child is forced to shut down, not feel, and consistently protect or defend the self against shame, rejection, and normal dependency needs, it causes a narcissistic injury.

Now I'm getting to experience some of the things that make everybody grow that I had never experienced growing up.

--- Hades' Angel Sara

Over a decade has passed since Angel Jo Anne married her prisoner and she says she is happy. She says, "I get something from him that you're supposed to get from your parents — unconditional love."

When first entering Hades, Hades' Angels expect to fix and feed an inmate's lost soul, not her own. She has no expectation of undergoing a reparative emotional experience.

Psychologist Heinz Kohut (1978) described empathy as "feeling understood by another human being while in a positively toned atmosphere." And that's what happens here. Time becomes a silent partner in the healing. Week after week, month after month, year after year, whether at first invited or coaxed, a Hades' Angel willingly descends into the "belly of the beast" to nurture the wounded part of an other. Committed to him, she offers her time and energy and her heart, ministering to her man through the simple gift of being there for him, empathically attuned. That empathic attunement is the emotional environment in which love grows and internal change, a transformative experience, occurs. Here, she works through her unmet needs for nurturing and mirroring.

> *It was like we read each other's souls.*
>
> --- Hades' Angel Lisa Heart

Angel Jo Anne feels a sense of attachment and connection that empowers a sense of self. Jo Anne stooped to meet her mother's idea of perfect; today she stands tall because her relationship is healing her wounded, unloved, unsafe, and shamed parts.

Angel PJ credits her inmate spouse for "helping heal a lot of my old war wounds, the wounds I grew up with, all those old terrors and fears and damage. In this relationship I can show my true colors and he sees the me that no one else sees."

Shedding Armor

One might think that a man contained inside prison walls offers a perfectly distanced relationship to ward off emotional closeness. However, the opposite is what actually occurs when these women find themselves shedding their armor and revealing their souls.

> *He is slowly turning that armor away from me and he is showing me what it's like to be loved; I never felt that before.*
>
> --- Hades' Angel Betty Jo

In all previous relationships, emotional distancing protected Hades' Angels' wounded core. In this case, against the backdrop of armed guards and the noisy clanging of prison gates, an empathic emotional environment develops; these men give back to them, and it feeds the soul. What they gave but didn't get in their families of origin, they get now from their partners: emotional nurturing, a sense of self, and a sense of a "we". The women feel they can talk with their inmate partners about anything and get heard, accepted, loved and are still wanted.

"I can be me and he's still going to love me," says Angel Callie.

From that interchange of empathic mirroring, the preciousness of the self gets gently coaxed out into the open. Hades' Angels hunger for nurturing gets satisfied by a man on the same wavelength, one who dealt with his own childhood narcissistic injury by acting out in a moment of uncontrollable rage.

Callie's history and fears of being shut down or swallowed up by another do not occur. She speaks her own mind, and stands her ground, and he is still there to love and appreciate her. Her change evolved in response to feeling loved, wanted, "held", and understood, building up her sense of self-worth and self-esteem. Having to achieve in order to belong no longer applied to relationships. Needing to justify and be legal has been replaced with loving reciprocity.

Dimples was trained to be afraid: "That's something I got from my father, because growing up it's like, I'm the dad, you're the child, shut up, don't say anything. You do what you're told. You don't argue. You don't have a voice. You don't have rights. You're nobody, you're nothing, just shut up and do what you're told." She is no longer programmed to shut down or fear authority! Recalling the many times she was told "you can't do that," she now knows she has a right to complain and is empowered to take action. Fighting for her husband taught her how to stand up and fight for herself. She wonders about the work God has in store for her. "Is God going to have me up before the Senate or the Assembly to fight for prisoner's rights?"

#2 Shedding of "Assigned" Family Role

Hades' Angels say they felt different inside, isolated -- like outsiders. Through sheer circumstance, some were forced into a caretaker nurturer role by external necessity, others by the family dynamics. Even though that role didn't suit them, it gave them a sense of importance and belonging in their family of origin. Because of it, they earned acceptance, and kept the family glued together. Later, that caretaker persona became their identity.

> *Both of us (inmate and spouse) sacrificed our own wants and our own selves to help somebody else. Today, I am past the point of doing things because it makes me special to people. I stand up and fight for what I believe is right.*
>
> --- Hades' Angel Jamie

To survive, a child adapts to an emotionally traumatic, and totally helpless position any way it can. The helpless child hides her emotions, creates a mask of certainty, a false self, and keeps quiet about her own needs. The strong caretaker/peacemaker role is a clever and adaptive survival tactic – take charge and be indispensable! It is a defense against not feeling wanted, or the fear of abandonment. The child takes on an indispensible role, and in Jamie's case she was "the hub of dad's wheel". Kalshed points out that though useful in childhood, this clever psychological mechanism that protects the traumatized part prevents "a potentially corrective influence" for the adult. An overly self- sufficient false self, as caretaker/protector of the wounded part, kicks in at the expense of individuation (Kalshed, 1996).

Though feeling fragile and shattered inside like Humpty Dumpty, externally these women present a pretty strong facade, glued together. Initially, Hades' Angels went into the "belly of the beast" prepared to do what they always do – "fix" the broken parts of someone else.

> *My role has always been to hold everything together. If someone's got a problem, anybody, it's me they come to.*
>
> --- Hades' Angle Lynn

For a Hades' Angels, the prison relationship begins to heal all that. The early parental role, which is to help the child develop a sense of self, didn't happen. The selfless energy of the nurturer/peacemaker, which got put into reclaiming others, now gets invested in re-parenting the self and in finding a self. Hades' Angels is involved in a reparative experience with one who is empathically attuned to her, and within the confines of that supportive emotional environment, she finds and becomes a self.

#3 Discarding of Dysfunctional Beliefs

Dysfunctional beliefs are the silent internalized *shoulds* and should-nots that we accept as part of family expectations. Many of these women understood they "need to have a man to be complete." Hanging onto your man when you are in an abusive relationship because "the women in our family don't get divorced" is a dysfunctional family belief that perpetuates the dynamic of dominance and submission.

Jo Anne heard: "I'll only love you if you do as I say." This held her to a rigid standard, a facade that was meant to protect the family from shame. The real shame was being unloved for who you are, then accommodating it by shutting down. Defiance was Dimple's way of reacting to rather than working through the noncommunication, and controlling family beliefs. Within the dynamic of an inmate/freemate relationship Hades' Angels learned to question and assess of what value, if any, are historical beliefs, and discard those that feel abusive or repressive in their current lives.

> *Showing anger is equated with being bad even when there was a good reason to have anger.*
>
> --- Hades' Angel Callie

Dysfunctional beliefs sometimes guard and control the family secrets: "What will the neighbors think?" creates facades, walls, and a pretense of acceptance. Prison presents a stigmatizing environment that is anything but acceptable. Here, pretense is discarded, dropped outside prison portals long before entering through razor wire fences and clanging gates. In this emotionally primitive environment, self-protection is the key to survival. Here the facades and the beliefs that protected the family against the shame and stigma of affairs, abuse, alcoholism, and womanizing are finally held up to the light and questioned. With no place left to hide, prison becomes the backdrop, the container, for this reparative emotional interchange. Such an interchange with a man who walked the same line helps these women open up Pandora's box, revealing the destructiveness of family secrets such as: peace at all costs; you're not supposed to think for yourself; or I need to shut up to survive.

What rises from the ashes is awareness that these beliefs were imposed on everyone in the family except the dominant, controlling, critical parent. The resulting top dog/under dog positions polarized the family with shame and fear. Home, like the prison setting, did not welcome the tension of the opposites. Rather, the rule of thumb was "my way or the high way". Home was an unsafe place to feel or think, an unsafe place where a child was victimized or securely attached to the pole of the victimizer. A child raised in that emotional environment internalizes the dysfunctional beliefs that keep that system well oiled. Though they may have inwardly rebelled, Hades' Angels perpetuated such dysfunctional beliefs by outwardly shutting down and now they question them.

The negativity in Angel Callie's family belief "You're higher than a kite!" sent a clear message that shut her down: don't feel. Callie's mother admonished her when she exhibited any show of emotions, be it anxiety, anger or even joy. As a result, feelings got masked, hidden, repressed, or denied.

Change occurs for these women who use the prison and prison relationship to go into the system and yet do not submit to it; instead, they learn to be centered within it.

#4 Creating a Relationship of Reciprocity

Time served, is time well spent for Hades' Angels who learn to bear anxiety, and sit on it, rather than jump in to fix it. From this relationship is also born the capacity to bear the tension of opposites, differentness, separateness and conflict. "Being understood" then expands the self to include the other as opposed to being swallowed up by the other. 'You are me', an emotional merger, is recognized as a boundary violation and no longer valid; thinking and feeling become an interactive two-way street.

I like the walking beside of -- and I feel that happens today.
>   --- Hades' Angel Jamie

Reciprocity is a two-way street and is most evident when one expects input rather than permission. It is felt when two people connect in a sharing dialogue, respecting differing thoughts and opinions.

He gives as good as he gets.
>   --- Hades' Angel PJ

Emotional mergers, a learned family dynamic, occur in enmeshed family systems where only one voice, one mood, one thought prevails. Mergers manifest as dominance and submission and the person on the submissive end of the pole is prevented from having a voice or developing a healthy sense of self. These mergers, often embedded in fear of abandonment or retribution, get replicated later on in unhealthy adult relationships. "Mother would do anything rather than rock the boat," says Angel Cretia. Indeed, Cretia learned how to be a very dutiful, corporate wife while submitting to the humiliating experience of her first husband's weekly "weigh-in" when he criticized her for gaining even a fraction of an ounce.

Even though Angel Danielle is no longer committed to her inmate, she believes she is changed dramatically. "I'm more of a person. I don't need anyone to tell me what to do or control me. I don't need him; he serves no purpose in my life now. I tried to help somebody and I got kicked instead. I felt I needed to have someone to need me. It has always been my role to take care of everyone. Now, I've learned it's not my job to pick up and rescue another person. Now I can see it coming. I went in to fix him and instead I got fixed."

Polarized win-lose dynamics – splits of dominance and submission occur when one person turns one's self over to another, willingly or not. In previous relationships, outwardly confident Hades' Angels had difficulty maintaining their otherwise strong identities. They allowed themselves to be dominated, used, objectified, and abused in previous demon lover relationships. Survival had a price tag of taking care of others her whole life. What Hades' Angels didn't know was how to stop being treated as an object or change relationship dynamics characterized by dominance and submission. Most Hades' Angels never needed a man financially because they had their own job and their own money. That ability to take care of the self materially in the world of the patriarchy did not translate into caring for the self emotionally, nor did it alter patterns of emotional submission in previous relationships. Hades' Angels paired up with a demon lover who sucked them dry. Their transformation somehow occurred as the result of lessons learned while in relationships with their inmate partners:

> *"He has taught me more in two years than I've learned my whole life. I no longer get upset because someone doesn't like me or said something about me. Now, I choose to please myself and I am no longer bound by the illusions of facades, or scared or shamed into doing what others expect of me just because it makes them more comfortable," says Angel Danielle.*

An internal, soul-to-soul connection has cut the cable, freed many Hades' Angels from the shackles of control that have been a large part of other relationships. Unmasked from their inner prison of feeling different, weird, shamed, and isolated, they now expect to enjoy reciprocity in their relationships. A transformation from dysfunctional relationship patterns has occurred during the course of these inmate/freemate relationships. "What's inside is what really counts, not what we look like on the outside," says Danielle. Hades' Angels have connected with the partner based on who they are inside, not because of appearance.

The only barriers left are the walls of the prison.

#5 Integration of Psychological Splits

A split is a psychological cut-off that pushes away or ignores part of the self. It is a common internalized tactic among the general population to deny or wall off uncomfortable or anxiety provoking feelings. This split occurs as a response to repeated rejection, retribution or psychological abuse. The child subjected to such rejection splits off the pain of shame or humiliation and then defends against remembering it. The pain exists but it is pushed down, separated from affect and out of awareness. It is a survival tool.

Angel Sherry puts it succinctly, "I had to hide part of myself."

To please a parent, Hades' Angels cut off the true self in favor of the false self. A false self replaced a well concealed, shamed, not-good-enough true self. Because the parent was unavailable to offer empathy or mediate the child's pain, emotions, too, were cut-off. The more acceptable intellectual aspects of the self replaced emotions. Callie says, "I learned to justify, not feel."

> *The part of me that got thrown away got redeemed in this relationship.*
>
> --- Hades' Angel Stephanie

A third split was from the feminine aspects of the self, which values attachment and emotional intimacy. This split, too, occurred to please a parent who experienced the world from polarized positions, discounted the feminine and valued more masculine, achievement-related goals. This split has a huge impact in later love relationships.

States Hades' Angel Jamie,

"With other men, I was always in charge. I know I'm a woman, but I didn't really feel feminine." With her current husband, she doesn't have to always be in charge because "I trust the way he handles things, his take-charge way." In conjunction with his caring, protective energy, it allows her to take off her professional hat.

The ways one views the self are powerful determiners in our life choices. What lies split-off, hidden, or repressed are powerful, though unconscious, factors in our life choices, particularly in love relationships. In previous destructive relationships, the Hades' Angel ended up being submissive to a critical, controlling, and emotionally abusive partner. Hades' Angel saw past the label inmate and connected with the man she saw inside, the man she believed strong enough to empathically mediate her pain.

We've both been wronged. We both walked up to the edge; he jumped and I didn't.

--- Hades' Angel Lady Honeybear

The wall between Hades' Angel Betty Jo and her inmate spouse is a physical wall. Earlier in her life she learned to create invisible emotional walls to protect a shamed, defenseless self:

Before, I felt hollow. I had very cold feelings. But now when I see him I get this warm feeling all over. My husband is bringing out things I never knew I could feel. It's very scary for me, but it's also wonderful. And I think that because of it I am able to communicate better with my father now.

Today, Betty Jo is armored with love and is determined to let go of family secrets. She climbed that invisible wall between herself and her father and told him about her inmate husband. He said, 'If you need my help, I'm here.' This broke through the barrier, encouraging her to talk about other secrets about her mother, her abuse, and her incredible pain. Today, she no longer hides part of herself from her father or her husband.

#6 Owning of the Shadow

This relationship has allowed me to explore my shadow.

--- Hades' Angel Ann

Everyone has a shadow. That which is deemed unacceptable, for whatever reasons, is pushed into the unconscious, forming what psychologist Carl Jung called "the shadow." The "shadow side" basically consists of those qualities or traits that individuals push down or refuse to acknowledge about themselves, both good and bad. Sometimes what gets pushed down is the buried gold, meaning our unborn potential.

Psychologists speak of "owning" or "not owning" the shadow parts of the self, not "owning" one's feelings of anger or shame, or even talents or strengths. When we can't accept parts of ourselves, we may unconsciously project these rejected qualities onto others: "He is angry." Hades' Angels are no different. Hades' Angels found "my soul mate", or "just meshed" with a part of the self they couldn't recognize: their own shadow. Ann says of her inmate spouse, "He was my evil twin." An attraction to the destructive energy in "bad boys" may also speak to the inability to recognize or acknowledge that shadow side in the self.

Beth acknowledges that she was a rebellious little girl, "I just didn't get caught." Beth valued and respected her inmate-spouse because she saw the "survivor" in him. What she could not see or acknowledge was the value of her own survivor part, her strength. Instead, she searched for the perceived strength in someone else. Through this relationship, she sees herself differently, accepts her strengths, including the survivor part, and values what she perceives as her wild yet submissive qualities.

Angel Lynn says, "My inmate husband fulfills some of that attraction to the wild side. Outside, I am very, very shy and introverted, and you wouldn't have guessed about my wild side. By looking at me, you would think that I'm little Miss Innocent, and that's the way I want it." She says she has incorporated the church into the wild side of her nature – and still finds "the wild side" exciting. She also gives life to words of the church by speaking up for those who suffer the results of a wild life.

In Angel Danielle's case, her ability to stand up for herself and do verbal battle was banned to shadow territory, yet she quickly observed this same submissive tendency in her partner. Seeing it in him angered her. She boldly "chewed him out" for timidly looking at the ground when the guards spoke to him, and for allowing himself to be treated as "a nothing." She was awakened and transformed by this realization. His submissiveness forced her to take a look at her own tendency to "let people do whatever they wanted to me." Today, she acknowledges and cares for the victimized part of herself, and forces herself to speak up and do battle when it's necessary. By speaking up, taking action, and getting her partner's case reviewed, for example, she got him removed from death row. Then, she let go of him.

7 Awakening of the Feminine

With him it's safe enough to lean on somebody and he won't buckle under. I can finally let go. That's the ultimate of femininity.

--- Hades' Angel Jamie

The transformation for Hades' Angels is in discovering a balance of feminine and masculine energies. Previously, the feminine, seen as sexual, manipulative, and submissive, played out in love relationships that replicated the polarized parental marital dynamic: emotionally submissive mother to a critical, controlling father. It resulted in enmeshment and merger at the threat of retribution or abandonment. Hades' Angels can now discern gentle from weak. The more communicative aspects embodied in the feminine is understood as a strength that strives towards connection and emotional intimacy, not a weakness. They struggle to balance the energies of the outwardly tough, self-sufficient "ram" aspects of their personality, and the equal toughness in their intuitive feminine without the fear of merging, losing the self, or losing their partner (abandonment). The feminine energy transformed the relationship into one characterized by emotional intimacy, which had been lacking in previous relationships. Unlike their mothers, being in a relationship no longer means playing dead emotionally to a critical, controlling partner.

Angel Cretia, whose previous husband required her to weigh-in weekly to be acceptable, says, "For twenty years I was hungry; I'm not hungry now." Her current husband says, "My love for you is not measured by the numbers on the bathroom scale."

The long dominant masculine energy and the submissive-though-ascending feminine energy are striving for balance within. That is a transformation for Hades' Angels.

8 Lessening the Sense of Shame and Stigma

That which doesn't kill me makes me stronger.

--- Fredrich Nietzsche

Shame and stigma are responses to chronic early narcissistic injury. A lack of empathy, frustration, and chronic rejection during childhood results in narcissistic injury and a depleted sense of self. In adulthood, when in the presence of rejection in relationships, Angels experienced a deep sense of shame about the self. In the outer world, their learned survival tools, perfectionism and achievement, kicked in to combat that shame. When those things don't work, anger is sometimes a fall-back measure. Angel Sara says, she feels no sense of shame or stigma about being married to a prisoner and has strong family ties with his family, which is additionally nourishing for her. Angel Bianca says, "On the plus side, this relationship presents an opportunity to work through my problems and stop caving in to others' demands." Again, her partner's devotion and willingness to commit is an important factor to her. "I spent years trying to get my parents to approve of me, and it got me nowhere."

The confining prison walls force Bianca to deal with old issues, such as anger, in a new way. She says, "I've noticed that up to a certain point he controls his anger, but beyond that it's like a wall goes up." This yo-yo dynamic hurts because it's reminiscent of her mother's way of handling anger: walls and cut-offs. She says, "I feel like I have to endure it, like I have no option. There were a few times I came close to leaving." Though she knows he doesn't want her to leave, he will say, 'Go ahead, run away from your problems.' If I could just get up and leave the table and walk around the room or get some distance and come back later, that would help but because of the physical setting, knowing that once I walk out I can't return that day, I can't do that. So, what I've learned to do is just let him cool down and then we talk about it like two adults." Peacemaking and pleasing, rather than confronting her fear of anger, colored her old relationships.

The hot waters of the prison visiting room is Angel Bianca's "bath". She has to sit in the situation and suffer through it and she comes out changed, empowered. Her transformation is a conscious understanding of her destructive life patterns and owning her role in perpetuating them. Her boyfriend holds a mirror in which she views her shadow parts and she consciously addresses them: she can sit in the midst of tension and anxiety and not choke on it, swallow it, or run away. Addressing such emotions in the heat of the moment is an empowering position for anyone.

Falling in love with an inmate, a man stigmatized by society, is for many Hades' Angels like a step backward into a childhood without control. Nearly all the Hades' Angels deny shame about their prison relationships, even though others often try to make them feel that way. Prison is a cold, shaming, demeaning environment and with each prison visit, that deadened childhood shame is vividly remembered. Their transformation lies in the fact that they now actively address what shamed them rather than keeping it snugly wrapped under their persona of perfectionism, self-confidence and external achievement. They see choices instead of fixed, submissive, or outmoded childhood response patterns.

What most Hades' Angels do acknowledge is stigma by association. Although it is present and is deeply felt, it is not taken in as fact but as a perspective, which they refuse to internalize. Often family members, church members and friends attempt to stigmatize them for their "crime by association". They are subjected to it each time they make a prison visit, so they work hard to fight it and keep from internalizing it. Their refusal to accept stigma by association is based, in part, on having "felt different and having had to build walls of toughness" to survive early narcissistic injury. The backdrop of prison becomes a stage set for growth and attempts to stigmatize are utilized as opportunities to try out new behaviors. Though "caught in the emotional dynamics of the system, just like at home," says BJ, the transformation begins when, unlike home, they deal with it and with authority figures (guards and wardens) differently.

Lisa Heart speaks for herself and other Hades' Angels:

> *"I want everybody to understand that we are not the scum of the earth. And we are not different. Our lives are lived a little differently than a lot of people, but the more of us there are, the less different it becomes."*

9 Finding One's Own Voice

> *I learned how to say no.*
>
> --- Hades' Angel Bianca

> *I learned to stand up for myself.*
>
> --- Hades' Angel BJ

Finding your own voice is about being centered and facing your fears and anxieties, then doing something constructive to remedy things.

Hades' Angels have established emotional and mental boundaries that define them. They no longer fear emotional abandonment if they speak their mind. They believe it a right to verbalize their own thoughts and feelings. Sara is proud of the growth and changes she made while in her inmate/freemate relationship, although that relationship has ended. She changed. She states, "Initially, I was fluffy and soft with him. Now I'm more confident. I realized he can't help me but he listened and it helped me grow, therefore I'd do it again." Falling in love with him encouraged her to take better care of herself and her health, which gave her the recognition that she could move on.

Hades' Angels say that through the experience with their lifers, they woke up, found their own voice, and use it to redefine the self: questioning, speaking up, and speaking out. They share a common desire to gain insight into their own behaviors and relationship choices.

"No More Mousy"

Rather than continue to submissively endure emotional and psychic pain, these women, "kissed by connection", fight back by speaking up. Danielle, haunted by the fact that her mother shut down and couldn't speak up for herself, wonders if it had any relationship to her death from cancer:

"She just shut down." Her current relationship has been a major catalyst in breaking her fear of speaking up. "I find that I am no longer afraid to speak up for fear somebody somewhere might get mad at me," she says.

Angel C.C. dares to speak up and write letters to attorneys on behalf of her husband, something she couldn't have done before: "If I want my husband home, I guess I have to be his advocate," she says.

Stephanie, "a diamond in the rough", has moved "from scared to confident." She views the social injustices of the prison system on a larger scale. "My personal mission is to bring light into this world of darkness and ignorance," she says.

Lisa Heart no longer swallows everything. She speaks out about her experience, tells people what she thinks, questions authority, is controlled by no-one, testifies at senate hearings, and advocates for others outside who need her help. She learned there are innocent people in prison for life, and she believes her husband is one of them.

She states:

Christ didn't come to save the perfect; He came to save the needy. We are all warty human beings; we just have different warts. I never would have thought that there would be an innocent person on death row or a person in prison that wasn't absolutely guilty.

In the laboratory of the prison, the Hades' Angels have learned to acknowledge their emotions and their pain, find their voice, channel their internalized anger, and use it to do service in the world. They do positive things that are satisfying to the soul.

On a global scale, "world soul", these women give voice to the Judeo-Christian message to fight injustice and indifference. As Louise states, "To those to whom much is given, much is expected in return." This global concept applies to …anyone in need. Some write articles about prison life for local newspapers, or become prison watch-dogs and document unacceptable behavior on the part of guards and report it to the warden. Others join advocacy groups, even putting themselves in the public eye by speaking out about the injustices of the system. As for Beth, "One side now refuses to get into chaos, drama, or squabbles affecting other people, but when it affects me or my husband directly -- the gloves go right back on and I'm ready to fight."

> *I speak up, which is new for me. I'm no longer afraid of authority.*
>
> --- Hades' Angel Callie

10 Taking Action and Effecting Change

Three levels of empowerment: personal, interpersonal, and societal.

> *For the last six years or so I've lobbied senators and assemblymen on inmate bills of rights. I've been trying to teach my kids you do what you do to change things to make them better, but you also do what you've got to do to survive.*
>
> --- Hades' Angel Lynn

Activism

Having to deal with both the prison system and a difficult boyfriend has made Angel Bianca tougher and more outspoken. As a result, Angel Bianca feels aliveness inside: "I guess I never really had a purpose or a direction or a place to direct my activist energy before."

Bianca comments,

> *"I've become an activist as a result of living this lifestyle. The whole prison issue is such a hot bed of injustices. For example, since the break up of AT&T there has been a*

> *growth in prison phone business and these companies agree to pay commissions to the prisons—a legal kickback for every call made. I recently spoke at a Public Utilities Commission hearing on the issue of the steep rates ($3.00 for each call from a prisoner in addition to the normal fees for a collect call). MCI charges families of California inmates for collect calls from state prisons. Surcharges are justified based on the cost of recording, branding, and monitoring calls made from prison. There are rate charges and approved legal kickback, and some companies round up phone calls up to the next minute. It was a big deal for me to get up in front of a large group of people, stand at a podium with a microphone and a camera, and talk about having a loved-one who is incarcerated – letting people know that I'm speaking from personal experience. But I got very positive feedback from a State Senator and a writer with the L.A. Times."*

Stephanie witnessed a lot of suffering and indignities in her life but felt inadequate taking action. Today, this "diamond in the rough" is the picture of commitment, follow-through and responsibility. "I got that way as the result of my relationship inside. He challenged me to grow and I learned how to effect change. He has made me feel like I'm a viable, important person. He has taken me from being a very scared individual into a very confident individual who is unwilling to turn her power over to anyone. He takes pride in my advocacy work," she says.

Danielle's new self-confidence has also added a dimension to her identity. She says, "His attorney will call me and say, 'I need you to write a letter to these people,' -- because he knows I'm not afraid. I mean, what are these people going to do to me? Nothing. I'm not doing anything illegal by advocating for him. I have no reason to be afraid. I've called the governor's office and the attorney general's office. I'm not going to just let him sit there. No, my advocating isn't going to get him out of prison, but he did get off Death Row, and that's better than nothing at all. But if I'm going to sit here and be afraid to stick up for him, what good am I to him or myself?"

For Angel Callie, her prison relationship gave her the love and respect she hungered for, and the partner she'd never had. She also got a rude awakening about prison justice, which has taken her out of her protective shell and given her a cause to focus on. She sees herself as a "good girl" who deals with "bad issues". Her husband, due to have been released some years ago, was one whose parole date got revoked when her state governor took a tough political stance on crime. This quiet, shy woman tossed old survival tools, transforming herself on multiple levels: giving voice to her internal world, putting herself out in front, courageously standing up for her man, and speaking at senate hearings about the abuses and the depravity of prisoners' conditions.

The process of finding the true self requires each of us to expand our consciousness. In the case of Hades' Angels, developing worldly consciousness means that she must be willing to emerge from innocence, see the realities rather than live a sheltered existence walking around in rose-colored glasses. The task of emerging from the domination of achievement and goal-oriented masculine consciousness is not about killing or conquering the masculine that enslaved her, but about the capacity to integrate and use it in behalf of the self, learn to bear the anxiety of separateness and conflict, trust her own essence, and then step up to the plate and take action.

Hades' Angels want to tell their stories about being prisoner's wives. Their action demonstrates that even though people make mistakes, people change. They are changed. Hades' Angels, though outwardly self-sufficient, are transformed inwardly from emotionally submissive, compliant victims into more than they ever thought they could be. Crises became turning points and opportunities for change, then empathic attunement and the reciprocity in their love relationships chipped away at emotional walls and deepened their sense of self. They are gracious, friendly, open, articulate, insightful and assertive women.

As a society, our collective consciousness is changed by their actions, and by their love.

It All Comes Down to Love

The powerful, but invisible, force driving Hades' Angels individuation is the transformative energy of love. Believing, feeling loved, heard, and understood -- held emotionally rather than sexually – becomes a safe container to birth, then blossom their inborn potential, including the dormant, split-off feminine aspects of the Self.

Hades' Angels say they moved from emotional submissiveness to feeling empowered on multiple levels: personal, interpersonal and societal.

Two Stories: Michele, Betty Jo

Portrait: Hades' Angel Michele

"I don't remember much about my childhood, except feeling badly that my brother got spanked so much so long and so hard." Michele, 45, has an older sister and a younger brother. Her father, a military man controlled Michele through verbal abuse -- with criticism, fear, shaming, and religious dogma rather than love. "I got the silent message from my dad that I wasn't worth listening to, and from my mom that I wasn't intelligent enough or good enough. My dad used religion in a misdirected attempt to save my soul – 'God's going to get you if you don't do it my way; if you're not loving and doing things for others, you're not a Christian.'" As a result, Michele believes she developed learning disabilities, low self-esteem and a conviction that she could never achieve.

Her parents expected her to attend college, but she was discouraged about her ability, and thinking she couldn't do the work. She remembers being told that her mother gave up a college scholarship to marry her dad. "I think I learned from my mother many of the characteristics I had, including not standing up for myself, not meeting my own needs, and sacrificing myself."

In spite of the mixed messages, Michele completed school after her daughter was born, and today is a therapist with two professional degrees. "I spend a lot of time listening to others. I have always been the champion of the underdog. I remember when I was in high school thinking that I'd like to do special education work with kids who are really severely physically handicapped. Maybe that was just me trying to find a way to earn being good enough; if I could just do enough for other people, then I could be good enough."

Early Relationships

Shame controlled much of Michele's life. Michele married twice but was ambivalent about her partners each time. Sex, guilt, and religion were always prominent relationship issues. She says of her first husband, the father of her daughter, "I wasn't in love with him, but I felt guilty because we were having sex and that was something you're not supposed to do in my religion. Marriage gave me outside legitimacy. Internally, I still felt very ashamed. Even after I got married, I still felt a lot of shame around sex. It was my belief that I had to please my husband so I quietly endured the shame of sex."

Each husband took advantage of her naivete and deceived her. Her first husband told her he was of her same religion: "After we got married I found out that wasn't true. Religion was my life, so to me that was a huge thing. I went to church three times a weekend, read the Bible every day, and taught Sunday school from the time I was 18 until I was 36. I really resented him for deceiving me."

"I was dismissed from my church for marrying my second husband. Church elders said we didn't have a scriptural divorce, meaning his wife hadn't committed adultery. He convinced me she had committed adultery so it was okay to get married again." Shame surfaced again when he ended up sexually abusing her daughter. "He sent out all kinds of red flags and warning signs that he did not respect my daughter, but I ignored them. He would buy things for her and do things for us that made him seem caring. Looking back on it, I think he was just grooming us. I don't know if that was in the front of his mind, but it was like he was thinking, 'I'll get this woman who has a daughter to marry me so I can have my way with the daughter.' I think he had pedophile tendencies before he married me, and he saw my daughter as a positive part of the package. I betrayed my daughter by not protecting her from him."

The submissiveness Michele learned growing up carried negatively into both these marriages. "I was a codependent and sacrificed my inner self." It was a very low point in her life. In a group therapy session, she became aware of a core belief that she had to be with a man in order to be a good and worthwhile person; to have a place and be someone's equal. Michele continues, "As time went on, I kept hearing, 'He's not the one' in my head, so after about a year and a half I talked to him about it and he said, 'Well, if you can find someone better than what we have, you should have it.' We broke up and he found someone he liked better."

Six months after Michele's breakup with her second husband, she met the prison inmate she is still with today.

How They Met

Michele says, "that while I was an intern in a correctional facility, I was drawn in by a man whose poetry and songs touched my heart." He gave her a tape of a recent song he had written and she realized that all of them were about her. He had memorized every conversation they ever had and put some element of it in his songs, which scared her. She told her supervisor about his apparent obsession with her, and he suggested she talk to the man's doctor, which she did. A meeting was held and he was questioned about his intent. He told Michele that he just wanted to share some creative things that he had done with her because he thought she'd be receptive to it. Michele told him that she respected his willingness to open himself to her, and she took that seriously. She told him she didn't want to abuse him by leading him on.

Michele was intrigued by him. "He felt like a kindred spirit to me. It wasn't love at first sight; it was comfort, a knowing at first sight."

As time passed, Michele became more interested in this man. "When I met him, he had a couple of months left before his scheduled parole hearing. If he left prison on parole then I'd have no way to talk to him so I said that when he got out I would like us to have coffee and get to know him better." Apparently, he was thinking along the same lines, but kept telling her that this parole might never happen. He'd been up for parole many times and was always told to meet with the parole board "next month, next month, next month."

Their relationship began with telephone conversations for hours at a time: Michelle relates, "You can only talk for thirty minutes and the phone cuts off. Once we realized that we loved each other, it all grew quickly."

At one point, a rumor went around the prison about Michele and another female intern. She recalls, "It was said that both of us were having sex with different inmates, which was untrue. I didn't want to ruin my schooling or my career. He had been under the impression that the rumor was true and he still cared about me anyway. He didn't let that change. At that point I knew inside that he was the right person for me."

But it wasn't that easy for Michele and her inmate to get married. "The Department of Corrections is not letting me visit. It won't let me marry, perhaps because I was a really good student and they feel I betrayed them. I was on the visiting list one weekend when they terminated me permanently. The reason they presented is that I was a contract employee, which I wasn't. I was an unpaid intern." Michele is fighting this injustice in court "for conspiring to violate civil rights". Initially, he was sentenced to life, then two weeks before he was supposed to get the parole date, the sentencing judge wrote to the department and said, 'I sentenced this guy to life without parole,' although it doesn't say "without parole" on his sentencing papers. Michele is also in a legal fight over him being re-sentenced to life without parole. "That's illegal that they did that."

What She Likes about Him

Michele confides, "Unlike anything I've ever felt before, I am involved in a relationship where I feel respected, heard, and supported. It's like when you're swimming, the water's not inside you but all around you, and it's supporting you, and you feel free within that support. I feel like I belong. I'm not as strange as I always thought I was because this is one person whose soul vibrates the same way mine does." She says that this relationship has grown to the point where today they team up to work together helping inmates get their grievances addressed; he inside the walls and she on the outside. She believes that's why prison officials cut off her visits. She continues their relationship through correspondence and phone calls.

Michele also believes that they have a spiritual, even psychic connection. She explains that he told her the first time he saw her that he saw a white light around her. "That afternoon I was telling him about my rushed afternoon, and he said, 'Yeah, and you had to get that dog out from under the bed and that didn't help.' I believe we are spiritual people having a physical experience." Instead of scaring her, Michele says these experiences drew her closer: "There's nothing about spirit to be afraid of."

His compassion for others is a big attraction. She relates that there was a prisoner in the health unit whose body was filling up from a liver disease and the authorities were not helping him. For two weeks the man lay in bed, disoriented, crying, and grossly swollen. Michele's inmate told her about it and she wrote a letter on the internet begging, "Please, someone who has any connections, please help this man." She also wrote to the governor of her state and to different organizations. Finally the governor directed him moved to an outside hospital and he got some relief, but he died soon afterwards."

Michele sees dual aspects of her inmate love. His intelligent, loving, gentleness is an appealing quality, but she also can see his very rough side from a very difficult past. "He's the most healed person I've ever met. He used to be a mean son-of-a-bitch. I think if he hadn't been incarcerated he would have gotten killed because he was on a bad path. I think he probably wanted to get caught."

How does she deal with his "dangerous" side? "I let him take care of it. That's his job, not mine." She connects with a different part of him, that which is intelligent, gentle, loving, and healed. She says this healed part co-facilitates men's groups, teaches anger management classes, and has earned the respect of the men inside. She doesn't think he's dangerous any longer and tells the following story:

> *"Last year, he was attacked by a psychotic prisoner. The man hit him on the head with a pillowcase full of batteries. In the old days, he would have broken the guy's neck right away and killed him. Instead, he got his arms around him and held onto him until he came out of it and stopped hitting him. The other men in his unit were watching this happen. On the inside, if someone disrespects you, especially if he hits you, you have to kill him. He talked this over with the men afterwards and said, 'you know, there are other ways of saving your honor besides going back and doing to them worse than what they did to you.'"*

Slow But Steady

Michele has worked hard on her own psychological awakening. She states, "I was awakened even before I met him, but now he's my compass and I'm on a new path." Michele says that as a child, her parents' treatment of her "diminished her ego's ability to maintain contact with her soul, which separated her from seeing how precious she is." She has moved past her fears of parental rejection and over the past eight years has confronted her father about the way he talks to her.

She has also been able to confront people at work and within the prison system.

Michele has found her own voice within her inmate relationship. She confides: "The cool thing is that we both worked on changing ourselves separately, and I think we found each other when we were ready to have a functional relationship. I got into recovery when it wasn't called recovery; he started to change about twelve years ago and gave up violence which used to be his way of life."

Michele tries to stay positive, but her life circumstances are momentarily shaky. She says she is anxious because she has dire financial difficulties, but she has enough to eat. She moved in with her divorced daughter and grandson, which is working out well. Meanwhile, she is upgrading her work skills, including training for litigation work and getting a private detective's license.

Commitment to her inmate remains strong, no matter what is happening in life on the outside. Michele says, "I never thought two people could connect the way we do. I have a person in my life with my highest good in the forefront of his mind, and part of why it works is that he's not responsible for me and I'm not responsible for him."

Michele's Update

Hades' Angel Michele and her inmate married in 2001 and have been visiting ever since, as well as counseling together while visiting with other inmate families who are having difficulties. Their intention is to work together creating "centers of healing". She says, "I'm a more loving person because I know him, and he's a more loving person because he knows me."

Michele's Transformation

Hades' Angel Michele found a way of putting her Christian values into practice. She honors her father by practicing her religion. Unlike her father, she does it out of love, and without criticism, control, blame or shame. By furthering her education she honors her mother, and in the process she has discovered that she is intelligent, has a lot to speak out about, and is worthy of being heard. Unlike her mother, she no longer allows herself to endure emotional or verbal abuse. She has self-respect and the respect of others, and has learned to give respect when it is earned. This relationship has brought her greater respect for the parts of the self she thought had no value: the intellect; and the part of the self that got used and abused, the body. She feels strength from both masculine and feminine energies. She believes these changes have occurred because she is "an equal, totally understood and accepted."

PORTRAIT: Hades' Angel Betty Jo

Betty Jo, 47, a claims supervisor, was an only child raised in an extremely abusive home. Life with her alcoholic mother forced her to learn very early in life how to stand on her own two feet. She ran away from home a lot, the first time at the tender age of five.

Her mother's abuse when drunk was horrific. She remembers an instance at the age of three when she cried about something, and her mother said, 'I'll give you something to really cry about,' and she grabbed her wrists, held them up, took hold of her two pinky fingers and broke them. After that, Betty Jo says she promised herself she'd never cry again. She never knew if her mother would beat her or hug her. She would pound her head into the wall, and then turn around later and hug and kiss her and say she was sorry.

Her mother had other men over when her father left for work at night. Betty Jo was abused physically, sexually, verbally, spiritually, and emotionally by her mother and by her mother's secret boyfriends. She says, "I was living a nightmare and had no idea what it was like to have parents who loved me. I had nobody to turn to except for my dog."

Betty Jo's emotionally distant father was unaware of the abuse in the household until one night he witnessed her drunken mother beating her head against a wall. "My dad rushed in, grabbed her by the neck and threw her out of the room. He told me, 'If that bitch ever touches you again, I'll kill her.' He was my only possible protector, but I never felt I could go to him because we had this emotional wall between us which I gave up trying to climb over." Had her father known about her mother's secret lovers and their abuse, "I think he would have killed her, or they would have divorced". Miserable as she was, "I didn't want my parents to divorce."

Betty Jo always wished for a mother who loved her, instead of one who kept telling her she was never wanted. It wasn't safe to let anyone inside, especially her mother. She learned to protect that "inside" self by facing the world encased in a good-girl persona and by doing what was deemed right. Inside she felt ripped off and angry.

Adulthood

At 17, Betty Jo graduated from high school, moved out, went to college, quit college and went back home twice. Each time she managed to break away, something would happen to bring her back. Then she moved in with a boyfriend, a Vietnam veteran who had been subjected to Agent Orange. She says he would wake up at night and, still thinking he was in Vietnam, pick her up and throw her across the room like she was the enemy. After that, she became involved in a number of destructive relationships that cut her off even more from her feelings and her true self. She was drawn to outwardly strong and rebellious men, thinking their strength would protect her and allow her to feel secure enough to let down her guard and take off her armor. Inevitably, she got hurt.

Betty Jo's shadow showed up when, at 27, she married a good hearted man who she thought wouldn't hurt her. But she says he was immature and they broke up because she thought his parents were trying to control her marriage.

Their divorce led Betty Jo into therapy and a 12-step program. Unaware of her inner rebel, her anger or her loneliness, she resisted psychological help. She admits she didn't recognize her anger until she started going to counseling sessions. She became defensive and angry at the counselor for drawing out her repressed feelings, so she quit. Now she thinks it was the best thing the counselor could have done. As she says, he was opening up that package, bringing out the anger and all kinds of memories she didn't want to remember anymore.

Prison Pen Pal

Several years after her divorce, loneliness drove Betty Jo to respond to a man's letter in a Friendship Booklet that came in the mail. "When I saw his name and address, I thought he might be in prison and I didn't want anything to do with that. But his handwriting kept drawing him to me."

Wanting "a relatively safe way to connect with a man", not a love relationship, Betty Jo began corresponding with him. She says, "He was someone I couldn't see, and as our friendship developed, I discovered I could confide in him and tell him my innermost feelings without feeling embarrassed by having to look him in the face." This was totally foreign to her: "I was very shy and very much a loner, walled off in my protective prison, but he began chipping away at it." Her feelings became stronger through their correspondence. She says there was warmth about him that kept radiating from his letters. She was also drawn in by his honesty, openness, and sense of humor. Their correspondence led to love and marriage. "There is a magnetic field that draws us together," she says.

Betty Jo says, "I see many similarities between my father and my husband: their mannerisms; sense of humor; off beat expressions; and even their skinny builds." On a deeper level, they both value honesty and straightforwardness. Betty Jo has always felt emotionally connected with her father, but wasn't able to tell him she loved him. "Like me, he keeps things bottled up inside. We both keep people at a distance." Her inmate husband is one of the only people she has let inside her walls.

The Dangerous Part of Him

Initially, safety was primary on Betty Jo's mind: "The fact that he was in a prison very far away felt safe. Mileage-wise, we were so far apart that I knew he wasn't going to be knocking on my door." Getting to know him in depth has changed that fear. Now, she insists she's not afraid and has no concerns about his release: "I don't feel he's dangerous at all. An accident while fighting in self-defense landed him in prison."

The Upside of the Relationship

Before meeting her prisoner husband, she says, "I was hollow. I had cravings. I had very hard feelings, very cold feelings." Betty Jo believes that she has changed since meeting him. She says that, "He fills up that emptiness, that void inside of me. I know he loves me. He shows, tells, and writes me that he loves me. When our visits are over and I kiss him goodbye, he stays on his side of the room and I go to the door – and then that emptiness creeps in again. But when I'm with him, he's part of me. Nobody has ever been able to do that for me. Nobody. It's almost like we were born to be together."

Betty Jo says this man, her Rock of Gibraltar, is setting free the feminine within her, which scares her. She says she's been in her own prison for so long that when he does come home she's going to feel very vulnerable; she won't be in control.

Talking, rather than putting up walls of silence or physical reactivity, is a new lesson for Angel Betty Jo. She says, "We spend quality time getting to know each other; we're not afraid to really talk and to explore each other's feelings. I realize it is important not to take each other for granted."

The Downside

Hades' Angel Betty Jo admits that this kind of relationship often drains her emotionally, spiritually and physically. She mentions, "My health and finances have suffered. It's a living hell, but I feel hopeful. I know he is coming home, but sometimes I have to take one moment at a time. I fear when the phone rings for I wonder if someone is calling to tell me either my dad has passed away or the prison telling me my husband is coming home in a plain box -- because there is a lot of violence going on behind those walls. Once I get him home safely, maybe I can ease up on that terror." His parole hearing is coming up soon which sheds some "light at the end of the tunnel."

Visiting Day

Visiting reminds her of all the chaos of her early environment. It is also heartbreaking because she wants so badly to bring him home. She admits, "It's just very cold and heartbreaking: we can't have a private conversation and can't show any love or affection. I'm so tired of the whole thing sometimes I don't want to go, but I do because it's the only time we are together and it means so much to both of us. When he first comes into the visiting room, it's like I fall in love with him all over again. I can tell he loves me just by the way he walks into the visiting room, and I hear it in his voice. We sit there in our own little world, clinging together, blocking out everybody else and don't let little petty things get to us."

The cold prison environment parallels her childhood emotional environment: the guardedness, anxiety, conflict, abuse, tension, and distancing; even the ritual of leaving after visits reminds her of her dad leaving her alone at the mercy of her abusive mother. Although the situation is heartbreaking, Betty Jo feels warmed inside and no longer feels so alone.

Advocacy Work

Today, Betty Jo invests her anger righting wrongs on behalf of herself and others: Betty Jo uses her time and energy helping prisoners, including her husband, by doing advocacy work. She makes trips to her state capitol on behalf of prisoner's rights, and she writes many letters and makes phone calls. She does as much for him as she can with her limited resources. She gets angry when doors get closed in her face, and she says she will camp out on the governor's doorstep if necessary.

The Stigma Problem

She sees both visitors and inmates being treated by the prison staff as if they are the scum of the earth. Betty Jo refuses to let the staff treat her like that. She says that she stands up to them and practically tells them that they will respect her, and the staff leaves them alone. When something degrading is said to her, she calmly tells that they cannot speak to her in that way.

Initially, the stigma caused a deeper split. Betty Jo is cautious to whom she discloses that her husband is in prison. She is sensitive to the stigma of it, and does not let co-workers or friends know, fearing she could lose her job or friends. She told her father only five years ago that her husband is in prison, not knowing how he would react. Her father said that he shouldn't be in prison, he should be home and that it was a 'trumped-up charge'. (Her husband was in a drunken brawl and killed someone in self-defense). Her father told her to tell her husband to contact him, and they've been communicating ever since; her husband calls her father monthly and they write to each other. Betty Jo is very happy that she made the effort to be open with her father. It is more than she had hoped for!

Prison walls to emotional walls very much form a part of Betty Jo's history. She says that the emotional wall between her father and her is slowly crumbling. Determined to let go of all her secrets, Betty Jo finally told her father what it was like for her as a child and what happened at home when he left for work. She told him about her mother's secret men. She says he "had no clue" what had been going on at home when he wasn't there. He asked why she'd never told him, and she had to tell him about the emotional wall he erected, and she didn't know how to reach him. She let him know she couldn't climb over that wall he created. Telling him brought them a little closer and her father's wall has been coming down.

Big Change

Today, Betty Jo's father is ill and she has made many trips home to spend time with him: She calls at least once a week to see how he is doing and let him know that she loves him. She says she was 37 years old before she could tell him, "I love you." He was taken by surprise when she told him. "I could hear his voice cracking like he was trying to hold back tears. After we hung up, I felt so good that I had done that because I don't know how much longer I am going to have him. I thought at least he'll know I love him and I'm never going to regret that I didn't say that."

Betty Jo doesn't buy the public's assumption that prison relationships don't last. She says, "I think mine is one of the rare ones that will last. When he comes home I'm sure there will be adjustments to be made, but down deep I believe we were meant for each other and this marriage is going to last." She says her husband agrees that they will make it work.

Chapter Twelve

The Future for Hades' Angels

Excerpted from a commencement address to the graduates of all-female Spelman College in 1993:

It doesn't matter what you've been through, where you come from, who your parents are -- nor your social or economic status. None of that matters! What matters is how you choose to love, how you choose to express that love through your work, through your family, through what you have to give to the world. Be a queen. Own your power and your glory!

--- Oprah Winfrey

There are many more Hades' Angels out there, as well as women in the general population, each one with a story to tell about early childhood emotional wounding, demon lovers, life crisis events, and turning points.

Hades' Angels made a connection with a particular prison partner that created an interpersonal bonding that changed her life, challenged destructive internalized beliefs, and altered her sense of self -- forever. Hades' Angels, whose sometime traumatic life story was written by others, are making adroit use of it to reclaim their own narrative. In a search for meaning, they unconsciously rise above life's challenge to change their 'fate' into a new found 'destiny' of their own choosing, which enables them to reclaim their potential and be the drivers of their own destiny.

Future Uncertain

These twenty-six women, honest, intelligent, articulate, and outspoken, forthrightly present challenges to the status quo. Though it is tough for Hades' Angels to retain a buoyant sense of optimism, they are mindful that commitment plays a big role in their slippery future. "There's a certain peace knowing you'll be together always," says Lisa Heart. Angel Maria emphasizes the point, "He feels he owes me the rest of his life and is distraught that he's not there to take care of me."

Is there a future for Hades' Angels, one that includes a life of harmony, emotional intimacy, and stability outside the prison walls? It is difficult for Hades' Angels to consider that kind of future when the reality of their partner's life sentence sets in. Rather than focus on the ugly truth of a life sentence, most choose to focus on "term to life", meaning he's eligible for release when the term is up, and getting him out on parole.

Real Success

Hades' Angels confront the reality and brokenness of their lives, but hope, internal change, and second chances come from their relationship dynamic, not whether he's in or he's out. Hades' Angels real life transformative journey describes one of descent, suffering, and redemption as they move along the path of individuation. The real success here is about experiencing that catalyst for deep, transformative change: connection, bonding and attachment experienced in the interplay of Hades' Angels' relationships. From a Jungian perspective, an attraction to the opposites and the integration of the split is part and parcel of that individuation process. These women, who have been in their current relationships for varying lengths of time, each stated they feel that their inmate-spouse "fills that void inside". Rose is committed to her husband who still lives "inside" because, she says, "he gives me strength." Various metaphors revealed they always felt that a piece of them was missing. "I grew up with a huge, huge, huge emptiness. Like I'm screaming, somebody love me, somebody tell me who I am, tell me that I'm somebody important," says Dimples. They say that this relationship has lent meaning to their life and helped them "learn to live from the inside out."

After decades guarding her emotional privacy, Maria shed the uniform that protected the self, opened her heart, and looks forward to someday being taken care of. She is clearly both reinvesting and reinventing aspects of the self. Her future is one of expecting reciprocity. "I just want to have a partnership where he takes care of me, where he looks after the bills and the insurance and the car and stuff like that."

Their men, whose dangerousness is locked behind bars, hear them, mirror their unspoken pain, and offer the empathy that helps them move towards wholeness and reclaim their potential. In an article in the New York Times about marriage behind bars, Tammy Moreland (not a Hades' Angel) said in reference to her lifer husband, incarcerated for murdering his wife, "This man, who has never touched me sexually because of this situation that we're in, has treated me better than any man I ever met out there," (Lyman, R., 4/16/2005). Whether or not these relationship dynamics can cement that same agreement outside prison probably needs to be assessed on a case-by-case basis.

> *This above all: to thine own self be true...*
>
> --- William Shakespeare

What has evolved along their transformative journey is a strong sense of an "I". With the healing of the early childhood narcissistic injury, an "I" is no longer invisible. Eve has gotten to know herself through this relationship. She says, "seeing myself through his eyes has allowed me to appreciate the generous, hardworking, understanding and lovely person I am. My husband has accomplished many things including completion of a book that WE are working on getting published."

As for Stephanie, whose life was presided over by chaos, this relationship has been a win-win of healing and self-discovery. Feeling filled-up, kissed by connection, she let go of him, choosing to put her life time and energy into further developing the relationship with her son and herself. The "throw away" part of Stephanie got redeemed in her inmate/spouse relationship: "I really didn't think I was worth shit. There are still some remnants of that; I still have these opinions of myself that aren't always great. At this point, however, I don't care what other people think of me. I am true to who I really am."

Ann rode this relationship roller coaster for the last time, changed inside…and gained a sense of self. Ann mortgaged her home to raise the money to fight for her husband's release, hoping to maintain "outside" the communication, and stability she felt with him "inside". Enlightened, then hurt by the experience, Ann learned about his dangerous, manipulative part the hard way: although her efforts did win his release, she lost him. She wrestles with her feelings about his deception and betrayal, believing he has no remorse for the loss she feels. Outside, he cut a flash figure and maintained only an abbreviated stint at commitment and reciprocity. When his needs got met, he lost interest and turned away from the relationship without remorse or sense of loss. Ann's agenda no longer hinges on sharing that "pain tape" (Loomis, 1995). Ann has become intimately familiar with the "evil twin" that dwells within, her shadow part: "I no longer need to live any part of my life vicariously through someone else," she says. She embraces a legitimate inner courage to put herself "out there" on the forefront. Ann's relationship expectations have changed: she believes it her "right" to love and be loved, not be abandoned.

Louise's life turned out differently. She fought for her husband's release like she taught and fought for her "boys" whether they were in school or in prison. "I gave them a sounding board, stayed connected through correspondence, encouraged them with their education, and became a prison activist "watch dog". My husband was first released to a halfway house, until the then-governor called him back." Today, they live together outside prison walls – she never let go and he will never let go of her love. In a community imposed by fate, their emotional bonds are strengthened through their work, which fulfills mutual goals and ambitions. He honors her and their marital vows, teaming their energy and commitment into mentoring efforts and political activism in the organization Citizens United for the Rehabilitation of Errants (CURE), which paves the way for rehabilitation for many young men upon release. They reach out, befriend, and support young men who struggle rechanneling their "warrior" energy and the underlying rage that put so many of them behind bars.

Sherry's rural upbringing taught her to trust, especially authority figures. "I'm not naive anymore and I don't have do things all alone." Convinced her husband was wrongfully convicted they are pursuing a wrongful conviction. Not knowing what's beyond the bend they, nevertheless, relish the reciprocity of "walking beside" while pursuing their legal journey for justice.

Location, Location, Location

There is a bigger picture for these women warriors who fight the system, fight for fairness and justice, and fight for their inmate spouse than whether or not their relationship has a future outside prison. The luminous reality is that uncertainty is their future outside prison. For the Self that resides inside the soul, it's a different story; it is a transformational experience. What the past did not provide for them, the present does: love, nurturing, and acceptance. And it is a healing energy. These women live in the *now*, transformed because of the nurturing they believe they get -- whether or not they have a home "outside" with their prison partners. For Rose, home is not a location; it is where the heart lives out loud, "My home is with him," she says.

Hades' Angels have unearthed a sense of personal empowerment that overrides a legal system heavily scripted with anxiety and frustration. For example, prior to his release, Callie's husband overpaid his time by more than a decade because the system demands that which cannot be guaranteed, that he won't return to using drugs. What healthy families teach through a nurturing model, the kind of caring ethic that guides most people, he and Callie learned inside: mutual support; good couples communication; and how to verbalize uncomfortable feelings without shame, blame, shutting down or acting out in anger. Though old habits are hard to break, her relationship dynamics changed. "Our relationship has helped me learn to be me," Callie says. Her future is not about the location of her love. What her previous relationships lacked, she has: emotional security, commitment, hope, and a strong sense of self because "I have found someone who truly loves me for me. I no longer try to please to be loved."

If changed by our choices, we can transform an existence of compulsion to becoming drivers of our own destiny. The templates, the belief systems we acquire growing up play a key role in our lives. Some, like counterfeit currency, have no value. We need to know when to break free of them.

Hades' Angels Callie, Bianca, C.C., Lady Honeybear, Danielle, Rose, Sherry, Stephanie, Cretia, Sara, Lisa Heart, Jamie, Betty Jo, Beth, Jo Anne, Dimples, Lynn, BJ, Eve, Sabrina, P. J., Michele, Louise, Ann, Bonnie, and Maria, know their early childhood wounds justify having personal issues around trust and emotional intimacy. Angel PJ says, "I grew up in a field of roses with thorns." She credits this relationship with helping her deal with those ghosts within, helping her "heal a lot of my old war wounds, the wounds I grew up with, all those old terrors and fears and damage." Sara has learned to take responsibility, confront and talk through the issues. "There's also a catch 22. Only what I allow to happen, can happen, because I can still turn around and walk away. I'm on the outside." Jamie transformed her peacemaker role as "the hub of her dad's wheel" into a relationship of caring for the self, speaking up for herself, and achieving her husband's release. Seeing the man past his label inmate, going against the grain, she says, "Today, I am past the point of doing things because it makes me special to other people. I stand up and fight for what I believe is right."

Hades' Angels, though outwardly strong, achievement and goal-oriented women, faced dire emotional poverty by becoming emotionally submissive in previous relationships. Lynn is not the old submissive self: "I don't give up my integrity about what needed to be ironed out. I don't submit or be a doormat but I have learned to "shift gears" and go a different route. I'm not a spore. Spores are plants that protect themselves. I'm more like a regular plant and I'm thriving, not just surviving."

A self-reflective state can lead to making changes so that our lives will become more worthwhile. A real-life snapshot of submissiveness jolted Danielle from living life as a doormat. She was forced to reflect at her own submissive ways after a challenging moment while visiting that caused her to rage inside. She boldly chewed out her partner for meekly accepting the guards' treatment. In that moment, she faced her shadow, the meek and vulnerable part of herself, and took action: "Now, I open my mouth and do not let people do whatever they want to do to me." Danielle found a self, released him, and moved on emotionally. "I attract idiots. Whatever it is that makes up this type of person who is a manipulator or a controller; I don't need that anymore."

Through their unorthodox love relationships, Hades' Angels have become more than they were: "With him I am better"; "I have waited my whole life for this kind of loving, nurturing and caring." Angel C.C., who refers to her self as "independently owned and operated", declared it "time to turn the page". Awakened from her submissive sleep, she fights for his release, and feels freed: from medication, from being stuck, from walking behind, and now stands up for the self and takes action towards getting him out.

Reaching Out to the Least of Thy Brethren

A whole person is one who has both walked with God and wrestled with the devil.

--- C.G. Jung

"There but for the grace of God go I" can develop into a challenging opportunity, interlocking us with those in need, encouraging us to use the strength and drive of our warrior energy to help out, extend, and support the discouraged, lost, or soul-dead aspects of an other. As understood in Twelve Step programs, healing energy emerges from harnessing the kind of caring ethic that reaches out, does service, and helps others. That helping hand keeps us facing the self reflective mirror, seeing our own shadow part in the reality and circumstances of others.

Angel Louise internalized the family belief that "to whom much is given, much is expected in return" and it moved her to take action. For her love, and for herself, she fought with the law, and won. "I didn't give up on or stop caring about my inner-city students because they got in trouble with the law." Nor did she give up on her inmate-husband's case for release. In both she welcomed the opportunity to put herself in a position of rebalancing an often unfairly stacked deck, thereby helping those to whom little has been given.

Hades' Angels give their inmate-spouses the hope, motivation and opportunity to repair the brokenness of their life and achieve something on the outside. Though Angels have lost credibility in the court of public opinion, their overriding success is the gift they give themselves which translates into a succinct and positive message as a step-up, a "corrective emotional experience".

So, they question why they are so often stigmatized and treated as if *they* had committed a crime?

Outside, they fight for their lifer-partners but on a larger scale they fight for those who cannot speak for themselves. In 2002, in Sacramento, California, 150 women with loved ones in prison gathered before a panel to share their experiences, thoughts, and opinions about the proposed changes within the California Department of Corrections (CDC) and California prisons. Those proposed changes are due to the pressure on corrections officials to reduce spending. The prisoners' families bear the brunt of these budget cuts in the way of reduced visitations -- including a three-hour wait to get from the front gate to the visiting room. Stephanie comments that, "Sly, degrading remarks, verbal abuse and physical harassment from some guards is encouraged behavior, and the decent people who work there must walk a thin line to maintain their humanity."

Against this backdrop of victims and survivors, Angel Eve brings a tone of dignity and a sense of urgency in the fight for her husband's release. "My husband believes he can wipe the slate clean of his prior offenses by performing good works. The things he has accomplished, artistically and with Houses of Healing, were done with the compassionate support of a very few brave individuals who were willing to risk the ire of the administration by occasionally allowing him to work with his artist's tools. This has enabled him to present many showings of his works. He has a large creative spirit which rarely allows him to give up." The same creative spirit holds true for Eve whose inmate-love "inside" altered her destiny.

Indifference and Injustice

Our obligation is to give meaning to life and in doing so to overcome the passive, indifferent life.

--- Elie Wiesel

Trauma shuts us down in body, mind and spirit.

War photos, and the response to the Iraqi prison abuse have startled and shocked many. A crisis that extends beyond American prisons got recognized with the tragic treatment of the foreign prisoners: torture, isolation, sensory deprivation, and physical abuse. Americans say, 'How can this be? Americans are so morally conscious!' Is this an American persona, the mask we wear?

Closer to home, and on the mellower end of the spectrum, what is brought to awareness is varying degrees of inhumanity that sometimes goes on inside some abusive American families and inside some American prisons. What Hades' Angels seek, what they become torchbearers for, is outside intervention to end this abysmal revolving door of danger and abuse. Angel BJ voices her opinion about the misuse of authority, "There is an entirely different psychology that develops when you are put in charge of other people. We've been dehumanizing other people for years and have become very good at it. I don't think the behavior in Iraqi prisons was so different or unusual; they just let cameras in and they got caught."

We want to portray ourselves as a morally conscious society. Yet, through their personal experience, Hades' Angels and other inmate families say they know abuse, in varying degrees, goes on inside our homes and also, they say, gets perpetuated in American prisons to varying degrees. Prisons simply become warehouses for unfinished family business: neglect and emotional abuse in dysfunctional family systems become the building blocks for a bumper crop of men whose community is imposed by fate; it gets relived inside some American prisons. The shame and stigma of incarceration is often carried by those who "jumped over the edge", felt trapped beneath the weight, rather than walk the line in a broken family system.

Our failure to educate and rehabilitate is one tragedy. Violence, humiliation, mistreatment and abuse are another American tragedy. Attitudes about prisoners and those who visit, have been shaped by the public's belief that inmates get what they deserve. And so the cycle of abuse continues, and it trickles down over multiple generations. To break the cycle of violence, lower the rate of recidivism, or expect different results, we need to alter our thinking and revisit existing policies.

What bothers Hades' Angels the most is what they see all around them: indifference and injustice. How is it, they ask, that we view such a large portion of the human population in our democratic country as throw-aways? How is it that this Judeo-Christian country sees incarceration and abuses of power, rather than justice, education, prevention and treatment, as the solution of choice to the ills of our society? Is it possible that we, the nameless, blameless members of society, can't see our own shadow parts in those we choose to discard?

What gets worked through, rectified, even healed, through Hades' Angels inmate-freemate relationship is their vulnerable and victimized, yet repressed shadow parts, and their internalized felt need to "right the wrongs". Many women, including those in the general population, grow up silently bearing injustice, closing down to protect and to hide the self — a dynamic which provides the perfect fit for a narcissistically injured man who angrily lashes out in response to a similar wounding.

Personal Power

Hades' Angel Stephanie, 44, is an accountant, a paralegal and a very tenacious person. She sees her inmate husband as a political prisoner who needed an advocate; she's been just that for the past thirteen years and it has unlocked the potential of this "diamond in the rough". The relationship dynamics has enabled her to get to know her long-held-captive shadow self. She says, "I have come to know myself better and therefore I am able to give more to people around me. He has given me confidence and I'm not scared of anybody."

For Stephanie the contrasts of fear and empowerment are stark. "There are people who are scared because they are afraid. When I first started visiting there was an elderly lady who had fallen and broken her hip because the dirt area in which she was walking had not yet been cemented in. She said they told her, 'if you file a complaint, we are going to move your son so far away from you, you'll never see him.' She said they told him the same thing. So he begged his mother, 'Mom, please don't do anything.' I told her, "If it had been me, I would have owned the prison." Her rebel part would turn a broken pavement into a playground for her newly-found guiding principle: "Nobody out there has any power over me if I don't give it to them."

Stephanie sizes up her understanding about power, caring, and control. "Visiting prison was very upsetting because I saw a horrendous amount of suffering, even to the point of including the correctional officers because they are very damaged individuals. I know there is suffering there and if I can do something about it, I will."

Empowerment

Stephanie also has very strong views about society's stigma of people in prison and the "horrible stigma it puts on people who visit" inmates. "The Bible says you are supposed to visit the people in prison. There are Christian people running this country, but they want to throw people away if they go to prison. I have a problem with that. I think the people in prison are all our brothers, our sisters, our mothers, our fathers, and our children. Unless we start caring about them and start caring about people that we perceive as less than ourselves, we can't care for ourselves. If God put a human being on this planet, he is not worth throwing away," says Angel Stephanie.

Stephanie can now acknowledge and care for the part of her that once got thrown away. From a broader perspective, on a soulful level, her actions revolve around her belief that we need to be treated like human beings by adults who care and want to help. It, an action that repairs the world, is a cost-effective blueprint for change.

Viable Options

"Pay your debts. Everybody gets another chance," says Hades' Angel Maria. Considered soft-headed and ineffective, rehabilitation has not been the "in word" for some time. However, it doesn't take a budget analyst to figure that it is cost effective to prepare inmates for life on the outside. It's a win-win situation because it lessens the number of people who commit new crimes, reduces chronic prison overcrowding, and redirects funds towards job programs that speak to attitudes of compassion along with the expectation of self-sufficiency.

> *He who opens a school door, closes a prison.*
>
> --- Victor Hugo

The general public is unaware that Hades' Angels, and other good women like them, are often the watchdogs of public prison policy and advocates of reform and rehabilitation. Hades' Angel Stephanie wasn't consciously aware she was attempting to heal her emotional scars when she started going into the prisons. She saw others that needed help and that's how she learned to help her self. She speaks for those who have a hard time with the idea that the people who are running the country are the same people who want to throw people away if they go to prison.

The concerned presence of Hades' Angels, and others like them, gives an emotionally healthy, viable option to an inmate's helplessness and hopelessness as the result of his incarceration.

To Self Advocacy

Through their relationships, Hades' Angels have unearthed painful memories of early childhood narcissistic wounding. Similar toxic environments and harrowing situations created rage-warriors of their inmate spouse. Working through this early wounding within their relationship dynamics pushed out all the stops. Hades' Angels are aware of the emotional, mental, sexual, and spiritual boundary violations they experienced in their families of origin, yet they do not seem to hold grudges. They rectify those wrongs by tapping into their inner "wild man" and channel their long repressed anger and their fighting instincts to take responsibility for changing their own lives.

On a personal level, they fight emotional injustices and fight to release themselves from their inner emotional prisons. Their voices speak out on behalf of the previously disowned part of the self. On an interpersonal level they have engaged in a win-win situation where fairness to all is actively pursued to work through their inner anger of historical personal injustice as seen in the injustices secreted away behind prison walls: punishment, retribution, cell searches, suicides, and codes of silence among guards. They have become prison reformers, fighting the injustices of the system for those inside. They have, in some cases, become the vigilant guard dog, watching and advocating for reform so that there should never be an innocent man in prison.

> *The conclusion is always the same:*
> *Love is the most powerful and still the most*
> *Unknown energy of the world.*
>
> --- Pierre Teilhard de Chardin

Portrait: Hades' Angel Sabrina

Sabrina, 54, lived her life feeling invisible. She gravitated to her mother because she was afraid of her alcoholic father -- a rager. Not having any good examples of how a man should treat a woman, Sabrina was naïve when she married at age eighteen. "Right out of high school, I picked a man who was just like Daddy – an emotionally unavailable rager." Even though there were serious problems from the beginning, Sabrina thought she could make her marriage work. She hung in for eighteen years and had three children. "I felt like I was in prison. He was just never there and when he was, we were all concerned about making him happy, careful not to make him mad. I felt helpless about this, then felt a turning point. 'I thought, eighteen years in one bad home, and another eighteen years in this bad home.' In that moment I decided I wasn't willing to give him any more years of my life. So we divorced."

Meeting Her Man Behind Bars

Sabrina got involved with her prisoner after writing him when he was in jail awaiting trial. But what drew her in were his letters in response to hers: "He wrote from his heart." What also appealed to her was his kindness. After corresponding for a while, he asked to become closer.

It's True Love

"Once I made a list of the qualities I wanted in an ideal man; that list covered two pages. It was important that he be Christian; that he believed in God and Prayer; that he be loving and caring: I didn't want a "rager". I wanted someone who took a shower! When I was married, my husband took a shower once a week, maybe twice. I wanted someone I could feel safe with. I feel blessed that we are alive, and he will say the same. When he holds my hand, I just feel loved and respected."

The Prison Visits

When asked how she deals with the fact that her man is incarcerated for killing somebody, Sabrina defends his actions: "His wife of almost thirty years was having her third affair and he went to talk to the man. The man had a gun. They both got shot. But his being shot was not brought out in the trial. He felt he had to do it to save his life. And if the facts had been brought out better, it would have been different, I think. But it's political. They are being "tough on crime" right now. He was sentenced under the Reform Act of 1989, and what they decided was if the states would be tougher on crime and give longer sentences, the federal government would give them money to build more prisons. Twenty-seven states accepted that."

The Change

Eager not to repeat earlier mistakes, Sabrina spent two years in psychotherapy. It helped her assess her boundaries and make some important changes in her life. "It got me to the point where I will not tolerate a lot of things, like being mistreated." Outspoken, but in a soft way, she says, "I have come to a place where if someone mistreats me, I'm not going to stay."

Sabrina feels strongly about thinking her own thoughts. "I speak my mind freely – even though at times my children have reacted badly to it. Right now, my son's not speaking to me – for almost two years. My youngest went two years and didn't speak to me. And my oldest went a few months not very long ago because she was mad. I've told them that we can agree to disagree. Different is okay. We don't have to not speak; we don't have to be angry forever. We are different, we have our opinions, and they may not always be the same." Her family finds these changes in her unsettling because they don't know who she is anymore, "But they are learning," Sabrina says.

Sabrina discloses, "Another thing I have been working on changing is my relationship with my father. It has improved slightly. Now two or three times a month he will call me on the phone or I will call him and we will talk for maybe half an hour. I do not allow him to talk about my mother, because he's got his own sense of reality on that subject, so we get along okay for now." The relationship with her mother also changed. "We were always close, even after I got married -- perhaps too close." Sabrina is aware of that enmeshment, has pulled away such close contact, and the restraint seems to be working.

It Keeps Me Busy

Sabrina has come a long way from a time when only one mood, one feeling, and one way of thinking was tolerated. These days she uses her voice and her pen to express her thoughts, beliefs, and feelings. "I belong to a prison support group, and I belong to an internet group, and I write a newspaper. When I'm feeling certain ways, I just contact them. I also am on the Board of Directions of Reconciliation; I go to many committee meetings, write about prison issues to help reduce the public's ignorance about the system, and I work for prison rights and for families."

Why Stay?

Sabrina gets appreciated and validated by her inmate: "He gives me unconditional love and when he holds my hand, I just feel loved and respected. At times I can't believe he really loves me. And then I think, 'I am worthy to be loved. I am not super-woman, and I've got my faults, but I think I'm a good person, an okay person. His dad will say things like how he is proud of me. I have never had a male, not even my brother, say, 'I am proud of you.'"

Sabrina is always thinking about her love behind bars: "The kind of life he has in there is heartbreaking. I worry because things happen. One time we were on the phone, he suddenly said, 'They're searching my cell,' and he hung up."

Update

Eight days prior to their wedding date, Sabrina's inmate-partner was found dead, hanging in his cell. The Department of Corrections said that he had committed suicide. Sabrina doubts their findings.

Transformation

Still soft spoken, Sabrina is living out loud today. She learned much from this relationship, particularly that there are loving, caring, romantic, affectionate men out there that can be trusted. She and her prisoner "grew to love one another" and it moved her from the wounds of fear and distrust. Like a flower, she opened up, stopped doing for those that stepped on her, and reached out to those who appreciate her. Believing herself loved translated into finding her voice and using it advocating for the self and others. She has established a support group and writes a newsletter that goes out to 150 prisoners and members over the United States. This freemate and this inmate became "dad" and "mom" for more than a few prisoners whose family abandoned them. She says, "I am an advocate for family and friends of prisoners and sign petitions when I can for changes in our prison system. I find prisoners so grateful for any time I take to communicate with them. We lock up millions of people in our system, which costs billions of dollars. "I was on the board of directors for two years of a local prison nonprofit group, went to meetings with the commissioner of prisons, attended weekly support meetings, and belong to a lot of groups online."

Even though he is no longer here to hold her hand, their relationship and what she learned about prison unlocked her from her own: she changed. Today, Sabrina is not constrained by the templates that locked her into helplessness and emotional abuse. She uses the power of her pen to write about injustices to help reduce the public's ignorance about the system. Her writing keeps her empowered, her deceased inmate partner's memory alive, and informs others about their rights. She is doing the work that the larger society won't do or doesn't know how to do.

Proactive Policy

Hard sentencing has not "cured" the rise in violent crime or lowered the explosive prison population. The Economist (August 10, 2002), reports that 600,000 American inmates will be leaving prison in the next few years. Are they prepared for this? Are we prepared for this? The answer is no. What does it take to invest emotionally and financially at the front end? Correction without the benefit of rehabilitation and training seems short sighted, meaning that we are simply warehousing our human potential.

Marriage Programs for the Already Married

Prison officials in more than twenty-four states inaugurated marriage programs hoping to keep traditional families together. "The Bush administration proposed to spend several hundred million dollars a year for five years on marriage, fatherhood and sexual- abstinence initiatives, a plan that has wide support among religious and conservative groups. The proposal calls for $100 million in annual grants to the states, plus an additional $100 million in grants that the states would have to match," (Lyman, 2005). Such programs, while hopeful signs of positive change, would not apply to inmate marriages after incarceration.

Where We Go from Here

Hades' Angels have become emboldened in-your-face advocates for prison reform and their voices are being heard. These women, and others like them have a sense of universality, intuitively seeing the larger picture, and when they advocate for change it is not blocked by color or religious beliefs. The foundation of their code of ethics and morality and advocacy work is based solely on *how can I help?*

Through continuing their inner journey of getting to "know thy self", Hades' Angels have altered their destiny. They have transformed 'fate' into 'destiny,' a passive "inner" existence into an active and empowering existence that expects reciprocity. They expect to be seen and to be taken seriously.

As a psychologist, my focus is creating a corrective emotional experience within the therapeutic setting, helping women awaken an invisible "I", find their voice, and move beyond self-destructive patterns to a position of empowerment and healthier relationship choices. To create that shift in consciousness, hungry-for-life women (men too) who struggle to define themselves as individuals, need to learn new tools, tease out the weeds of shame and blame, and unearth the undiscovered self.

As a researcher, I used Hades' Angels lived experiences and the prison as a laboratory to investigate what makes a woman bind herself to or build a nest with a man in prison; and to bring their experiences and stories to light. My purpose was to understand what goes on in the dimension of this dark, alchemical container. I questioned what fertilized the emotional soil where the archetypal splits live and breathe, and what kinds of relationships grow in it. Although emotionally prepared to "meet the wolf", meaning deal with whatever subtle body entered the interview space, in Hades' Angels stories I felt their life-changing situations as both a challenge and an opportunity which led me deeper into my soul than I ever thought possible.

The outcome and implications of this work have immeasurably enriched my understanding of what helps people change. It translates into work with the general population of women who submissively live out their lives in destructive "demon lover" relationships. Hades' Angels felt healed because, through relationships, they finally got back what was short-changed them in their parental emotional environments, and what they have generously given to others: mirroring, holding, and empathic attunement which translates to love... and that is an empowering energy that nurtures the self, others and world soul.

The Real Deterrent

The correctional system is obviously a faulty system but it is not the cause of the problem; it simply warehouses the problems resulting from increasingly emotionally-removed parental and family systems and the unmet need for an emotionally present parent. Children cannot get heard without a caring parental ethic that guides and models a strong sense of self in the developing child. These unnurtured children, lost souls, who hold so much unrealized potential, are our very own children who have been tossed about by the winds of divorce, slipped through the cracks in our educational system, and been led astray by substitutes for nurturing parental role models: drugs and alcohol, gangs, and the media because they soothe their unnurtured and anxious souls.

Perhaps it is these imprisoned lost souls, particularly the male population, who have found their home in prisons and with whom Hades' Angels find their soul mate.

I'm angry at the situation that got him there.

--- Hades' Angel Betty Jo

Healing individuals and families' invisible emotional wounds addresses reform proactively and has a multi-generational trickle-down effect. As a psychologist, I am an advocate for emotionally healthier family functioning and family relationships. My concern comes from working with families in which children grow up not having appropriate boundaries and guidance, and lack a sense of family values and a sense of self, and frequently without a father figure to harness and channel that warrior energy.

Often a missing link within a broken family system is the partnering of a strong male protector and guide who functions alongside the strength of a nurturing, devoted, achievement oriented maternal figure. This masculine energy molds and influences a son through affection, direction, structure and involvement. Sadly, through his absence and disregard, a father can also mold and influence his son negatively. Acting out their anger and hostility, it seems "normal" to turn to gangs for a sense of family and identity, to drugs and alcohol to fulfill an emotional hunger, and even to suicide for peace.

A basis for my advocacy is a profound fear that we have become a polarized good guy/bad guy society that perpetuates multi-generational dysfunctional family systems in prison. The more inappropriate societal "problems" are simply warehoused in another type of family---prison. Here, sometimes there occurs an interesting phenomenon of teamwork and reparenting: Hades' Angels and some inmate spouses use this as an opportunity to reparent the self; and within the system an inmate "Dad" mentors from inside and "Mom" from the outside.

Immediate Gratification Junkie

In our fast-paced technological society, wants and needs often get confused. The family gets caught up in focusing on achievement and on the acquisition of material goods, leaving little time and energy to tend to the family's emotional needs — the primary need being the sense that one belongs within the family system. Material objects offer little feedback to the child as to his/her value within that system, and no sustenance in times of crisis. The emotionally hungry child becomes an immediate gratification junkie who develops into a pseudo-mature adult without a sense of identity and unable to cope effectively with stress and anxiety. The true self is drowned in a sea of material things.

Why wait for this disaster story before providing a secure base for balanced family emotional functioning? There is a hunger for an interdependent system that integrates these polarized extremes.

The Message

Emerging creative energy driven toward wholeness was born from this "work". The birth takes form as this book, women's psycho-educational empowerment groups and workshops that address core narcissistic injuries and their polarized acting-in and acting-out defenses; and rebalancing the internalized feminine and masculine energies. The result is a sense of personal empowerment, wholeness, and healthier relationships.

Individuals and families need support creating healthy emotional boundaries, learning to communicate straight, rather than from top-dog/under-dog, victim/victimizer positions, gain insight as to the source of their pain and anxieties, and make some changes. Knowing the true self and its potential, achieving a healthier balance between internal and external goals integrates polarized extremes and moves one towards wholeness and healthier relationships.

Empowerment groups offer support while traveling "the yellow brick road" towards life change. They also offer women (men, too) new tools that give them confidence to see their strengths and their worth. We may not like looking into the "magic mirror" but it enables us to view ourselves, and our life situations from a witness perspective, step out of our comfort zone, and step into our potential. Women gain the freedom to visit the "graves of their fathers", break away from and reexamine what they have been taught to believe, the faulty beliefs and internalized messages about the self and the family belief system that keep them feeling helpless, stuck, and emotionally imprisoned. Hopefully, the strength inherent in the archetype of the feminine will be understood and appreciated as an empowering, creative feminine consciousness that will be released into the larger consciousness. It is called soul.

We have viewed Hades' Angels transformative journey... of descent, suffering, and shifts in consciousness from a multitude of lenses, including soul. Their journey along the "yellow brick road" has been an internal quest for self-realization and redemption: awakening them to unconscious forces, wholeness, and a new stage of life.

We were so well trained to listen and obey, and found it easy to go into self-protective, altered states. It's time to learn new tools! You cannot change the world without first changing the self.

Chapter Thirteen

Help and Self-Help

He who has health has hope; and he who has hope has
everything.

Arabian Proverb

Just get out there and never give up sounds too simple. True change is an inner journey, a descent, a search for what gives your life meaning. The spiral on the cover of this book indicates that growth and change is a moving process. It is not a straight shot, rather it moves in and out, round and round, reassessing and continuously evolving. Home is not a fixed place. It is a place inside that can accept a state of evolving. Consider that a rose never dies; its essence simply lies fallow until the "right" conditions bring it to form. For some, perseverance is the essential tool to achieving a personal goal. Your difficulty can become a challenging opportunity for growth that will push you past your fears and out of your comfort zone.

Most of us need the support of others, so this section includes people and resources to help you get from point A to point B. I encourage you to persevere in your search and you will no doubt find additional resources that will be of help to yourself and others.

EXERCISES To Help Identify Your Invisible Wounds

He who knows others is wise; he who knows himself is
enlightened.

--- Lao-Tzu

The greatest tool we humans have is the capacity for self-reflection. By looking at the past events of our lives, the history we lived, the patterns that got created and our private analysis of them, we can choose to change them. Thus, we can decide to make our present and our future look differently. The following exercises are meant to help you identify your invisible wounds by redeeming and empowering the internal sense of self. Some of these exercises are simple. Others may require help sorting through what you discover. Therefore, I suggest that they be undertaken with the guidance of a professional or as part of a group.

Following are some exercises to help you make those changes.

A Good Look in the Mirror

Start by taking the time to look into the mirror. What do you see? Reflect about how you see yourself, your life choices, your life experiences and what has given your life meaning. In so doing, do not look for blame. You are confronting the past in order to move forward. How we got through early life experiences, the messages we internalized, and the tools we used can form the basis of our sense of self, our identity, today. There is no denying a deep need to make meaning out of our lives. During adolescence, mid-life change, and crises, the need is stronger; it can become a motivator for growth and deep change. Now is the "right" time. Let today be a new birthday, one in which you give birth to a new self. Light a candle and honor this journey you are choosing to travel.

Creating a Personal Mirror

In this exercise we are going to discern real time from emotional time. Begin in a factual, cognitive way, by sorting through your mind's eye to form an image of yourself at different ages. Write out, cut out, or draw that image. An old photograph at each stage or time frame will also work. Beside each image identify your age, the people closest to you, a special memory about each person, and how each one affected you at that stage of life. Can you identify any related events in the external environment that surrounded you at that time?

Next, return to emotional time to reflect on the emotional landscape. Identify the greatest joys and the stressors over time. Joyful celebrations and rituals can carry us through times of stress. How were joyful times celebrated? How did you manage to get through difficult times? What coping mechanisms did you use? What were your survival tools? Do you still use them today? Were you taught to open up and talk to someone (who?) or shut down, grin, and bear-it? What childhood messages give you strength, which cause you more pain? Is there a feeling or a pattern as to what draws you, or what you push away? What worked and what didn't?

To honor the past and then release it, place images of yourself during childhood, adolescence, adulthood, and crises into north, east, south and west positions. Identify your strengths during each time frame, becoming acutely aware of the energy from each source and draw it into yourself. Welcome that which warms you and say good-bye to that which makes you feel devoid of life energy and meaning. Create a poem that honors the memory yet helps you release it. You can choose to save the negative images in a scrapbook or put them in a basket and burn them. Close your eyes, and breathe in deeply, begin to internalize this new energy as a part of the self.

Now, create your own future mirror that reflects the person you are choosing to become, today. Look into the "mirror of the mind" to establish a whole new identity, redefine parts of the self, alter belief systems, or seek new ways to lessen your emotional isolation. You can do it. But first it is essential to look squarely into the mirror.

Start by giving yourself a new "birth-day," meaning honor this day as the first day of the new you. Celebrate it in a way that brings you into harmony with an image of the wholeness you want to create for yourself. For example, gather together items that bring you strength and courage and reflect how you want to be viewed. Make a circle of them and sit in the middle, identifying how each is some part of the new you:

a candle for awareness, music that speaks to your soul, a prayer, a poem, a rock that symbolizes a solid core, a blossom from the garden to symbolizes your earthiness or the flowering new you, etc.

Your Own Personal Story

Start with the present time and to the best of your ability, work your way back in time. Reflect, take a good look at the blessings and the events that you remember most fondly. Begin to write about them freely without fear of an inner critic or a critical parent supervising your work.

My favorite exercise for beginning to get in touch with your history is to gather all the old photograph albums and sort through them by ages beginning when you were a small child. Use a straight line as a timeline or create your own format. It can be horizontal or vertical as long as there is room for dates and events. On this time line, ask questions, reflect, then write or draw your information on the developing time line. It is interesting how you view your life when you see it laid out in front of you. Now, write or tape record your story.

Music and song has a tremendous impact on the developing child and on love relationships. Write down the song that fits best with each photo. What songs did your heart learn to sing; what song does your heart long to sing now? Was there a particular song that plays in your mind during these different developmental stages? Did your parents sing to you, or lull you to sleep with a lullaby you remember? What was your favorite song as a teenager? What song played at your wedding? How do you include such meaningful emotional music in your life today?

Write down the members of your family of origin. Cut-out or draw pictures of animals that you can identify with each member of your family then, write about the characteristics you see in each one. Is there a particular animal that symbolizes how you saw yourself? Think about your place and how you were in the family of origin. What are the dynamics between the members of your "family?" For example, who was the controlling top-dog, what made him/her be that way? Which members of the family played into his role, which ones rebelled against it?

Sex Roles and Identity

It is informative and fun to find out how our thoughts about gender came to be. In a very simple exercise, divide your paper in half, the left pertains to women, the right pertains to men. As a child, our views were often formed through actors and actresses. On the left, write down your favorite male and female actors and on the right, the roles they played. Continue this process with family members or teachers who may have impacted your thinking. See how their role may have unconsciously served as a model for you.

Early Emotional Alignments

Values. Without judgment, take a look at the attitudes and the values of each parent. List them under each parent's name. Whose attitude and values do you feel most connected with emotionally and in your work-world? Is it the same parent or does it vary? Begin to question how you formed those values and that parental bond. From whom did their values develop?

What is the influence of the father? To explore how you view him, find a metaphor, an image of how you see him. For example, was he your rock or your safety net or the thorn that kept digging at you? Paste the metaphor in the center of a paper and search magazines for words that describe this metaphor of him. Was he an absent or a dominant figure in your growing up years? What kind of father was he? In what ways has he influenced your choice of men in relationships? Find a photo that depicts your relationship with him. Make a collage of photos of all the ways you see him from childhood into adulthood.

What is the influence of the mother? Think about how you view your mother and her role in the family. Find or create a metaphor that describes how you viewed her as a child, and how you view her now.

What was her predominant attitude in the family? Was she dominant, controlling, submissive, passive, nurturing, or all of these in the family? What role did she play in the family/nurturer, peacemaker, martyr, victim, or mediator? Which of these characteristics did you take-in and which did you reject?

In terms of temperature, i.e. hot, cold, etc. draw or find pictures that exemplify how you describe her emotionally and physically. This should open up an emotionally descriptive territory that leads to feelings about the relationship itself. It is productive to write about both negative and positive feelings that come up for you.

In retrospect, how did you internalize the dynamics between your parents? Here we explore the parental marital dynamic from your mind's eye. The first model of how a partner should treat you comes from what you witnessed growing up. Explore this without shame or blame. Were they supportive of one another or critical? Were they close or distant? How did they show respect for one another, etc. How has their relationship impacted your own?

Identify Early Shame

Start with the present and to the best of your ability, work your way back in time. Reflect, take a good look at the blessings and the events that you remember most fondly. Begin to write about them freely without fear of a critical parent supervising your work.

Shame is a controlling mechanism. "What will the neighbors think" is an attempt to keep shameful things from coming to light. Healing occurs when this early shame is identified and the child's imagined but felt role in bringing shame to the family gets reevaluated.

To get in touch with your history is to gather all the old photograph albums and sort through them by ages beginning when you were a child. For this exercise, ask questions of yourself and then reflect on the different time frames as you developed. Music and song has a tremendous impact on the developing child and on love relationships. Write down the song tht fits best with each photo. What songs did your heart learn to sing; what song does your heart long to sing now? Was there a particular song that plays in your mind during these different developmental stages? Did your parents sing to you, lull you to sleep with a particular lullaby? What was your favorite song as a teenager? What song played at your wedding?

To Identify the Sense of Shame

First trace the shape of your hand with fingers extended. Inside your palm, write down when you felt shamed for wanting and needing love and attention. How old were you and what was the situation surrounding it? Outside your hand write down or sketch what your parents said to you. Inside the shape of your fingers identify the actions you took to compensate for feeling shamed. Repeat this exercise to bring all the early shame memories to awareness. Remember, what is not brought to awareness often gets repeated in the present. That was then.

Repeat the same exercise, from a here-and-now position, i.e. identify the shame you feel today as a result of that early wounding. Then, inside the shape of each finger write down what your options are today.

Identify How You See Yourself Now

1. Draw the shape of your face. Cut and paste words and/or pictures from magazines that identify the way you see yourself now: the feelings you hold inside, the thoughts you think about now, the way you view your world, are you serious or playful, the memories you have in your head. Do you see yourself as a compliant victim? Do you use your femininity: to rely on men to help you out?, to protect and defend you?, or do you rebel against that aspect of yourself by doing it all by yourself?

Create a self-portrait to continue to identify how you view yourself: Do you do for others, or even get used by them, and still expect nothing in return? Anne, a previous group member, visualized herself as a weightlifter. Her arm muscles held all her best qualities and helped her support a new self-image.

After you complete your own self-portrait, write down, without editing, the feelings it stirs in you. What do you want to change about yourself and what strengths you see in yourself that you want to keep?

2. Draw the shape of a rainbow. Put in colors that are meaningful to you: yellow might indicate cheery, red, passion, and blue, cool. Identify how these colors make you feel. For example, purple reminds me of one of my first party dresses. I felt fat and thought I looked ugly. Today, however, velvety-purple is how I feel when I am lost in states of self-reflection. Continue creating your own personal rainbow and relate it to how you see yourself today. When you get angry what color are you, red hot or black? When you feel used, do you see yourself as black and blue? Get into this exercise and discover what colors stimulate a sense of personal empowerment.

The Ideal Image You Hold Of Yourself

1. Draw it or inside a circle write the words that indicate how you want to see yourself. Do you think of yourself with the strengths of a certain animal?

2. Awareness is often a frightening and lonely trip. Once on this journey, there really is no turning back in time; sometimes old friends choose not to travel alongside you, so in the process we make new ones.

To help you along this path, fill a small overnight bag one by one with loving memories of objects you will need and meaningful transitional objects while on your journey. Look through your drawers, find and wrap special items such as a flashlight or certain songs that light the way. Carefully put these items into your overnight bag. If have to push yourself to connect with people, and want to change that, carry a little hard candy around as a reminder to reach out with a different attitude: "Life is dandy, sweet as sugar candy."

Find a song whose melody or words give you strength to "carry on" when you are feeling anxious or alone. Imagine, by John Lennon is my favorite song. I carry this song in my head and on the tip of my tongue and when I feel afraid. When anxious or afraid, draw on the energy of your own favorite song or poem. Reach out and connect.

Family Historical Patterns Through Genogram Work

Genograms were first used by Murray Bowen (1988) to graphically illustrate historical family patterns. Genograms are diagrams of family emotional patterns and are an outgrowth of his family systems theory. This systems perspective views the physical, social and emotional functioning of family members. By viewing an event, both the event and the viewer are changed. Your purpose is to use an objective lens that brings you a deepening of consciousness.

Use the genogram format below to record historical data and emotional events: births, deaths, marriages, divorces, illness, occupation, critical events and addictions (drugs, alcohol, affairs), incest.

Now, reflect on the principal emotional dynamics within the family, then record the family emotional alignments using different lines to show the relationship patterns: close, fused, distant, very distant, conflicted, hostile, emotional cut-off.

To show dominance and submission: use an upward pointing arrow to indicate dominance and a downward pointing arrow to indicate submissiveness among the parental and marital dynamics.

What do you see? This process allows you to stay fully present while taking a long, hard look at the family emotional dynamics.

Use this genogram format to assess patterns of family functioning. Place your family members on the genogram. Use a circle for females and a square for males.

Genogram Format

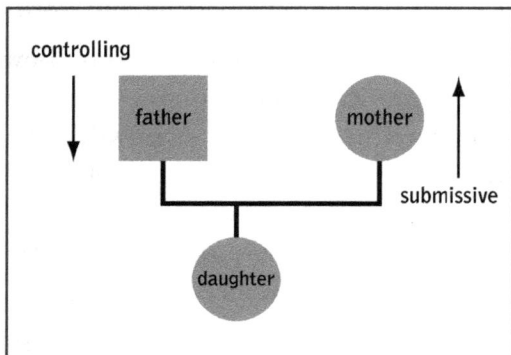

controlling

father   mother

submissive

daughter

Close: _____

Very Close: ==================

Distant: ....

Cut Off: _____| |_____

Conflict: /\/\/\/\/\/\/\/\

Creating Boundaries in Relationships

Our personal boundaries are safeguards that protect our sense of self, our personal and our emotional space and give us the breathing room to make competent, well-thought out decisions without being pressured by a partner or an inner critic, or a critical parent. Learning to say your mind, to bear separateness, and dialogue about it when in a relationship keeps the relationship alive: 1 + 1 = 3. No more my way or the highway!

Define Your Boundaries

To get clarity and define you from me, versus you are me, have a little fun doing the following exercise. Draw a large circle. Inside it, name the qualities you believe are you, and outside what is not you. Make a second circle and this time focus your attention to what is and is not you in relationships.

Do you change who you are or become different when you are in a relationship? Where did this message of accommodation come from? What happens to "You" when you lose "you"? What are your silent expectations of the other? Do you think he "should magically know" what you want? You can expand this exercise by cutting out pictures from magazines and placing them in the inner and outer circles. Take the time to write about your revelations.

Create your checklist of boundaries in a relationship

Cut pieces of paper into squares then write on each one what you believe are clear boundaries in a healthy relationship, i.e. asking clearly for what you want or need, or when you trust yourself and your intuition.

On a second set of paper write down what happens to you when you give up those boundaries, i.e. when you give more of yourself and expect little or nothing in return. Put them side by side as you string them up to form a circle or wreath. Paste a picture of yourself in the center. Keeping this circle of boundaries close at hand is a good, concrete way to support an emerging sense of self.

Unearthing Family of Origin Beliefs

We all tend to seek connection and belonging, particularly within the family of origin. Family beliefs are the unspoken, silent messages we get from the family about the family and how we should function within it to belong. As we grow into adulthood, it is the inner myth(s) we live that have great impact on our lives, our interactions, and our relationships i.e. the women in the family don't get divorced. One woman in my Women's Group drew herself as attached to the hip of her husband. Her inner myth was: "stand by your man". To illustrate "smile at all costs", another group member drew the traumatic events and a huge smile that covered it up. She understood the smile was a "cover-up" for negative emotions. Find your own myth and cut pictures from magazines to try to illustrate it.

Discovering your inner myth is a gentle way to unravel the negative impact or the power it has had over you. Freedom from that inner myth means confronting the void of no myth to guide you through life. It is not uncommon to have a sense of dread at the emptiness of no myth and our need for structure. Today, you have the freedom to choose how you live, and in creating new messages to guide you along the way. Though you lacked control as a child, you have choices today. Next, create a new inner myth that serves you and your goals today.

Family Roles

In families, each member takes on a particular role and responsibility within the family system. Do you see yourself as a little dog with a big bark? Draw a picture of yourself among your family using caricatures that also identify each family member's responsibility. Questions to ponder: How has your personal role evolved through the years? Has it changed, matured, or do you still adhere to the assigned childhood role? Perhaps you are compensating for its negative impact.

Identify family roles. Who is the glue that holds everyone together? Who is the most reliable, the most dependent, the most emotionally fragile, the most powerful? For example, are you heroically sitting astride a white horse waiting to rescue faltering family members?

In order to move forward into newly defined roles, examine the old and let go, then make room for the new. Orpheus, a tragic figure in Greek mythology symbolizes the resistance to accepting loss. In great despair over the death of his bride, Eurydice, he descended into Hades to plead with the gods for her release. With pity for his despair, the gods released her on the condition that he not look back to see her until they reached Earth. Unable to contain himself, he looked back and lost her forever.

We are looking back in order to make room for the new. Make a list of the roles you've taken on over the years that formed your sense of identity or that have been valuable, i.e. mother, wife, teacher, nurturer, babysitter, workhorse. Rank them by priority. Imagine letting go of the least important one. If no longer in this role, where would you put that time and energy? What does it mean to be giving up important aspects of yourself?

Your Personal Metaphor

Finding a metaphor for the way you see yourself is a playful and interesting way to create a visual impression. You can use it to elicit feedback from close friends. Are you like a bird in a nest or do you see yourself hiding under a leaf or being stepped on like an ant?

Based on your innermost sense of self, what is your personal metaphor? For example, do you picture yourself as a rocket with a great deal of power and energy that can't get off the ground? Do your friends see your stuckness or your power? Victoria had an abusive childhood; her metaphor brought insight as to how she remained a victim. She visualized herself as a wad of play-dough: being too pliable and easily rolled over by authority figures. Finding such metaphors are fun and offer a lot of food for thought and self-reflection. It is also helpful to understand how others see you.

Shadow Work

What symptoms speak to you of shadow content? Do they appear in your dreams, in your body, in your relationships, in your interactions at work? Do you seek out friends who are your opposite? The following exercise may inform you of your shadow.

Dream work is highly respected and of enormous value to help you move towards your personal enlightenment. You may want to consult a psychologist to help you interpret your dreams. Dreams talk to us in the quiet of the night when our ego defenses are down. Our dreams may compensate for what we dare not feel or think in waking hours. We need only to listen and learn their language; symbols and metaphors. One thing may imply another because looking straight at the truth is too painful. What, if any, are the symbols in your dream i.e. money, stairways, fences, walls, open doors? What are the characters in your dreams: warriors, lovers, gods and goddesses, kings and queens, that lead you on a new path?

Keep a dream journal to keep track of your dreams, dating each one. Consult a psychologist to help you discover the meaning of your dreams. You can work on and gain enlightenment from them by looking for a common pattern, a theme that ties them together. First, identify the characters and the objects in your dream, and label them. Next, describe the setting of your dream, where it takes place? What feeling did you get from it, i.e. fear, anger, hope, death? When you awaken, how do you feel: energized or drained? What are the positive and negative aspects of the dream symbols and characters? Go back and look at the interactions of the characters. What might they describe the differing about you? To learn more, say your dream again using "I" for every aspect in the dream.

Movies, such as *Chocolait*, are a lovely way to be entertained while you look for the shadow parts in the characters portrayed in this film. For example, the lead character is a chocolatier. She is viewed as a temptress because she brings a different energy, a sweetness and frivolity, into a cold, frigid community. Dormant, hidden within the coldness of the townsfolk lies their own individual sweetness. The main character, in essence, represents their shadow. Watch for other shadow characters.

The Masks You Wear

Begin by drawing two different circles on a large piece of paper. Label one my inside self, the other my outside self, meaning the mask you show the world. Now, draw or write words that represent how you present yourself to the world and how you really feel inside. Do they match, are they different, or are they flip sides of one another?

Releasing the Persona

Bullworth is another film that exemplifies the persona and what happens when it is held too tightly. As you watch this film look for the masks that the lead character Warren Beatty begins to shed. What he digs into and discovers is the strength embodied in his shadow parts.

Create a graph with lines on it (a plaid) and large enough squares so that you can see inside it. Use colors to identify how you feel inside and then cover it with a color that indicates how you present yourself to the world. In a corner of your paper make a little legend that shows your colors and what they mean to you.

Blocks

Search for a belief that blocks you from moving towards new, healthier ways of interacting in your life. Write it down, meditate with it, walk with it, sit with it. When you feel ready to let it go, to release it, light your paper with a match, burn it and drop it into a fireplace or metal basket. Look at the fire as the paper burns. This fire symbolizes a desire for change. If you find yourself buried in negativity and it no longer serves your ideal image of yourself, you are ready to let it go. Write it down. Wear a rubber band like a bracelet as a conscious reminder of the blocks that bind you. Snapping that rubber band on your wrist as a personal reminder that you can let it go. Having released the old belief into the universe, visualize your change now and live as if it has already taken place.

Your Personal Myth of Romantic Love

Draw or write what it looks like to feel love. Our myths about love come to us by way of fairy tales, stories, and experiences in our family of origin. Create your own story of your ideal "love" relationship. If you have been in addictive or unhealthy relationships it is a good idea to explore what you believe a healthy one "should" look like. Our relationship myths come from unspoken messages in the family, what we see and hear in the media, and from stories. All our story "princesses" are maidens waiting…to be rescued.

A woman's expectation and concept of romantic love is often borne from movies and fairy tales characters such as Cinderella, Snow White, Sleeping Beauty, Beauty and the Beast, etc. Their messages tell us to whistle while we work, wait patiently to be rescued, that "Someday My Prince Will Come", do what the father tells us, and be good girls. Therefore, the message learned and often lived-out, is to wait passively for a special someone who will magically do for us what we need to do for ourselves, actualize our potential. I am not aware of any fairytale that informs a female child it's okay to be alone in life and be happy.

Previous Relationship Dynamics

Think about and then list those men you have been attracted to and with whom you have had a serious, committed love relationship. Are any of their traits similar or emotional reminders to those of the father? Look for commonalities to identify any patterns you are drawn towards. "I'm always attracted to the bad boys," or "I know I don't want anyone with a lot of money," informs you of unfinished business about shadow issues, money and self-esteem. Once you identify them, they can be worked through. What attracts you to a particular person, his qualities, and then start considering what caused you to leave him or he to leave you. Did you seek out relationships with these "type" of men or did they chase after you? Did you change after you were in the relationship? Did he?

Turning Points

Turning points can come from insights or from external events. Opportunity is always knocking but we don't always hear it because we are either not ready or attuned to meeting the needs of others.

Poetry, words of wisdom, or inspiring words from a song or story offers courage and may also create an insight. For example:

Being challenged in life is inevitable, being defeated is optional.
--- Roger Crawford

All you need to do to receive guidance is to ask for it and then listen.
--- Sanaya Roman

Trust in yourself. Your perceptions are often far more accurate than you are willing to believe.
--- Claudia Black

Holy Moments: These are the "aha's", the moments of awakening because the light bulb goes on and you really get it. Such moments bring a sense of release because suddenly you see the old in a new way! When what someone says "rings a bell" or has a great impact on you… that is a Holy Moment!

EXERCISES that may help you define a turning point in your thinking:

Cut yourself a very long piece of string. Beginning with the present time frame, move backwards towards your childhood while you tie knots representing the points of crises in your life. If two crises came close together, then tie those knots close to one another. If there was a long gap between life crises, then the string should reflect that gap. Now, get a piece of paper and pencil and write a little about each particular crisis. How old were you when they occurred? What impact did they have on your life? Did they become turning points? Were you open to a different way of thinking or a new perspective, or did you continue on the same path without making any positive changes.

Illness can be the body's way of handling suffering during a crisis. With any severe illness we go down, we suffer, and then we may heal. Marriage, divorce, birth of a child, addictions, and death are all events that can create mixed feelings: joy, suffering and change. How did you handle these moments? Did any of these events cause you illness, depression, to self-reflect, or were they turning points?

Looking for Your Lost Part

Draw a circle with lines stretching from it like rays of the sun. You are the circle, born whole. On each line-ray, write down the part of yourself that is not acceptable to you. Where did that come from? When? What would your life look like if these parts were integrated back into the whole?

Finding Your Inner Voice

What old messages and/or emotional needs are you willing to release so you no longer have to carry it forward in your life. When you are ready, speak your intention out loud, then write it down on a piece of paper, and put it into a trash can and burn it inside the can while you joyfully let it go. You can release the following:

Release your dependency on a spouse

Release any unwillingness to fully embrace your own destiny

Release old messages about money

Release your fears about being swallowed up by another

Now, replace that old message with a new one. "I do a good job caring for myself" speaks of emotional and physical independence. If you have a fear of being swallowed-up by a partner's strong energy, then it is time to find your own energy. If your partner is feeding off your strength you are therefore, being drained of life blood in order to fill his emptiness.

Start by using the word "I" which clearly defines one person from another. Observe yourself during a conversation with your partner. Does he complete your sentences, interrupt you, or cut you off? Know that you are entitled to your own mind, your own thoughts, and to voice them. Perhaps it's time you think and say what they are from an "I" position. As you move along this path, start to identify any deeper fears, such as separation, aloneness or abandonment that might occur if you do your own thinking. Know that awareness and observation is an important first step that preceeds action. You are on your way. The next step is to plant a few seeds from an "I" position and become aware of what grows from it.

Singing Your Own Song

A song can be far more powerful than the money that lines your pocket. Find a song you can carry in the pocket of your mind, one that helps you get through each day. You might discover how early songs influence our thinking. One of my all-time favorites, *I Believe*, has carried me through many dark moments.

Thoughts on Relationships

The following "gems of wisdom" are thoughts to carry with you while you travel along your "yellow brick road". Perhaps one will touch you in an especially soulful way that resonates with the rhythms of your heart. Such pearls offer connection with others who have journeyed on their own path of enlightenment. Search for your own pearls to help set the tone for a day with less turmoil and more peace.

> *One does not discover new lands without consenting to lose sight of the shore for a very long time.*
>
> --- André Gide

> *Do not fear mistakes__there are none.*
>
> --- Miles Davis

> *What shakes the eye but the invisible?*
>
> ---Theodore Roethke

Love Relationships and Boundaries
THE THIRD CANDLE IN RELATIONSHIPS: 1 + 1 = 3

Who am I without you?

In a healthy relationship, the right answer is me. I am who I am, and with you I am more (and so are you). I am not diminished by you, nor are you, by me. We are we. For many couples, the process of defining appropriate emotional boundaries in order to create a healthy sense of a "we" in their relationship can be tricky. Couples enter therapy for guidance on how to define and articulate their boundaries, how to learn to distinguish between negotiable and nonnegotiable needs, and how to raise awareness about destructive family patterns and belief systems that may be impacting their union.

The Third Candle

In the Judeo-Christian marriage ceremony, the father walks his daughter down the aisle And turns her over to the awaiting groom who is then expected to take on the job of caring for her and protecting her. The daughter's identity as her own person is ignored. In some marriage ceremonies, when a couple walks down the aisle, each one carries a candle. At the altar, they light a third candle to symbolize their union – their we. Then, they blow out their own individual candles.

The trouble with this ritual is that symbolically it perpetuates the cultural idea that in marriage, two individuals should fuse into one —the third candle: "I am my beloved and my beloved is mine." But this can be destructive because one day somebody wakes up (usually it's the woman) and realizes that her individual candle has been snuffed out.

How much healthier it would be if the couple getting married could not only light that third candle (which symbolizes their union), but also keep their own individual candles lit: 1+1 = 3. This represents two independent individuals uniting to enrich one another -- but without either one of them giving up pieces of themselves in the process.

Here's a case in point: When Joe and Evie fell in love, it was wonderful—at first. Each felt they'd found the perfect partner, a kindred soulmate who'd meet their innermost longings. As in most early romances, they were deliciously "high" on each other, with great hopes for the future. At that point, they were at the fork in the road where the relationship could either lead them towards healthy individuation, or swallow them up. Joe and Evie nearly got swallowed up.

Joe got so caught-up in being the apple of Evie's eye that he forgot to get to know her as a person—what she liked, what she thought about, her dreams. It never crossed his mind that she had a mind of her own. While her need to be needed and his need to control felt like the perfect match at first, after a while it began to irk Evie. She started complaining that she felt controlled by Joe, that he never listened to her, that she felt she had no room to breathe. She realized that her candle had been snuffed out. Joe didn't understand what the problem was. He was confused: "What made her change?"

Setting Up a Win-Lose Situation

When one person unwittingly turns themselves over to another person (as Evie did with Joe) in order to fill up their own emotional emptiness, it sets up a win-lose dynamic. The "I" in the relationship gets lost or discounted, and the person starts to feel ripped off. Joe needed Evie's nurturing, emotional support and validation, which initially she was willing to give – until she began to realize that she had needs of her own, and Joe wasn't meeting them. Resentment and anger set in.

Keep Your Own Candle Lit

Romantic love in a relationship starts to dwindle when one partner is viewed as emotionally dependent on the other. Expecting our partner to be on call, to rescue us, to fill up our bottomless pit of emotional neediness, can destroy all good will. So in your own relationships, don't blow out the individual candles; light that "third candle" and keep it lit. Keep all three candles lit as a reminded that the "I" is as important as the "we". By keeping our individual candles lit, we are saying, "I am a person. I expect to be considered. Do not discount me. I need to state what I want to eat, where I want to go, and if I want some space from you. I need you to do the same with me. I need you to know what I am feeling, and I need to feel comfortable saying just that to you. I need to not withdraw or submissively lie down and play dead. I need a relationship that is reciprocally communicative without fear of losing you. I want and need that from you. That is the "I" candle. Don't snuff it out.

To those who choose to journey on a new path of self-discovery: I salute you!

Charlyne Gelt, Ph.D.

Contact The Author: Charlyne Gelt, Ph. D.
(818) 501-4123
Website: http://www.drgelt.com
Email: info@drgelt.com

For Information Related to the Book
Workshops: for information call (818) 501-4123
  or
Email: cgelt@earthlink.net

Women's Groups: Call for dates and time. (818)-501-4123.
Web Site: http://www.drgelt.com

Suggested Readings

Achterberg, A. (1990). *Woman as Healer*. Boston: Shambhala.

Bandele, A. (1999). *The Prisoner's Wife*. New York: Scribner.

Borysenko, J. (1999). *A Woman's Journey to God*. New York: Riverhead
Books.

Borysenko, J. (1988). *Minding the Body, Mending the Mind*. New York:
Bantam Books.

Bradshaw, J. (1990). *Homecoming: Reclaiming and Championing Your
Inner Child*. New York: Bantam.

Campbell, J., Moyers, B. (1988). *The Power of Myth*. New York:
Doubleday.

Casarjian, R. (1995). *Houses of Healing*. Boston, MA: Lionheart
Foundation.

Douglas, Kay. (1996). *Invisible Wounds*. Great Britain: The Women's
Press Ltd.

Engel, B.(2000). *Loving Him Without Losing You*. NY: Jon Wiley &
Sons.

Gibran, K. (1969). *The Prophet*. New York: Knopf.

Harris, M., Harris, B.(1969). *Like Gold Through Fire.* North Carolina: Alexander Books

Johnson, R. We. *Understanding the Psychology of Romantic Love.* San Francisco: Harper Collins Publishers.

Jung, C.G.(1957). *The Undiscovered Self.* New York: Mentor Books.

Jung, C. G. (1964) *Man and His Symbols.* New York: Doubleday.

Katherine, A. (1991). *Boundaries.* NY: Parkside Publishing.

Kipnis, A. (2004). *Knights Without Armor.* Santa Barbara, CA: Indigo Phoenix Books.

Kipnis, A. (1999). *Angry Young Men.* San Francisco: Jossey-Bass Inc.

Lerner, H. *The Dance of Intimacy.* (1989). New York: Harper & Row, Publishers.

Loomis, M. (1991). *Dancing the Wheel of Psychological Types.* Wilmette, IL: Chiron Publications.

Loomis, M. (1995). *Her Father's Daughter.* Wilmette, IL: Chiron Publications.

Love, Pat. (1990). *The Emotional Incest Syndrome: What to do When a Parent's Love Rules Your Life.* NY: Bantam Books.

Lozoff, Bo (1985). *We're All Doing Time.* Durham, NC: Human Kindness Foundation.

Miller, A. (1981). *Drama of the Gifted Child.* NY: Basic Books, Inc.

Miller, A. (1990). *Banished Knowledge.* New York: Doubleday.

Murdock, M. (1994). *The Hero's Daughter*. New York: Fawcett-Columbine Books.

Perera, S. (1981). *Descent to the Goddess*. Toronto: Inner City Books.

Pines, Malach, A.(1999). *Falling In Love*. New York: Routledge.

Pinkola Estes, C. (1992). *Women Who Run With the Wolves*. New York: Ballantine Books.

Shinoda-Bolin, J., M.D. (1984). *The Goddesses in Everywoman*. NY: Harper & Row, Publishers, Inc.

von Franz, M. L. (1972) *The Feminine in Fairytales*. Dallas, TX: Spring Publications, Inc.

Viorst, Judith (1986). *Necessary Losses*. NY: The Free Press.

Woodman, M. ((1982). *Addiction to Perfection*. Toronto: Inner City Books.

Woodman, M. (1990). *The Unravished Bride*. Toronto: Inner City Books.

Woodman, M. & Dickson, E. (1997) *Dancing in the Flames*. Boston & London: Shambhala.

Zweig, C. & Wolfe (1997). *Romancing the Shadow*. New York: Balantine Books.

Resources, Links, and Self-Help Groups

Domestic Violence:

National Domestic Violence hotline: thehotline.org.
(800) 799-SAFE (7233)

Jewish Family Service 24-hotline: jfsla.org.   (818) 505-0900

National Council for Jewish Women Talkline:
Ncjwla.org/community-services/women.helping.women.
                              (323) 655-3807 or (877) 655-3807

Batterers intervention Program:
openpaths.org/our-services/domestic-violence-anger-management.
                                        (310) 691-4455

Jewish Women International: jwi.org

Prison Activist Groups Online:
        PrisonNewsNetwork@yahoogroups.com
        Subscribe: PrisonNewsNetwork-subscribe@yahoogroups.com
        Unsubscribe: PrisonNewsNetwork-
        unsubscribe@yahoogroups.com
        Visit the NEW Prison News Network Website at:
        http://www.prisonnewsnetwork.us or
        http://www.vip-cali.com/pnn/default.htm

(numbers may have changed since publication)

For Families Of Prisoners:

1. Aleph Institute (Federal)
        www.aleph-institute.org   (305) 864-5553

2. Amnesty International   (212) 907-8400
        322 Eighth Ave. New York, NY. 10001

3. B'eit T'Shuvah (12-step program) Los Angeles

4. California Appellate Project   (213) 622-7890

5. California Department of Corrections:
    www.cdc-info.com

6. California Prison Focus   (415) 252-9211

7. Family and Corrections fcn@fcnetowrk.org

8. Friends Outside ---National   (209) 955-0701
    Los Angeles County   (626) 795-7607
    friendsoutsidela@sbcglobal.net

9. Nat'l Prison Project:
    Citizens United for Rehabilitation Errants Of CURE
                                              (202) 789-2126
    www.curenational.org   (202) 543-8399

10. Centerforce   (415) 456-9980

11. Church on the Way, Los Angeles   (818) 779-8000

12. Delancy Street, Los Angeles   (213) 6624886
    www.prisoners.com/delancyf.html   (415) 957-9800

13. Employment (Los Angeles County):
    Countywide Criminal Justice Coordination Committee
    www.bos.co.la.ca.us   (213)974-8398

    Chrysalis www.changelives.org   (213) 895-7777
14. Families Against Mandatory Minimums (FAMM)
                                              (202)457-5790

(numbers may have changed since publication)

15. Family Focus Resource Center   (818) 677-5575

16. Guide to Inmate Voting: Los Angeles County Registrar
    Recorder/County Clerk
    www.lavote.net   (800) 466-1310

17. Housing (Los Angeles County):   (323) 664-2200

    PATH (Persons Assisting the Homeless)
    www.epath.org
    Midnight Mission www.midnightmission.org (213) 624-9258

18. Human Kindness Foundation   (919) 304-2220
    www.humankindness.org

19. Incarcerated Fathers Library at FCN
    fcn@fcnetwork.org.   434/589-3036,
                                                434/589-6520

20. Incarcerated Parents' Manual
    info@prisonerswithchildren.org

21. League of Women Voters (inmate voting rights) (213)368-1616

23. Lionheart Foundation
    www.lionheart.org/   (617) 267-3121

24. NAACP Legal Defense and Educational Fund (212) 219-1900

25. National Institute of Corrections Information Center
                                                (303) 444-1101

26. Prison Ministry info@miraclesprisonministry.org

27. U. S. Department of Justice-Civil Rights   (202) 514-6255

(numbers may have changed since publication)

Locating Prisoners/Prisons/Jails

Prison Locators: (916) 445-6713
To locate an inmate within the California Department of Corrections, call prison locators. Available 24-hours a day. To receive information use the inmate's CDC number, or the inmate's full name and date of birth. The Inmate Locator/ID Warrants will provide an inmate's location, mailing addresses and relevant phone numbers. Please note that for new or transferring inmates it can take up to seven business days to update location information.

California Department of Corrections   CDC website

Locating Prisoners in Jail

Locating prisoners by the internet

> AnyWho
> The White Pages
> 411.com
> California Public Records

CONTACTS IF YOU CANNOT AFFORD TO PAY FOR A LAWYER:

National Legal Aid
Northern California Innocence Project
California Innocence Project
California Pro Bono Resources
California Pro Bono Directory

Resource links are the courtesy of Criminal Law Specialist
Faye Afra: info@bestdefender.com www.bestdefender.com

Hades' Angels Epilogue

Hades' Angels experience has given me knowledge and understanding, and has broadened my perspective about inmate-freemate relationships. This work deepened my awareness of certain common threads among the general population of women: a profound desire for love and belonging, a search for meaning, and a way to feel fully alive with purpose, sometimes at any cost.

My hope is that the impact of Hades' Angels Transformative Journey informs the reader more deeply of the interconnectedness of our human experience. Similar factors and dynamics can be applied to women in the general population who get caught up in destructive relationships with men who are not incarcerated. I hope that this work offers such women the insight and provides them with the knowledge and necessary tools to jump-start their healing, individuation, and transformation.

We were so well trained to listen and obey, and found it easy to go into self-protective, altered states. It's time to learn new tools! You cannot change the world without first changing the self.

ON MARRIAGE
Kahlil Gibran

The Almitra spoke again and said,

And what of marriage, master?

You were born together, and together you shall be forevermore.

You shall be together when the white wings of death scatter your days.

Ay, you shall be together even in the silent memory of God.

But let there be spaces in your togetherness,

And let the winds of the heavens dance between you.

Love one another, but make not a bond of love:

Let it rather be a moving sea between the shores of your souls.

Fill each other's cup but drink not from one cup.

Give one another of your bread but eat not from the same loaf

Sing and dance together and be joyous, but let each one of you be alone,

Even as the strings of a lute are alone though they quiver with the same music.

Give your hearts, but not into each other's keeping.

For only the hand of Life can contain your hearts.

And stand together yet not too near together:

For the pillars of the temple stand apart,

And the oak tree and the cypress grow not in each other's shadow.

The Prophet (1969)

ON CRIME AND PUNISHMENT

And how shall you punish those whose remorse is already greater than their misdeeds?

Is not remorse the justice which is administered by that very law which you would fain serve?

Yet you cannot lay remorse upon the innocent nor lift it from the heart of the guilty.

Unbidden shall it call in the night, that men may wake and gaze upon themselves.

And you who would understand justice, how shall you unless you look upon all deeds in the fullness of light?

Only then shall you know that the erect and the fallen are but one man standing in twilight between the night of his pigmy-self and the day of his god-self,

And that the corner-stone of the temple is not higher than the lowest stone in its foundation.

Kahlil Gibran

About
Charlyne Gelt, Ph.D.

Charlyne Gelt, Ph.D., CGP is a licensed clinical psychologist, and a group psychotherapist who works with "strong" women struggling with issues of submissive dependency and emotional intimacy in relationships. She is particularly committed to helping women move from emotional submission towards empowerment and healthier relationships: 1+1=3.

Dr. Charlyne Gelt received a doctorate in Clinical Psychology from Pacifica Graduate Institute. Her private practice includes individuals, couples, adolescents, women's empowerment groups, workshops, and families. It also includes families with someone in prison. Her experience facilitating groups for Friends Outside led her to delve more deeply into inmate/freemate love relationships. This work led to her doctoral dissertation, Hell's Angels.

As a clinician, Dr. Gelt is familiar with life crisis, the struggle to define oneself, and the transformative change that can occur with a "corrective emotional experience", sometimes outside the traditional therapeutic environment.

She is in private practice in Encino, CA, and has served as adjunct faculty at U.C.L.A. and Phillips Graduate Institute. Her articles have appeared in The Los Angeles Psychologist, The California Therapist and other professional publications, and Lifestyle.

Dr. Gelt is a member of: Los Angeles County Psychological Association (LACPA); California Association of Marriage and Family Therapists (CAMFT); American Association of Group Psychotherapists; Los Angeles Group Psychotherapy Association; California Psychological Ass., and the American Psychological Assn.

Charlyne Gelt, Ph.D.
cgelt@earthlink.net
http://www.drgelt.com
(818) 501-4123

REFERENCES

Alexander, F. (1961). *The scope of psychoanalysis*. New York: Basic Books.

Bandele, A. (1999). *The prisoner's wife*. New York: Scribner.

Barrie, J. M. (2008) - *Peter Pan in Kensington Gardens* - Peter Hollindale, editor. Oxford University Press

Beattie, M. (1987). *Codependent no more*. Minneapolis: Hazelden.

Benson, H. Love blooms behind bars. *San Francisco Chronicle*, July 1, 2007.

Bowen, M. & Kerr, M. (1988). *Family evaluation*. New York: W.W. Norton.

Butterfield, F. Repaving the long road out of prison. *New York Times*, May 4, 2004.

California Department of Corrections.(1996). *California code of regulations* (CCR). Title 15, Sections 3044 and 3174. Family Visiting, November 1, 1996.

California Department of Corrections. (1999, February 1). *CDC Facts*. Corrections Communications Office.

Campbell, J., Moyers, B. 1988. *The power of myth*. New York: Doubleday.

Capra, F. (1983). *The turning point*. New York: Bantam Books.

Casarjian, R. (1995). *Houses of healing*. Boston, MA: Lionheart Foundation Publishers.

Centerforce. (1999, April 28). Subcommittee meeting of proceedings with Senator Vasconcellos, Sacramento, CA.

Davies, R. P. (1980). Stigmatization of prisoners' families. *Prison Service Journal*, 40, 12-14.

Fishman, L. (1988). Stigmatization and prisoners' wives. *Deviant Behavior*, 9, 169-192.

Girshick, L. (1996). *Soledad women: wives of prisoners speak out.* Westport, CT: Praeger Publishers.

Goodyear, C. (1999, April 15). Deathly Afraid. San Francisco Chronicle, p. A3.

Grimm Brothers. 1972. *The complete grimm's fairy tales.* New York: Pantheon Books.

Guggenbuhl-Craig, A. (1995). *From the wrong side.* Woodstock, CT: Spring Publications.

Hurst, J. (1983). "Prison marriages: Why do they do it", *Los Angeles Times*, April 17, 1983.

Isenberg, S. (1991). *Women who love men who kill.* New York: Simon & Schuster.

Jung, C. G. (1961). *Memories, dreams, reflections.* (R. & C. Winston, Trans). London: Collins and Routledge & Kegan Paul.

Jung, C. G.1964. *Man and his symbols.* New York: Doubleday.

Jung, C. G. CW 14 p. 212; Seminars, i.p.121.

Kalsched, D. (1980). Narcissism and the search for interiority. *Quadrant*, 13(25), 46-75.

Kalsched, D. (1996). *The inner world of trauma.* London, NY: Routledge.

Kepford, L. (1994). The familial effects of incarceration. *International Journal of Sociology and Social Policy,* 14(3/4/5), 55-90. Kernberg, O. (1975). *Borderline conditions and pathological narcissism.* New York: Jason Aronson.

Kohut, H. (1966). *Forms and transformations of narcissism.* Journal of the American Psychoanalytic Association, 14, 243-272.

Kohut, H. (1971). *The analysis of the self.* New York: International Universities Press.

Kohut, H. (1977). *The restoration of the self.* New York: International Universities Press.

Kohut, H. (1978). *The Search for the self: Selected writings of Heinz Kohut, 1950-1978.* New York: International Universities Press.

Kohut, H. (1984). *How does analysis cure?* Chicago, IL: University of Chicago Press.

Kohut, H., & Wolfe, E. S. (1978). The disorders of the self and their treatment. *International Journal of Psycho-Analysis, 59,* 413-425.

Kupers, Terry. Behavioral Sciences and the Law. 15,4, Fall, 483-501, 1999.

Loomis, M. (1991). *Dancing the wheel of psychological types.* Wilmette, IL: Chiron Publications.

Loomis, M. (1995). *Her father's daughter.* Wilmette, IL: Chiron Publications.

Lozoff, Bo (1985). *We're all doing time.* Durham, NC: Human Kindness Foundation Publishers.

Lyman, R., Marriage programs try to instill bliss and stability behind bars. *New York Times*, April 16, 2005.

May, R. (1991). *The cry for myth*. New York: W. W. Norton.

Maynard, Joyce. True life stories. *Vogue Magazine*, February 2007.

Meador, B. (1992). *Uncursing the dark*. Wilmette, IL: Chiron.

Miller, A. (1990). *Banished knowledge*. New York: Doubleday.

Miller, David, L. (ed.) 1995. *Jung and the interpretation of the Bible*. Continuum: New York.

Naifeh, S. (1997, March 2). Lecture, Pacifica Graduate Institute, Carpinteria, CA.

Neumann, E. (1971). *Armor and psyche*. New York: Princeton University Press.

PBSONLINE. (1999). Angel on Death Row, in *Frontline*. PBS video retrieved April 19 from video@pbs.org.

Perera, S. (1981). *Descent to the goddess*. Toronto: Inner City Books.

Pinkola Estes, C. (1992). *Women who run with the wolves*. New York: Ballantine Books.

Shinoda-Bolen, J. (1995). *Crossing to avalon*, San Francisco: Harper.

Shinoda-Bolen, J. (2004). Transitions as liminal and archetypal situations. Lecture at the *Mythic Journeys* Conference, Atlanta, Georgia.

Steese, E. (1988, April 28). Wives of locked up husbands. *The Christian Science Monitor*, p. 23.

Tarnas, R. (1991). *The passion of the western mind.* New York: Ballantine Books.

Too many convicts: America's tough crime policy is having unintended consequences, *The Economist,* August 8, 2002.

Trillin, C. (1999, April 19). Paris and his sisters. *New Yorker,* p. 62.

von Franz, M. L. (1972). *The feminine in fairytales.* Dallas, TX: Spring Publications, Inc.

von Franz, M. L. 1980. *Redemption motifs in fairytales.* Inner City Books: Toronto, Canada.

von Franz, M.L.(1997). *Archetypal dimensions of the psyche.* Shambala, Boston & London

Warrick, P. (1997). *Los Angeles Times,* p. E-1.

White, E. (22 May 2006). 1 in 136 U.S. residents behind bars. *Associated Press.* http://www.commondreams.org/headlines06/ 0522-03.htm.

Winnicott, D. (1958). The capacity to be alone. *International Journal of Psychoanalysis,* 39, 416-420.

Woodman, M. (1982). *Addiction to perfection.* Toronto, Canada: Inner City Books.

Woodman, M. (1989, March/April). The conscious feminine. *Common Boundary,* pp. 10-17.

www.ingramcontent.com/pod-product-compliance
Lightning Source LLC
Chambersburg PA
CBHW072051020426
42334CB00017B/1467